RELATION AND RESISTANCE

ADVANCING STUDIES IN RELIGION
Series editor: Christine Mitchell

Advancing Studies in Religion catalyzes and provokes original research in the study of religion with a critical edge. The series advances the study of religion in method and theory, textual interpretation, theological studies, and the understanding of lived religious experience. Rooted in the long and diverse traditions of the study of religion in Canada, the series demonstrates awareness of the complex genealogy of religion as a category and as a discipline. ASR welcomes submissions from authors researching religion in varied contexts and with diverse methodologies.

The series is sponsored by the Canadian Corporation for Studies in Religion whose constituent societies include the Canadian Society of Biblical Studies, Canadian Society for the Study of Religion, Canadian Society of Patristic Studies, Canadian Theological Society, Société canadienne de théologie, and Société québécoise pour l'étude de la religion.

1 The al-Baqara Crescendo
Understanding the Qur'an's Style, Narrative Structure, and Running Themes
Nevin Reda

2 Leaving Christianity
Changing Allegiances in Canada since 1945
Brian Clarke and Stuart Macdonald

3 Everyday Sacred
Religion in Contemporary Quebec
Edited by *Hillary Kaell*

4 Convergent Knowing
Christianity and Science in Conversation with a Suffering Creation
Simon Appolloni

5 Seeding Buddhism with Multiculturalism
The Transmission of Sri Lankan Buddhism in Toronto
D. Mitra Barua

6 The Subversive Evangelical
The Ironic Charisma of an Irreligious Megachurch
Peter J. Schuurman

7 The Public Work of Christmas
Difference and Belonging in Multicultural Societies
Edited by *Pamela E. Klassen and Monique Scheer*

8 Identities Under Construction
Religion, Gender, and Sexuality among Youth in Canada
Pamela Dickey Young and Heather Shipley

9 Prayer as Transgression?
The Social Relations of Prayer
in Healthcare Settings
*Sheryl Reimer-Kirkham,
Sonya Sharma, Rachel Brown,
and Melania Calestani*

10 Relation and Resistance
Racialized Women, Religion,
and Diaspora
Edited by *Sailaja V. Krishnamurti
and Becky R. Lee*

Relation and Resistance

Racialized Women, Religion, and Diaspora

Edited by

SAILAJA V. KRISHNAMURTI
AND BECKY R. LEE

McGill-Queen's University Press
Montreal & Kingston • London • Chicago

ISBN 978-0-2280-0852-1 (cloth)
ISBN 978-0-2280-0853-8 (paper)
ISBN 978-0-2280-0973-3 (ePDF)
ISBN 978-0-2280-0974-0 (ePUB)

Legal deposit third quarter 2021
Bibliothèque nationale du Québec

Printed in Canada on acid-free paper that is 100% ancient forest free (100% post-consumer recycled), processed chlorine free

This book has been published with the help of a grant from the Canadian Federation for the Humanities and Social Sciences, through the Awards to Scholarly Publications Program, using funds provided by the Social Sciences and Humanities Research Council of Canada.

Funded by the Government of Canada | Financé par le gouvernement du Canada | Canada

Canada Council for the Arts | Conseil des arts du Canada

We acknowledge the support of the Canada Council for the Arts.

Nous remercions le Conseil des arts du Canada de son soutien.

Library and Archives Canada Cataloguing in Publication

Title: Relation and resistance: racialized women, religion, and diaspora/ edited by Sailaja V. Krishnamurti and Becky R. Lee.

Names: Krishnamurti, Sailaja, 1976– editor. | Lee, Becky R., editor.

Series: Advancing studies in religion; 10.

Description: Series statement: Advancing studies in religion; 10 | Includes bibliographical references and index.

Identifiers: Canadiana (print) 20210226900 | Canadiana (ebook) 2021022715X | ISBN 9780228008521 (cloth) | ISBN 9780228008538 (paper) | ISBN 9780228009733 (ePDF) | ISBN 9780228009740 (ePUB)

Subjects: LCSH: Women and religion—Canada. | LCSH: Minority women—Religious life—Canada. | LCSH: Feminism—Canada. | LCSH: Canada—Religion.

Classification: LCC BL625.7 .245 2021 | DDC 200.820971—dc23

This book was typeset by Marquis Interscript in 10.5/13 Sabon.

For Krishna
and
for Ann

Contents

Acknowledgments

This project has been a long journey, but a deeply rewarding one. As feminist scholars, we have been intentional in working from an ethic of care, empathy, and mutual support throughout this process, and have learned much from each other along the way. We are also grateful for the opportunity to work with and learn from all the contributors to this volume, and thank each of them for their commitment and engagement. We wish to thank Terry Tak-ling Woo for encouraging us to undertake this project. Many thanks also to James Warren, our astute and generous copy editor and indexer whose keen eye helped us to put this excellent volume together. Special thanks are owed to Kyla Madden, senior editor at McGill-Queen's University Press; Christine Mitchell, series editor of Advancing Studies in Religion; and all those at McGill-Queen's University Press who worked behind the scenes to make this volume possible.

We also wish to thank the following bodies at York University for their generous support of a symposium featuring the contributors at York University: the Office of the Vice-President Research and Innovation; the Faculty of Liberal Arts and Professional Studies; the Department of Humanities; the Centre for Feminist Research; the Graduate Program in Social and Political Thought; and the Office of the Master of Vanier College.

The Faculty of Liberal Arts and Professional Studies at York University provided additional financial support towards the indexing of the volume.

RELATION AND RESISTANCE

1

Introduction

Conceptualizing the Study of Women and Diasporic Religion

Sailaja V. Krishnamurti and Becky R. Lee

This book explores the stories and lives of racialized women connected with religious diaspora communities across the geographical and political space of Canada. Women have played a critical role in building these communities and maintaining transnational networks. They have been catalysts of change and transformation, working in relation with and in resistance to religious groups and the wider community.

Together, the essays we have collected here contribute to a broader conversation about women and religion in three key ways. First, they demonstrate that a deeper understanding of women's experiences of displacement, migration, race, and gender is critical for scholars studying religion in Canada. Second, they show how women have engaged with discourses of citizenship and multiculturalism as they shape identities for themselves within the settler-colonial space of Canada. Third, these contributions reveal how women are conceptualizing traditions in transformative ways, challenging some prevailing assumptions about diasporic religion as nostalgically entrenched in the past.

The volume arises from the nexus of diaspora studies, women and gender studies, and religious studies. We have approached this work as feminist scholars of religion who are interested in the intersections of religion, gender, and identity. Our project was sparked in part by a desire to move further in the direction of an earlier book of essays edited by Becky R. Lee and Terry Tak-ling Woo, *Canadian Women*

Shaping Diasporic Religious Identities (2016). That volume offers an introduction to thinking about women and religion in Canada. *Relation and Resistance: Racialized Women, Religion, and Diaspora* is an attempt at thinking more critically about the relationship between race, gender, and nation, and about the margins of these formations. We have brought together a number of scholars who study women in Caribbean, South Asian, East Asian, and Métis diaspora groups. Many of the contributors to this volume are women who are themselves part of diaspora communities, and some reflect on their own experiences in their work. They are located across Canada, connected with different histories and geographies. Explicitly or implicitly, all the essays included here trouble the multicultural Canadian imaginary and the prevailing narratives of diaspora in different ways.

The contributors to this volume also work in a wide array of disciplines, including literature, history, legal studies, sociology, anthropology, political science, and Indigenous Studies. They differ widely in approach and in the kinds of data they draw upon: some consider questions of representation, while others discuss material religion and social practice; some are concerned with literary analysis and historical records, while others address law, policy, and activism. What ties the essays together is an interest in showing how women's experiences, perspectives, and words matter. In this introduction, we seek to outline the volume's variety of approaches to the core concepts of gender, religion, and diaspora. In the last section, we provide an overview of the chapters.

APPROACHES TO WOMEN AND RELIGION

Religion and religiosity are gendered in critical ways; moreover, the space of religious and political institutions is mitigated by gender. Women exist in different relations of power than men within these institutions, and gain access to power in different ways. Women in some religious communities may be restricted from roles in ministry or leadership, but play a critical role in the administration of religious institutions. In other communities, women have been significant as spiritual and social leaders. Women's bodies carry a variety of markers of religion, from veiling to clothing styles and aesthetic practices connected with "modesty," femininity, tradition, and marital status. In diaspora, this often means that women who are visibly religious are also the targets of racist and xenophobic violence. This also means that in Canada, women's bodies are often at the centre of debates about religious pluralism, multiculturalism, and secularism.

This collection explores the complex ways that women in diasporic communities have shaped, challenged, and transformed diasporic religious practice in Canada's complex cultural landscape. Some of the women discussed in this volume see themselves as feminist, while others might resist or reject this identification; it is nonetheless possible for us to think about their experiences through a feminist lens. Many feminist and womanist scholars of religion have shown how religion and spirituality are important parts of the experience of racialized women in diaspora (Alexander 2006; Jesús 2015). Religious community, and particularly ethno-religious community, may be a place of safety or respite from experiences of racism and oppression in everyday life. For early migrants to Canada, religion was also a crucial way of building community and shared identity. For some contemporary women, it is precisely because of the value of religion for community survival that it is both possible and necessary to challenge some aspects of religion in feminist terms.

As editors we seek to make clear at the outset that our understanding of women as a category is inclusive of trans and non-binary identities. We approach the concept of "women" as a socially constructed and often contested category that is not generalizable or reducible to a set of physical characteristics. Our aim has been to look for linkages, contrasts, and relationships among women-identified people navigating religious spaces and identities. While our contributors have primarily studied cisgender women, they reflect diverse and varied perspectives on what it means to be gendered in different religious, social, and political contexts.

Gendered identities intersect in crucial ways with other vectors of social location. Intersectionality is a concept developed by Black feminists that has been widely adopted by scholars and activists (Crenshaw 1989; 1991). Sirma Bilge and Patricia Hill Collins (2016) describe intersectionality in this way:

> Intersectionality is a way of understanding and analyzing the complexity in the world, in people, and in human experiences. The events and conditions of social and political life and the self can seldom be understood as shaped by one factor. They are generally shaped by many factors in diverse and mutually influencing ways. When it comes to social inequality, people's lives

> and organization of power in a given society are better understood as being shaped not by a single axis of social division, be it race or gender or class, but by many axes that work together and influence each other. Intersectionality as an analytic tool gives people better access to the complexity of the world and of themselves. (25)

Working from this significant turn in feminist theory, our understanding of gender emphasizes its intersections with race, ethnicity, class, sexuality, and *status* – the latter referring to immigration status, citizenship, Indian status, or other forms of relationship determined by the state. We recognize that women's access to power and authority and expectations about their roles, both in religious communities and in broader society, are shaped by these other vectors. While contributors to this volume do not necessarily locate themselves in intersectional feminist theory, the book demonstrates these vectors at work. For example, as Rima Berns-McGown shows in her chapter, Black Muslim women report experiences of anti-Black racism in Muslim spaces where power rests with members of non-Black racialized groups. While all are Muslims of colour, complex intra- and intercommunity dynamics are inscribed by unequal relations of race, class, and gender.

DIASPORA STUDIES AND RELIGION

Diaspora is generally understood in sociology and social theory to mean a community that is "scattered" across one or more geographical locations, and which, despite distance, maintains connections across borders and across time. These connections might develop and be maintained through shared identities, languages, and cultural and religious practices. While some theorists have attempted to develop categorically limited definitions of this term (Cohen 1997), in recent years it has been used to describe a dizzying array of migrant social formations (Brubaker 2005; Tölölyan 2012). Diaspora is also often entangled with the concept of the "transnational," though these two terms have different implications and are not interchangeable (Goldring and Krishnamurti 2007). Transnational processes, exchanges, and movements take place across borders. Not all diaspora communities are transnationally connected in the contemporary moment, though migration might have been essential to their formation.

Khachig Tölölyan writes that diaspora is both "objective and subjective"; he understands the term to refer to "those communities of the dispersed who develop varieties of association that endure at least into their third generation" (2012, 8). For Lily Cho, diaspora is "first and foremost a subjective condition marked by the contingencies of long histories of displacements and genealogies of dispossession" (2007, 14). She writes that diasporas "are not simply collections of people, communities of scattered individuals bound by some shared history, race or religion, or however we want to break down the definitions and classifications. Rather, they have a relation to power. They emerge in relation to power" (15). Building on this understanding of diaspora as both deeply subjective and historically contingent, these essays consider how diasporic women's experiences of gender and religiosity shape, and are shaped by, relations of power, authority, and faith within their communities and in the broader Canadian context.

Many scholars working with the concept of diaspora emphasize the notion that diasporic communities retain a nostalgia for, or desire to eventually return to, a homeland. But as several of our contributors show, this is an outmoded approach to understanding how communities form in migration and how they conceptualize their relationships to "home." Indeed, for some people in diaspora, such a home does not exist, or is unattainable. Avtar Brah (Vowel 2017) conceives of a "homing desire," suggesting that rather than only looking "back" toward a lost, forsaken, or impossible homeland, diasporas "are also potentially the sites of hope and new beginnings. They are contested cultural and political terrains where individual and collective memories collide, reassemble, and reconfigure" (3). Our objective is to draw attention to some of the ways that racialized women's religiosities and strategies for resistance might be understood through this lens of diasporic "homing" on the contested cultural and political terrain of Canada.

In this light, one of the key tensions in diaspora studies in Canada in recent years has emerged around understanding migrant groups in relation to Indigenous people. Diaspora studies is by definition interested in social formations that move across borders and beyond nations. A problem in diaspora work is that it often takes for granted the histories of nationhood, territory, and belonging that are effaced by a narrative of diaspora groups making new "homes." It is a reality that in building communities, diaspora people have occupied Indigenous land across Canada. When we brought the contributors to this volume together in 2017 for a symposium at which we all had an opportunity to read and engage with each other's work, this set of questions emerged as critical to our discussions of diaspora. Crucially, the symposium began and ended with reflections on Chantal Fiola's call to "be good relatives." In chapter 12 of this volume, she writes, "Knowing how we are connected helps us understand our roles, responsibilities, and mutual obligations if we aim to be good relatives – whether our ancestors have been here for millennia, settled here in the last few hundred years, or are newcomers" (260). These conversations prompted a critical rethinking for us, as editors, about the ethical obligations of doing diaspora work in the context of ongoing settler colonialism.

As scholars of religion in Canada, working in various disciplines and institutions, our responsibility begins by acknowledging that Canada is a settler state and that diaspora communities here exist on Indigenous land; but it does not end there. We seek to remind ourselves that state policies on the management of immigration, religious pluralism, and cultural heritage that have encouraged the development of diaspora communities in Canada are part of the same state apparatus that manages the ongoing colonization of Indigenous people. In her book *Indigenous Writes: A Guide to First Nations, Métis, and Inuit Issues in Canada* (2016), Métis lawyer and writer Chelsea Vowel provides a nuanced perspective on racialized people and settler colonialism:

> Like European-descended peoples of the lower classes, who were more pawns than power-brokers in the early years of colonization in Canada and the United States, non-European peoples displaced by colonization in their own lands are folded into the settlement process when they arrive here – even as they are often denied equal social privileges. However, non-European migrants do not have the power to bring with them their laws and customs, which they then apply to the rest of the peoples living in Canada – no matter what some alarmists like to claim. The dominant sociopolitical structures in place remain European in origin and, as Indigenous peoples are well aware, they are not so easy to change. (17)

To make this statement is not by any means to deny the violence and displacement that underlie many histories of migration connected with enslavement, war, and terror. Vowel recognizes the complicated histories of trauma that underlie many experiences of migration, and makes clear that in her view, Black people in Canada cannot be seen as settlers. The argument she is laying out is that all these groups, shaped by various histories of migration, are in relation with Indigenous people here. They also carry the legacies of colonialism, violence, and displacement in other parts of the world. A few of the contributors to this book, particularly Chantal Fiola and Ken Derry, are attempting to think through these relations in their chapters. As researchers, we must all continue to think about how this shapes our understandings of diaspora in Canada.

CHAPTER OVERVIEW

Navigating Religion, Nation, and Identity

The three areas of focus we identified at the beginning of this introduction – migration and identity, Canadian multiculturalism, and transformative spaces and practices – are all addressed in different ways in each chapter. The book is organized into three sections. The first introduces readers to some of the ways that women in diaspora have worked to create spaces for themselves and for their communities in Canada. Over time, and across different contexts for migration, women in diaspora groups must contend with expectations about gender roles and religious norms that exist within the diaspora group and in Canadian society. The contributions in this section consider some histories and contexts for migration alongside the processes and policies of colonialism, nation-building, immigration, and multiculturalism. Women in diaspora fashion identities and relationships in response and in resistance to both state policies and religious community attitudes.

These four chapters are methodologically distinct, but together they offer a diversity of theoretical and disciplinary perspectives on women and religion. Sailaja Krishnamurti's study of women and diasporic Hindu religiosities looks beyond mainstream community spaces and practices to women who may not feel at home in such spaces. Krishnamurti asserts that the conventional narrative of diasporic belonging is tested by thinking about those who remain marginalized within diaspora, at the boundaries of both diasporic communities and the community at large. Through interviews with women who have grown up in diaspora, she explores how South Asian diasporic feminists and queer-identified people select and reject "Hindu" identities and beliefs in ways that allow them to think through issues of social justice and solidarity.

Ken Derry's chapter considers the marginalization and displacement of women through a different lens. The chapter considers two foundational works of modern Métis literature, Maria Campbell's *Halfbreed* (1973) and Beatrice Mosionier's *In Search of April Raintree* (1983), through the lens of Nêhiyaw (Cree) scholar Neal McLeod's concepts of "spatial diaspora" and "ideological diaspora" (2001). Recognizing his location as a white male settler engaging these texts, Derry turns to the voices of Indigenous women scholars and writers whose interventions illuminate how Campbell's and Mosionier's texts position Indigenous religions – and writings – as critical to the process of recovering a sense of home.

The next two chapters in this section look at different aspects of Canadian nation-building politics and their impacts on diasporic women. Cary Takagaki argues that although some scholars have suggested that Japanese women in diaspora played significant roles in religious community in the first half of the twentieth century, this assumption ignores some mitigating factors in Japan and in Canada. The little space that immigrant Japanese women negotiated for themselves in Canada prior to the Second World War was impacted by the pressure to assimilate into Protestant Christian Canadian culture, shaping spaces for women in both Buddhist and Christian Japanese communities. Takagaki discusses *fujinkai*, Japanese women's associations, as spaces where they were able to access some agency and participate in public life.

Shifting forward to the twenty-first century, Julie Vig analyzes how Sikh women in contemporary Montreal position themselves in relation to discourses on gender equality that are generated within their Sikh tradition as well as in the ongoing debates over the place of religious symbols in Quebec's public spaces. In addition to illuminating the subversive potential of religion within diasporic communities, this analysis demonstrates that discourses on women and gender equality are being transformed in the Montreal context, and that those reconstructed discourses have a significant impact on Sikh women's experiences, self-representations, and choices regarding their roles within the family, the Gurdwara, the community, and the larger society.

Women in Transnational Religious Communities

The second group of essays addresses transnational relationships, groups, and institutions and their role in women's experiences of religion. Chapters by Nadia Hasan, Lina Samuel, Henry Shiu, and Preet Kaur Virdi examine some of the transnational networks in which women have participated from the early twentieth century into the present moment. In each of these cases, the role and value of women within the community is connected with the performance of piety or traditional religiosity. But, evoking Saba Mahmood's landmark theorization of piety as a form of agency (2005), women in these communities are in some ways able to challenge religious ideas and community norms from this transnational perspective. These chapters thus complicate two conventional narratives about diaspora: first, that diaspora groups are inherently conservative and traditionalist on gender issues because they are "stuck" in a historical past; and second, that gains made by women in these communities are always attributable to immersion in Canadian or "Western" liberalism. Instead, these chapters show how gender attitudes in diaspora are affected by shifting ideas in homelands and other diaspora locations; these ongoing conversations about community identity may change religious attitudes about women, but do so in unexpected ways.

Preet Kaur Virdi's chapter examines dynamics of tradition and resistance within diaspora communities in her study of Punjabi Sikh marriage migration from India to Canada. She critiques the scholarly tendency to essentialize diasporic communities and women's experiences, and instead offers some models for thinking about the diverse histories and experiences within communities. Drawing on interviews with Sikh women and men in Canada, Virdi shows how marriage migration and marriage breakdown is experienced differently by Sikhs with varying relationships to India and Canada – especially in the case of women whose basis for migration is transnational marriage. Among what she calls trans-local subjects, Virdi argues that migration could enable new possibilities for women, both in marriage partner selection, and, for initiated Sikhs, in challenging cultural caste and kinship norms.

Tracking transnational connections in Chinese Buddhist communities, Henry Shiu argues that increased leadership roles for Buddhist nuns in Canada are attributable to ongoing transnational connections with Buddhist nuns in Asia. While scholars often conceive of diasporic religious communities as "frozen" in a particular historical movement and entrenched in tradition, Shiu shows that it is progressive organizations in Asia that are helping to improve leadership roles for women. Shiu also suggests that the motivations for pursuing gender equality in Chinese Buddhist communities are less informed by liberal approaches to gender in Canada than by shifting religious ideas in diaspora.

In a study based on interviews with members of three cohorts of Malayali women in the Syrian Orthodox Christian Church in Canada, Lina Samuel discusses how women's connections with the church can be both empowering and debilitating. She demonstrates that as the church grew from a small transplanted community to a well-established institution, women's roles as caregivers and as keepers of tradition were emphasized. While second-generation women that Samuel interviews are more ambivalent towards church participation, the more recent migrants in the study have relied on the church to find a sense of belonging, even if they find the church's patriarchal conservativism contradicts their own beliefs regarding gender.

Nadia Hasan analyzes the experiences of Pakistani Muslim women in Canada who are committed to developing their piety through participation in Al-Huda International, a transnational women's Islamic education organization that promotes a form of Islam that is seen as quite conservative, both in Pakistan and beyond. Hasan documents how her subjects find a way to frame their conservative Muslim piety as authentic, rational, and modern, dexterously reinforcing the trope of the model minority while simultaneously resisting the hegemonic Islamophobic ideas pertaining to that trope.

Building Relations, Imagining Futures

The final group of essays in the book encourages us to think about diasporic futures. If the earlier chapters problematize the notion of diasporas as always looking backward toward the past, in this section, contributors help us to imagine possibilities for the future, in which traditional and ancestral religious practices are part of women's solidarities with each other. We begin this section with Andrea A. Davis's analysis of Jamaican Canadian writer Nalo Hopkinson's novel *Brown Girl in the Ring*. In this work of speculative fiction, Hopkinson imagines near-future post-apocalyptic Toronto as a subversive city saturated by the stories of racialized migrants and shaped by their oral histories and spiritual practices. Survival in this city depends on the empowerment of Black people through African diaspora spiritual practices. Davis reads the novel as an anticolonial narrative that challenges questions of national origin, cultural authority, and class privilege. By situating Canada's entanglement in the histories and memories of the Caribbean, Africa, and South and Central America, Davis argues that Hopkinson radically expands our understanding of diaspora, religion, and multiculturalism. Through the lens of gender and religion, Davis shows how the novel "reconsiders African spiritual practices and Caribbean women as important sources of retrieved African memory and as a potential source of Canada's healing" (217–18). Hopkinson's novel characterizes state-sanctioned multiculturalism as an "empty" policy, a form of spirit thievery that legitimizes the appropriation of othered cultures while simultaneously zombifying individuals and communities by forcing them to conform to an imagined Canadian ideal. In *Brown Girl in the Ring*, Davis argues, multicultural relations are refigured as a radical interventionist practice of shared belonging.

In her contribution, Rima Berns-McGown shows the centrality of religion in young women's mobilization at the forefront of social change in Canada. She views diaspora as a space of connections that forces one to think deeply about "home" and "belonging." Drawing upon the voices of numerous young Muslim women, she demonstrates how their experiences of racism, Islamophobia, and social injustice in Canada have helped them to understand and to empathize with others who are marginalized – the victims of intolerance, inequity, abuse, and stigma. That empathy, in turn, prompts many to work for social justice, which they understand to be integral to Islam, not just for Muslims, but for the whole of the society in which they find themselves living.

The volume closes with a reflection by Chantal Fiola, whose chapter invites scholars of contemporary religion to think critically about diaspora religion on Indigenous land. Fiola suggests that some aspects of diaspora theory may be useful for thinking about Indigenous communities, but cautions against subsuming Indigenous experiences of displacement into the discourse of diaspora without thinking through relationships with land. Instead, Fiola argues for a decolonizing approach to diaspora, decentring the state and instead thinking through diaspora from the perspective of nation-to-nation relations. Recounting histories of precolonial relationships between Indigenous nations, and of colonial treaties intended to build relations between Indigenous and colonial nations, Fiola conceptualizes Indigenous communities and diaspora groups existing in "relational sovereignty" (271). This framework emphasizes resistance to the Canadian state as the manager of colonization, immigration, and settlement. Fiola's essay opens up a critical space for thinking through how we understand diaspora relations in the context of settler colonialism. We encourage all readers of this book to reflect on this intervention in their study of women, religion, and diaspora.

REFERENCES

Alexander, M. Jacqui. 2006. *Pedagogies of Crossing: Meditations on Feminism, Sexual Politics, Memory, and the Sacred*. Durham, NC: Duke University Press.

Brah, Avtar. 1997. *Cartographies of Diaspora: Contesting Identities*. London: Routledge.

Brubaker, Rogers. 2005. "The 'Diaspora' Diaspora." *Ethnic and Racial Studies* 28, no. 1: 1–19. https://doi.org/10.1080/0141987042000289997.

Cho, Lily. 2007. "The Turn to Diaspora." *TOPIA: Canadian Journal of Cultural Studies* 17: 11–30.

Cohen, Robin. 1997. *Global Diasporas: An Introduction*. 1st edition. London: Routledge.

Collins, Patricia Hill, and Sirma Bilge. 2016. *Intersectionality*. Cambridge, UK and Malden, MA: Polity.

Crenshaw, Kimberlé. 1989. "Demarginalizing the Intersection of Race and Sex: A Black Feminist Critique of Antidiscrimination Doctrine, Feminist Theory and Antiracist Politics." *The University of Chicago Legal Forum* 140: 139–67.

– 1991. "Mapping the Margins: Intersectionality, Identity Politics, and Violence against Women of Color." *Stanford Law Review* 43, no. 6: 1241–99. https://doi.org/10.2307/1229039.

Goldring, Luin, and Sailaja Krishnamurti, eds. 2007. *Organizing the Transnational: Labour, Politics, and Social Change*. Vancouver: University of British Columbia Press.

Jesús, Aisha M. Beliso-De. 2015. *Electric Santería: Racial and Sexual Assemblages of Transnational Religion*. New York: Columbia University Press.

Lee, Becky R., and Terry Tak-ling Woo, eds. 2016. *Canadian Women Shaping Diasporic Religious Identities*. Studies in Women and Religion/

Études sur les femmes et la religion 13. Waterloo, ON: Wilfrid Laurier University Press.

Mahmood, Saba. 2005. *Politics of Piety: The Islamic Revival and the Feminist Subject.* Princeton, NJ: Princeton University Press.

Tölölyan, Khachig. 2012. "Diaspora Studies: Past, Present and Promise." https://ora.ox.ac.uk/objects/uuid:b1aa700c-8285-43c6-87e9-649ca74ce840.

Vowel, Chelsea. 2016. *Indigenous Writes: A Guide to First Nations, Métis, and Inuit Issues in Canada.* Winnipeg: Portage and Main Press.

PART ONE

Navigating Religion, Nation, and Identity

2

Grounded Religiosities

Women Navigating Hindu Identity and Social Justice

Sailaja V. Krishnamurti

For many women in diaspora, religious community is an important space for affirming traditional identity, maintaining transnational family ties, and fostering cultural connections. But not all diasporic Hindu women's religiosity is conservative, nostalgically driven, and "homeward facing." The voices of "official" Hinduism in India and in the diaspora (Vertovec 2000; Kurien 2006) often reflect conservative attitudes, but diasporic Hindus represent a range of social and political perspectives.[1] Hindus have diverse and sometimes conflicting practices and perspectives, and, as every textbook on Hinduism points out, Hindus have no central leader or institution, no singular core text, and no universally shared worldview. Some researchers have likened this diversity to the great spreading branches of a banyan tree: "the Hindu banyan is not uniform to look at. Rather, it is a network of variety, one distinctive arboreal complex shading into another, the whole forming a marvellous unity-in-diversity" (Lipner 1994, 5–6; Banerjee and Coward 2009, 33). In this chapter, I want to consider this metaphor from another perspective: what is happening underground?

Research on Hindus in Canada has tended to focus on the diversity of "above-ground" practices that centre families and communities, and to emphasize maintenance of home puja and temple life (Banerjee and Coward 2009; Younger 2012; A. Pearson and Nayak 2016; Spina 2017). Like the banyan's aerial roots, these formations are visible to researchers and intelligible to the ethnographic gaze of religious studies. But below the surface, rhizomatic networks proliferate.[2] There are many who might be marginalized or excluded from normative religious communities because of their sexual identities or political perspectives. What kind of "underground" Hindu religiosity happens in non-traditional, personal, and marginalized spaces where these other diasporic subjectivities take root?

In this chapter I explore how feminist and queer women with commitments to social justice navigate their relationships with Hinduism and diaspora. For the twelve women who participated in this project, diasporic Hindu religiosity is a complicated negotiation between traditional spiritual practices and beliefs and their own contemporary critiques. For some participants, Hindu religion has been an important and affirming space for exploring feminist possibilities, offering a path, as one put it, to "feeling grounded" in diaspora. For others, Hindu communities are heteropatriarchal spaces that are hostile to their existence: they have felt excluded or marginalized in diaspora communities and frustrated by beliefs and practices that maintain social order. But this experience of non-belonging in normative spaces of diasporic Hinduism does not necessarily signify a rejection of Hindu spirituality or religiosity. Rather, it illuminates how a commitment to an oppositional social critique of Hindu community, or the experience of exclusion from these spaces, sometimes conflicts with the desire to maintain practices and traditions that are deeply important to one's well-being.

In *Impossible Desires: Queer Diasporas and South Asian Public Cultures*, Gayatri Gopinath writes that the archive of queer diaspora culture includes informal and "mercurial" spaces and practices – nightclubs, festivals, community events – that are difficult to document (2005, 21). The public and private spaces of queer religiosity are even less visible because of the complicated relationship between sexual and religious identities. These diverse perspectives on identity and sexuality have not been captured in previous studies of Hindus in Canada that are focused on organized communities and heteronormative family environments; conversely, studies of South Asian women's organizing or queer organizing in Canada do not address religious identity.[3] An exploration of these perspectives complicates the theorization of diasporic Hinduism. It forces researchers to ask what kinds of Hindu religiosity might exist *under*ground, and thus moves toward a more nuanced approach to diasporic religious identity and practice.

Through interviews with twelve feminist activists, all South Asian women in Canada with ties to the Hindu diaspora, this chapter attempts to make visible some of these complex perspectives. The participants represent a diversity of positionalities and experiences. They are academics, authors, artists, and activists. Seven of the twelve identify as queer (and one as "straight-ish"); one participant identifies as a queer woman and uses both she/her and they/them pronouns.[4] Each has developed their own ways of integrating Hindu religiosity into their lives even while feeling marginal in mainstream Hindu diaspora community. For some, the term "Hindu" itself is a site of contestation because of its association with Hindu nationalist politics. For others, it is an important (albeit fraught) term for self-definition and exploration.

The women in this group reflect distinct narratives of migration that connect them to Canada in different ways. Four are first-generation migrants: two are members of what diaspora researchers call the "1.5 generation" (migrated at a young age), and the remaining six were all born in Canada. Eight of the participants' families arrived from India or Sri Lanka. Four of the participants are what some scholars would call "doubly diasporic," meaning that they or their families came to Canada from previous locations of South Asian migration, including the Caribbean and East Africa. Some came with families as refugees, while others came as skilled migrants or under student visas. Participants also represent a variety of backgrounds with regard to language, caste, and subsect.

In our conversations, each participant talked about their own approach to spirituality, tradition, and religious practices. I refer to these as reflections on religiosity, taking my approach to this concept from Becky Lee and Terry Tak-Ling Woo, who write: "The concept of religiosity, with its attention on the religious feeling or experience of individual believers, renders the distinctions between formal and informal, official and unofficial, elite and popular religion irrelevant" (2016, xi). Religiosity may or may not be structured; it can also be highly individualized. Hindu religiosity can include conventional practices of home puja, temple-based rituals, and devotional gatherings, as well as informal prayer, mantra, yoga, ayurveda, astrology, meditation, music, and personal ritual in diverse forms. Each of the women that I spoke to talked about space in different ways – the space of the Hindu temple, of the home, of "back home" – but also about the need to create spaces for activist organizing and queer community. They described the spaces they have produced as practitioners outside mainstream spaces of devotion. I refer to the spaces these women occupy as radical spaces of religiosity, defined by commitment to social justice, building intentional communities, and working towards solidarity with other marginalized people.

ABOVE GROUND: HINDUISMS IN CANADA AND NORTH AMERICA

To contextualize the perspectives of the women in this study, it is useful to first look at the various branches of Hindu communities "above ground" in Canada and North America. Hindus and other South Asians have settled on Turtle Island/North America since the late nineteenth century. In most cases, early South Asian arrivals, largely men, were connected to circuits of labour flowing through the British Empire.[5] As agricultural and industrial workers, Hindus, Sikhs, and Muslim South Asians contributed to the establishment of the United States and Canada as white settler states on Indigenous land.[6] Then, as a result of policies in Canada and the US limiting Asian arrivals in the early twentieth century, migration virtually stopped and did not restart significantly until the 1960s when new immigration policies brought a second wave of Hindus from South Asia.[7] Hindu populations in Canada grew over the next decades, with arrivals from India and South Asia. Thousands of Tamil Hindus from Sri Lanka arrived in the 1980s and 1990s as refugees from the civil war. Hindus also arrived from other former colonies such as Trinidad, Guyana, Fiji, Mauritius, South Africa, Uganda, and Tanzania.

Thus, by the 1990s, Hindu communities across North America increasingly represented a diversity of experiences, traditions, languages, and migration histories. Shaiva Tamils from Sri Lanka, for example, utilize different kinds of spaces and practices of worship than Arya Samajists from Trinidad, or Punjabi devotees of Ram, even though each group would call themselves "Hindu." Hindu temples and religious communities, particularly in larger urban centres like Montreal, Toronto, and Vancouver, were now trying to accommodate diverse groups of practitioners. Vasudha Narayanan writes that in thinking about Hindu communities, "a general rule of thumb in North America is that the smaller the geographic area under consideration, the more inclusive the group" (2006, 661). In larger urban centres, increased diversity has led to the establishment of temples organized around particular sectarian, linguistic, or ethnic communities. Participation in this type of temple community is generally predicated on being an insider to an ethno-linguistic group, or a willingness to commit to the principles of a particular sect.[8] Still, some of the oldest and most well-established Hindu temples in North America have maintained an intersectarian approach. In a study of Hindus in the US, Prema Kurien (2007) describes how, seeing a need to draw in and represent diverse sects of Hindus in a context in which they were already a minority, Hindu temples and community organizations in the US became more "ecumenical." A similar development has been documented in Canada by Paul Younger (2012). But while congregationalism is a unique feature of diasporic Hinduism, it can also lead to a flattening of differences, the production of an "official Hinduism," and an increased marginalization of those whose practices, beliefs, or politics do not find an affinity in this manufactured mainline Hindu community.[9]

In Canada, relations between Hindus and other ethnic and religious groups are also mediated in a number of ways by the discourse of multiculturalism, and the notion of "preserving and enhancing" heritage practices through state intervention.[10] Because of the official policy of multiculturalism and the perception of Canada as a welcoming place for immigrants and refugees, patterns of Hindu migration and inclusion have developed somewhat differently than in the US. Canada's very large population of Eelam Tamil Hindu refugees from Sri Lanka's civil war and sizeable Indo-Caribbean population are examples of these differential patterns. Political advocacy tends to cohere around cultural or linguistic groups, or around a pan-South Asian identity. Hindus in Canada, as in the US, benefit from a "model minority" discourse, but Canadian multiculturalism also constructs Hindu religion as compatible with the perceived liberalism of "Canadian norms." There is no significant national Hindu advocacy organization in Canada, though small-scale local efforts have reflected a politics similar to the Hindutva organizations of the US. This is most recently visible in the Hindu-led campaigns against Muslim prayer spaces in Mississauga, Ontario schools (Bascaramurty and Alphonso 2017).

The latter case also illuminates one of the key differences in Hindu organizing and social identity in Canada. The Hindus involved in these campaigns argued that as a community of "good Canadians," they would never ask for the kinds of accommodations that observant

Muslims might request. The implication is that Hinduism is a religion that is compatible with multicultural life in a way that Islam is not. While this is an example of ultra-conservative Hindu thinking in Canada, other Hindu voices also portray Hinduism as consistent with liberal, pluralist views. For example, the grounds of the Vishnu Mandir in Toronto, one of Canada's oldest Hindu temples, contains a "peace garden" with a memorial to Canadian soldiers alongside a statue of Mahatma Gandhi. In this way, Hindu Canadian politics tends to orient Hindus as the ideal subjects of multiculturalism, while other groups (Indigenous, Muslim, and Black) are unfairly benefiting from, or abusing, state benevolence.

A significant but under-studied issue among diasporic Hindus is the problem of caste. In a study of South Asians working in Western Canada, Nishant Upadhyay writes extensively about how upper-caste Hindus are conceived as the normative South Asian subject in Canada; what is recognizable about Hindu religiosity – temples, yoga, deities – are markers of *savarna* or caste-Hindu practices that are not available to Dalit people (Upadhyay 2016). The dominance of these forms of Hindu South Asian-ness renders invisible Dalits and members of other marginalized South Asian communities in Canada. Differences of caste are often intelligible to Hindus and other South Asians through surnames. In temple communities, caste differences are often not discussed, but community members' names may still play a role in people's status within the community.[11] While little data on this social issue exists in the Canadian setting, a recent report by the US-based Equality Labs ("Caste in the United States: A Survey of Caste among South Asian Americans," 2018) suggests that caste-based discrimination among South Asians in the diaspora is a significant issue. While upper-caste Hindus in diaspora may claim to have moved "beyond" caste, the report shows that it is still a social reality for those from Dalit and oppressed-caste communities. In their study, Upadhyay shows how caste-based conceptions of social hierarchy and superiority among the South Asians are intermeshed with discriminatory attitudes towards Indigenous people in Canada. Thus, to return to where I began this section, the debates of the early twentieth century regarding South Asian Hindus' proximity to whiteness and their distance from Indigenous people of Turtle Island/North America are echoed in present social relations. The perception of Hindus as a model minority diaspora group is underpinned by social hierarchies that circulate through South Asian and Canadian colonial histories.

WOMEN AND HINDU COMMUNITY IN CANADA

There is limited research on Hindu women in Canada and the US. Some of the earliest studies in the 1980s and 1990s deal with immigrant women's health and social inclusion. In Canada, studies by Vanaja Dhruvarajan (1993) and Anne Pearson (1996) were among the first to focus on Hindu women and practices of religiosity. Vasudha Naryanan's work on Hinduism in America has been critical in developing this area of study in the US (2006). Bandana Purkayastha and Anjana Narayan (2009) have collected reflections from South Asian Hindu women in the US on experiences of religion, identity, and social issues. A recent chapter by Anne Pearson and Preeti Nayak (2016) about Hindu women in Canada explores some of the contrasts between first- and second-generation perceptions of Hinduism and experiences of settlement in Canada, focusing on family life. One of the most extensive studies of contemporary Hindu women in Canada comes as part of a study of second-generation youth presented in the volume *Growing Up Canadian: Hindus, Buddhists, Muslims* (Beyer and Ramji 2013). As part of this project, Nancy Nason-Clark and Cathy Holtmann (2013) analyze the data collected about second-generation Hindu women and their perceptions and experiences of Hindu religion and religiosity.

Both the *Growing Up Canadian* project and the essay by Pearson and Nayak present similar arguments that settlement in Canada has created opportunities for younger women to explore religion individually and independently; adopt hybrid or interfaith perspectives on religion; and critique traditional practices, including those which appear patriarchal in nature. In both studies, many of the second-generation women did not see themselves as especially religious in a traditional sense, and expressed that being in Canada facilitates possibilities that might not have existed for their mother's generation "back home." But at the same time, in their conclusion, Nason-Clark and Holtmann write:

> Some women were critical of what they perceived as a lack of depth in their family's religious practice. In their opinion, if they did not really understand what they were doing, how authentic could it be?
>
> While all of the women interviewed had learned about Hinduism primarily at home, none of them mentioned the

> pandits at their local temples as sources of information. If a significant proportion of the 39 women who took part in the study were only moderately engaged or unengaged in their Hindu religious world but indicated that later on, perhaps once they get married and have children, they would become more engaged and interested in teaching their children about the faith – where would they turn for answers and guidance? (2013, 163)

There are two striking features of this passage that I would like to highlight. The first is the women's critical view of the diasporic religious community, and the suggestion that they might turn instead to their own research for answers to religious questions. The second is the reflection that marriage and children are seen by the women as something of an inevitability, and that child-rearing necessitates an increased awareness of religiosity. Despite their critical perspectives, the young women in these studies – university students in scientific and professional fields, with expectations of heteronormative marriage and family life – also represent a fairly normative cohort of Hindu women in diaspora. If women in this conventional, middle-class group express this sense of disconnection from religious community, how might more marginalized women experience it? In particular, I am interested in the kinds of questions raised by women whose feminist political perspectives or gender or sexual identities might bring them into conflict with normative family and community views.

THE FRAGILITY OF "SOUTH ASIAN" IDENTITY

The interviews I draw upon here are part of a larger project on Hindu religiosity in radical social justice spaces. In the invitation to participants, I indicated that I was looking for South Asians who are part of radical, social justice-oriented, feminist, queer and/or QTBIPOC organizing spaces, who draw on or use religious or spiritual ideas and practices associated with Hinduism in their work or personal life. I sought participants for the project through word of mouth, working from my own community contacts. While the participants in the broader project include men and gender non-binary and non-conforming people in the US and Canada, in this chapter I focus on a set of participants who identify as women and as feminists, and are based in Canada. The twelve women discussed here were interviewed in 2016 and early 2017. Interviews were completed by phone, Skype, or email, following a structured list of open-ended questions.

The women in the sample range in age from twenty-two to forty-seven at the time of the interviews. As a group, they wear many hats, and sometimes several at the same time: four are health practitioners, and five are full-time community organizers or researchers. Three work in the arts, and three are teachers. In addition to these commitments, three are also graduate students, and one an undergraduate student – all in gender studies or humanities-based disciplines. Most of the women were based in Toronto or Montreal, but several had also lived in other Canadian cities. Their family migration histories connect them to five different South Asian languages and many countries around the world. All of the women were born into Hindu families though many of the women resisted this identity themselves, for reasons I will discuss later in the chapter. Almost all of the women were from savarna or caste-Hindu families. Some of the women described their childhood homes as working class. Having been raised with Hindu practices in various ways, the women I interviewed have developed different sorts of personal relationships with religion and spirituality in their adult lives.

I began each interview by asking the participants to talk about their relationship with social justice, feminist, and activist work in order to better understand how each participant viewed the importance of these politics in their lives. The women all identified as feminist, though some indicated that they had an uneasy relationship with this term because of its association with white liberal feminist politics. For example, RN,[12] an artist whose parents came to Canada as refugees from Sri Lanka, told me, "I still struggle to use the word feminist … I would usually use something like Tamil or brown or South Asian feminist before that or woman of colour. So I never use feminist as a word on its own." Some participants were hesitant to call themselves "activists," though the actions and commitment to social issues that they described might typically be understood as activist in nature. For others, notably the older women in the sample, activism was an important part of their identity, and they used the term to refer to a variety of actions and interventions.[13]

All of the women, in varying degrees, indicated that they felt disconnected from or unwelcome in traditional cultural and religious spaces in the diaspora.[14] For some, it was a direct result of their political views, gender, or sexual identity. TS, an undergraduate student organizer, told me, "I often feel out of place. I am often told that I am too liberal for the Tamil community … I find it difficult to balance myself in between both cultures." MS, a mixed-race queer woman born in Canada, said that growing up she was "seen as too outspoken, too political, too independent" to really be welcomed in her local Bengali community.

This sense of non-belonging was described by most participants in relation to the particular ethnolinguistic community of their families, but for some it also extended into the subcultural space of South Asian community organizing. TS and RN, both Eelam Tamil, problematized "South Asian" as a category that they felt they did not quite fit into. Similarly, JP, a queer woman who came to Canada from Guyana with her family, described feeling disconnected from various diaspora communities: "I actually don't see myself as part of the Guyanese community here and neither do I see myself as part of the South Asian diaspora community here." Her comments are a reminder of the complexity of framing configurations of "South Asian" and "Hindu" diaspora.

In Canada, particularly in urban centres like Toronto and Montreal, "South Asian" has become a category of social identification that has allowed diasporic people to navigate community inclusion and exclusion. As a category, it acts as the basis of a broad cultural coalition among Hindus, Muslims, Sikhs, and Buddhists of South Asian ancestry. This has been an important term for social organizing: for some women I spoke with, as in the example from RN above, "South Asian" was an enabling category. But embracing it can also necessitate a rejection of the "religious" in favour of the "cultural." Interviewing Pakistani Muslim youth in Toronto as part of a larger project on "South Asian" as an identity category, Sutama Ghosh observes that, "by avoiding practices that would inflict upon them certain conservatisms, the youth consciously embody and publicly express only benign aspects of the 'South Asian' culture, stripped of any religiously based normative practices" (2013, 47). These youth, argues Ghosh, resist public indicators of religiosity even when they might engage it privately; the experience of Islamophobia led to a perceived need to project a secular, non-religious group identity that cannot be misread as "fundamentalist."

The term "South Asian" is similarly employed by Hindus in diaspora as a non-religious identity claim to avoid being read by others as religiously conservative or Hindutva-oriented, and therefore in conflict with Muslim or Sikh peers.[15] "South Asian" then can refer to a particular kind of activist organizing space that centres secular identities, and some Hindus use it as an alternative identity claim (Rahemtullah 2012). For this reason, some of the women chose South Asian or even "brown" as an identity claim that allowed them to acknowledge affinities with other ethnic and religious groups.

This affinity comes with a great deal of negotiation across differences of race, ethnicity, and religion, and solidarities can be fragile. "South Asian" has been the basis for much secular social justice organizing (Shakir 2008; Sundar 2008; Ghosh 2013). But it has also, perhaps too often, become a proxy term for "Indian" and Hindu, the identities most predominantly associated with South Asians as an ethnic group. For this reason, some activist women from communities already marginalized within this coalition, such as Eelam Tamils or Indo-Caribbean people, may resist "South Asian" as an identity claim even though they might otherwise have a political affinity with it.

CLAIMING AND REFUSING HINDU IDENTITY

If navigating "cultural" identity claims is a struggle, religious identity is a deeply complex issue for the women I spoke with. All of the participants in this study engage in some way with "Hindu" or Hindu-adjacent forms of religiosity in their everyday lives – primarily, this takes the form of engagement with yoga, meditation, and chanting, but for some it also includes the maintenance of a home puja altar or visits to a local temple. However, when I asked each participant if they would identify themselves as "Hindu," six of the twelve resolutely said no (one participant said "Hell no!"). This refusal was often linked with political positionalities around "Hinduism": "Over the years, as I have learned more and more about the violence embedded in the Hindu stories with which I grew up (courtesy of comic books!) toward Indigenous people, and as my anti-casteist views have made so much unpalatable, I will never ever actually identify as a Hindu, while at the same time, I try to take responsibility/ accountability for what my last name, my family history and so much more represents" (MS, forty-seven, community activist). For AK, a queer woman who lived in the Middle East as a child before eventually emigrating to Canada, a reticence to claim Hinduism for herself was connected with perceptions of Hindus in global context: "There is enough kind of messiness

I think, that comes with this idea of Hinduism that makes me also want to keep my distance ... I just kind of think about fundamentalism. That's kind of like a very quick thing, like I hear Hinduism and I think Hindu fundamentalism." PS (thirty-one, researcher) described "Hindu" as a "default identity," but one that she increasingly does not claim: "On a form I might check it off because it's convenient or I'll say other or no religion or something. So, but increasingly, especially as I see what Hinduism is doing and the ways it's being mobilized, I really distance myself more and more from it."

I asked the participants if they felt that the category "Hindu" was capacious enough to have space for them, their perspectives, and their commitments. RN said that she recognized Hindu identity as important for her community: "Sri Lanka Tamils identify as Hindu or come from a Hindu tradition and so maintaining that I think is also part of a refugee experience too ... So I also see the political nature of holding on to religion or faith as part of a minority or a displaced or dispersed community as well." But despite the political significance of Hindu identity for diasporic Tamils, RN remained ambivalent about Hindu identity for herself: "I think a lot of my beliefs do resonate ... [but] I still don't know if that would convince me enough to identify with it ... But I definitely see how elements of what I consider to be my spirituality or my spiritual practice do coincide or intersect with things that are included in Hinduism. I think there is a place for me in there, I just don't know if I would still say I'm Hindu."

Other participants who identified as Hindu described their relationship with this identity as one of tension or ambivalence, often linked to relations with family and community. DL described herself as "culturally" Hindu and expressed difficulty with rejecting the term: "I don't think there is really any defense of Hinduism that would work with my political commitments, but I don't think it's as simple as a disavowal, because I have to negotiate these things with my extended family all the time." OS (forty-two, academic) also talked about connections to family: "I feel like I strategically identify as a Hindu sometimes, but I have difficulty with this term. I'm not sure what is left in Hinduism for me after I take out all the things that bother me about caste and gender inequality and systemic violence. But it is also the tradition of my grandmothers and my ancestors. So I feel like I need to hold on to it in some way, but there is also a lot that I want to fight against." CA talked about the perception of diasporic Hinduism as a more conservative form of religion: "I've seen

Hinduism in a very complex way knowing that at its roots it can actually be a very open faith but how it's practised in the West is very different, [practised by] by a Hindu middle class. It becomes a normalizing force within, you know, when you're in a non-dominant culture." For CA, the diasporic community's rigid conservativism did not reflect her broader philosophical understanding of Hinduism.

In contrast to some of the participants I have discussed here, JP, a queer Indo-Caribbean twenty-six-year-old student, felt strongly about claiming Hindu identity for herself. But she described some concerns about publicly acknowledging this identity:

> I think I am very afraid actually that … I don't know, there's a lot of right-wing Hindutva stuff from India, right, and I'm afraid that my experiences will be interpreted through that lens … a lot of folks I've met when I say I'm Hindu, they automatically assume that what I mean is that that sort of politics and those sort of principles and those sort of religious norms and behaviour, that's where I'm coming from … But a lot of those things got read onto me by virtue of saying the word Hindu … I struggle, I struggle with this right now because in the sense that I've always felt so much love and belonging in Hinduism as a child and I still continue to. I still feel, if I were to answer your question, actually I find belonging in Hinduism as opposed to a community.

When I asked her to elaborate on this last thought, JP distinguished between "Hinduism" as a spiritual practice, and "Hindu community" as a space she struggled to find belonging within as a queer Indo-Caribbean woman. She described a time that she was told to leave a temple by a Hindu priest after she approached him to ask questions about religious attitudes towards queer people. Even framed hypothetically, her question was enough to justify her immediate exclusion.

BELONGING, QUEERNESS, AND INTENTIONAL COMMUNITY

For all the participants in my study, feeling excluded or unsafe in cultural and religious diaspora spaces as feminist women was a common experience, but it was different in some critical ways for the seven queer participants. Only two of them said they would also identify as Hindu; in contrast, three of five straight participants said they were comfortable with this identity. For JP, a queer woman who expressed a desire to feel at home in diaspora community, being excluded was a source of some anguish, anger, and frustration. She described the "emotional and mental work" involved in being in community spaces, such as a neighbourhood Caribbean restaurant, with her girlfriend, and having to be careful not to touch each other. For others, some distance from the mainstream diaspora community is necessary and productive. AK, who like JP came to Canada on her own as a young adult, described a degree of freedom as a queer woman who is not tied to the local Hindu community: "I live in a city where I don't have the pressures of family and close community, you know, and I think that allows me a degree of flexibility and independence that not everyone has access to."

Much attention is paid in diaspora studies research to feelings of belonging (Braziel and Mannur 2003). Studies of diasporic religion often emphasize the ways that religious community can facilitate a feeling of belonging and homeland affinity in those who are perceived as "outsiders" (Kokot, Tölölyan, and Alfonso 2004; Hausner and Garnett 2015; Lee and Woo 2016). But the comments of the women in my study reflect a central problem underlying this chapter: what happens when you are an outsider as a diasporic, racialized minority, but you are also an outsider to that very diasporic community?

The narrative of diasporic belonging is challenged by people who remain marginalized within normative diaspora formations and fall outside of heteronormative conventions; those who are at the boundaries of the diasporic community and also at the margins of the community at large. Queer people in diasporic communities experience this particular form of marginalization in a number of ways. Rinaldo Walcott (2007; 2015) writes about the formation of a kind of "queer black diaspora," where queer-identified Black people find affinities with each other that transcend narratives of national belonging within particular communities, and find belonging in the shared experience of isolation or rejection by those communities.

In the South Asian diaspora, this kind of community formation on the basis of queer affinity rather than along religious or ethnic divisions is a form of resistance to diasporic narratives of cultural (and sexual) purity. Gopinath writes that "a queer diaspora mobilizes questions of the past, memory, and nostalgia for radically different purposes ... queer diasporic cultural forms work against the violent effacements that produce the fictions of purity that lie at the heart of dominant nationalist and diasporic ideologies" (2005, 4). This is very much reflected among the study participants, many of whom described how they felt that they didn't quite belong in "the community" – meaning mainstream Hindu, South Asian, or ethnolinguistic diasporic communities.

Each participant suggested that "belonging" for them was more often conceptualized through "chosen" communities of allies, and this was particularly important in the cases of queer participants, for whom family and community ties were often fraught. CA and MS, both in their forties, recalled queer South Asian spaces such as the Desh Pardesh festival[16] as creating a sense of belonging among others on the diasporic margins, for what MS calls "a home away from home."

> It was indescribably important to be in connection with folks who were brown, queer, deeply political and so much fun. (MS)

> Do I belong in the mainstream South Asian middle-class Hindu Punjabi community? Probably not because who I am and my ideas are so different. Do I belong in the communities in Toronto that are carved out of queer, progressive … you know, non-normative community? Yes! (CA, forty-six, community organizer)

Participants in their twenties and thirties and those who grew up outside of Toronto did not experience Desh Pardesh, but described the importance of other similar spaces for queer and social justice-oriented community. Several participants talked about connecting with intentional communities around sexual, racial, or political identities. For some this also overlapped with South Asian, Tamil, or Indo-Caribbean identities, but for others, like RN and MS, it was also about making connections with Black, Indigenous, and other people of colour doing activist or social justice work. For all the participants, and particularly for those who identify as queer, accessing queer and social justice subcultural spaces and building community with South Asians and other racialized people with similar perspectives was a critical approach to diaspora.

HINDU RELIGIOSITY: GROUNDING, UNDERGROUND

In the interviews, the queer participants and others for whom this kind of intentional political community was important also described resisting normative religious spaces. But despite the resistance against Hinduism as an organized space of religious community, all the participants talked about religiosity in different ways that were connected to their own histories, families, and beliefs. In some cases, it was important for participants to make clear how separate their personal sense of religiosity was from what they understood as "Hinduism." All of the participants engaged in different ways with aspects of Hindu religiosity, though these were often reframed as healing practices that helped them to manage traumatic experiences. To develop these practices, all of the women described processes of learning that did not rely on Hindu priests, temples, or family members. Instead, they described coming to their own understanding of Hinduism through personal study; this often came in the form of reading, taking university courses, attending yoga or meditation classes, and engaging in conversations with friends and allies.

Several participants described a prayer practice linked to pujas, bhajans, or mantras learned as children, or pranayama (breathing) and meditation practice. Some participants described the altar spaces they kept in their own homes. Some of the participants, mainly those who chose to identify as Hindu, also talked about attending temple. Some of the participants engaged in the study of yoga and Ayurveda, and four completed yoga teacher training.

AK, a queer health practitioner who uses yoga and meditation in her practice, told me, "I guess technically I'm Hindu, and my parents are Hindu, and I don't subscribe to any other religion … and I engage in certain rituals, but when I am engaging in those types of rituals I don't necessarily do it with that identification." Similarly, RN a media producer and yoga teacher, told me: "I don't identify as Hindu but I definitely am honest about being raised with many parts of Hinduism and that influencing I guess parts of my spirituality, I would say, but I don't identify as Hindu." RN and AK are among a number of participants who acknowledged a connection between their practices and the traditions they had grown up with, but were cautious about naming, or not naming, themselves or their chosen forms of religiosity as Hindu.

CA noted that her non-South Asian partner, a dedicated yoga practitioner, "is probably more of a Hindu than I am." For her family, yoga and its connections to Sanskrit chanting and meditation is connected in some ways with Hinduism, but is also something distinct: "So it's funny, it's through that association through the yoga that I've probably come closer to you know, a certain kind of Hinduism, um and when I go there [to the yoga centre] I do meditate … I do chants, the kids chat with (my partner) … but I don't think of it as a religious practice so much as a broader spiritual practice."

Among those participants who did identify as Hindu, JP described feeling a strong connection between diasporic ancestry and her own forms of religious expression. JP described keeping an altar in her home with images of Hindu deities that are important to her. She prays regularly each day, often using Sanskrit prayers learned as a child. Her perspective was different from some other participants, perhaps because she had also experienced exclusion as an Indo-Caribbean woman in some South Asian community spaces. She described her Hindu religiosity as directly connected to feeling grounded and belonging to something larger than herself: "I see my practice as being connected to Hinduism. Actually, the way I think about it is being connected to a legacy, and that is very important to me in terms of feeling connected to, like, my ancestors or feeling connected to a space and a place that maybe in reality I won't be connected to. Because if we think about belonging, so much of belonging and non-belonging is about not finding groundedness in any way. So with Hinduism, it grounds me in something, somewhere, in an imaginative sense." This notion of groundedness emerged in other discussions of the connections between family, ancestry, and religious spaces. TS, an Eelam Tamil woman whose family experienced trauma as refugees, said: "I feel that it gives me a sense of peace when things feel overwhelming and a sense of community when I go to the events together with my family." TS noted that although she does not always feel welcome or accepted in her community, the experience of going to the temple or community events is important for her well-being. For some participants, the connection with family and community through participation in religious ritual was important for their sense of identity and well-being despite the feelings of exclusion. DL described participation in some Hindu religious activities as necessary to maintaining any connection to her family, even if she "disagrees with them on religious and political grounds." But she also explained that these religious activities were not the ones that reflected her own sense of spirituality; her own religiosity includes a daily meditation practice.

Like TS and DL, other participants described various strategies for taking what they needed from the spiritual or religious practices and spaces to which they had access. MS talked about making space for her own self in community religious spaces that are not welcoming to her as an unmarried woman, let alone a queer woman in polyamorous relationships: "During the pujas held in community, I usually give *anjali* in the name of my lovers and the kids I helped raise and other family I have chosen, which is my way of seeming to participate, but on my own terms. I often shake my head at the mostly silent queering/re-naming." As she describes in her reflection, this act of making a space for herself as a queer woman is "mostly silent," and not necessarily visible or intelligible to others. It is a strategy that allows her to bring some of herself into the practice, a way of claiming ground.

RELIGIOSITY AS ACTIVISM AND COMMUNITY ENGAGEMENT

Participation in certain forms of religiosity, particularly yoga, meditation, and Sanskrit chanting, was discussed by several participants. Four of the twelve participants (AK, NS, GN, RN) had trained as yoga teachers; all four also work as alternative health practitioners in various fields. For several other participants, including CA, DL, and MS, yoga and meditation were important everyday practices. But despite a clear commitment to these practices, all of these women described a complicated relationship with yoga's Hindu connection. For some participants, a resistance to identifying their practice as "Hindu" was also complicated by the perception of yoga as a practice that has been appropriated by a consumerist, white culture, or as MS describes, "the shitty hippy ways white folks grabbed onto Indian things." CA pointed out that the yoga community that is a core part of her family routine is dominated more by white Canadians than by Hindus. For some, a hyperawareness of the deracination of modern commercial yoga practice is inescapable: "I go to a studio where all the teachers are white, and pretty much everyone there is white and like you know, that's also the nature of doing it here [in Canada] you know. They pronounce all the Sanskrit words really funny – I laugh inside a little bit. But I really appreciate that form of exercise."

The use of Sanskrit in yoga and prayer spaces was discussed by several participants. NS and GN, both trained yoga teachers, use Sanskrit in their teaching and also in their own personal prayer practice. For CA, Sanskrit chanting is a regular part of her practice. JP also discussed using Sanskrit in her daily prayer routine. AK and

RN both described a more complicated perspective on Sanskrit, yoga, and chanting. Since Sanskrit has a complicated history in South Asia regarding gender and caste restrictions about its study, using this language in South Asian community spaces could be seen as a kind of casteism. It also signifies the valorization of one form of Hindu and South Asian culture. In her teaching, RN explained, "I don't force people to use the Sanskrit words because I am Tamil and using a Sanskrit word doesn't feel right for me as well ... At the same time there are very real reasons to reject English, but I don't have access to any other language." AK noted that she might change her approach depending on the composition of the group with which she was sharing her yoga practice.

Crucially for some participants, spiritual practices were an important site of community development. RN and GN each have a yoga and alternative health practice that prioritizes working with Black, Indigenous, and racialized women and queer people. RN also told me about her commitment to teaching yoga to newcomer women and women in social housing. For these practitioners, community building around social justice principles is connected to a practice of healing that transcends conventional community boundaries defined by belonging as "Hindu" or even as "South Asian." AK described how her yoga practice, as a learner and as a teacher, allows her to practice a form of solidarity with other people of colour. "For me, healing justice is about having access to care, well-being, services, and looking at barriers to that, whether that's economic or other types of access needs."

Even for those women whose activism is not directly connected to yoga or meditation, there is a strong link between activism and the personal forms of religiosity they describe. CA, for example, explained that her yoga and meditation practice is important for staying "grounded" in her activist work:

> I do feel like a regular yoga practice definitely helps me feel physically much, much better and grounded, which then will enable me to have more energy to do social justice work. The meditation is very good for grounding when I can do it. It's very much a way to find that inner peace and calm and I would say that overall having a yoga practice for the last eleven years has definitely allowed me to have some balance in my life ... the pranayama breathing that comes via the yoga has allowed me to find a sense of balance in life too which I think helps me as an activist.

Although CA was very clear about the importance of these practices for her own well-being, she was equally clear about the need to distinguish between her own yoga practice and the forms of Hindu religiosity she had been raised with.

HINDU RELIGIOSITIES UNDERGROUND

These interviews unearth some important perspectives about diasporic religion, traditional practices, and the desire for resistance and creativity. All of the women in this study emphasized their conception of diaspora as a space for building solidarities. This is reflected in their critiques of mainstream Hinduism as nationalist, casteist, misogynist, homophobic, and anti-Black. It is also represented in the elements that they felt were recoverable or claimable as tools, especially prayer, yoga, altar-making, and meditation, as these are practices of religiosity that can be solitary, but can also be shared as part of a collective healing practice. In both the critique of mainstream Hindu diaspora community and in the discussion of community building, there is an emphasis on making connections with allies in other religious and racial communities. The criticisms the women made of Hindu religiosity concerning racism and casteism were aligned with their experiences of racism and cultural appropriation in Canada. As a group of feminist and queer activists, the ability to make connections across differences is key to supporting social justice, and this commitment is reflected in the forms of Hindu religiosity they have chosen, modified, or adopted.

Even among those women who did not identify as Hindu, there were acknowledged connections between their own practices and Hindu traditions. These connections were sometimes the site of ambivalence, challenge, and critique, but were also important for healing and well-being for all of the women, as ways to feel "grounded" and connected both with themselves and with their chosen communities. Although practices like yoga might be associated in contemporary culture with "mindfulness" or "self-care," the participants recognized the connection of these practices with South Asian ancestry. Many of the participants worked to deepen their own personal understanding of practices and traditions beyond what they might have learned from families or their religious community. Some participants felt that it was really important to distance themselves from normative or "official" Hinduism. Despite sometimes-strong feelings of exclusion from mainstream Hindu community, several participants also felt that continuing some traditional religious or spiritual practices associated with their families, communities, or ancestors was important to them. In different ways, these are all iterations of Hindu religiosity that grow underground.

What enables these emerging forms of religiosity to flourish underground in the diaspora in Canada is not the official policy of multiculturalism and state support of cultural diversity; these have allowed "official" diaspora communities to develop while others have been pushed to the margins. Rather, it has been the particular histories of women of colour activist and feminist and activist organizing, public engagement with advocacy for Canada's Indigenous people, and participation in solidarity networks to resist racism and homophobia that have enriched these women's perspectives on religious community. Through these rhizomatic connections, women are resisting the homogenizing, reductive tendencies of normative diasporic religious community, and are developing new forms of religiosity that reflect the complexity of their diasporic identities, histories, and locations.

NOTES

1 Steven Vertovec uses the terms "official" and "popular" Hinduism (Vertovec 1994, 2000) to distinguish between Hindu religious institutions and practices. "Official" Hinduism refers to large, even transnational organizations with structured leadership; it is state-sanctioned, supported, or complicit; and it claims to speak for Hindus. By contrast, "popular Hinduism" might describe how everyday Hindus actually practise in their own communities.

2 I use this term here in reference to Deleuze and Guattari's concept of the rhizome in *A Thousand Plateaus* (1997). While I do not elaborate on this theoretical framing in this essay, I use it here in relation to the discussion of the Deleuzian concept of assemblage in Jasbir Puar's essay, "I'd Rather Be a Cyborg than a Goddess" (2012).

3 There are a number of essays that discuss South Asian women and political organizing (Bannerji 2000; Thobani 2007), but when religion is discussed, it is primarily as part of cultural and racial identity.

4 Most of the participants are cisgender women. The participant who uses she/her and they/them pronouns uses the word "woman" and notes that they "present as a cis woman." While the study was open to trans women,

gender non-conforming, and genderqueer people, these groups are not represented in the sample. This is a limitation of the study that I would like to explore in further research.

5 One of the challenges of tracking this early phase of migration is that the term "Hindu" (or even "Hindoo") in historical documents refers to any South Asian, including Sikhs and Muslims. The first South Asians on Turtle Island were collectively called Hindus or "Hindoos," though many were in fact Sikh. They settled first on the west coast where many became agricultural labourers; later, some became land and business owners.

6 Among South Asians, it was desirable to be seen as more proximate to the colonizers than to the colonized Indigenous people, Black people, and other racialized groups. In 1923, Bhagat Singh Thind unsuccessfully claimed the right to settle in North America because, as a "high caste Aryan," he should be seen as white. Thind's case hinged on connecting the concept of "high caste Aryan" with "Caucasian," thus mobilizing logics of caste supremacy and white supremacy. A detailed discussion of this case is found in *White by Law: The Legal Construction of Race*, by Ian Haney Lopez (2006).

7 Migrants from British India, Ceylon, and the West Indies tried to enter Canada as British subjects but were effectively barred through the implementation of Canada's white supremacist Continuous Journey policy of 1908 (Hasan et al. 2019). Those who had already settled in western Canada and the US thus encountered much animosity from white settlers who saw them as threatening to the social order for a variety of reasons (Kazimi 2012; Shah 2012). As these communities grew, so did public debate about whether to allow the migration of South Asian women; proponents of a "white Canada" insisted that bringing families would only encourage Asian workers to stay in Canada, rather than supplying a temporary source of labour (Dua 2007).

8 Spina's book *Women's Authority and Leadership in a Hindu Goddess Tradition* (2017) provides a good case study of this kind of community in Canada, the Tamil Adiparasakthi community.

9 Kurien uses "official Hinduism" to describe "the articulation of Hinduism by leaders of organizations that claim to speak for all Hindus" (2007, 9). Since the late 2000s, the Hindu American Foundation has become a prominent "official" voice in the US, issuing press releases on issues of public concern, launching "awareness" campaigns promoting Hindus as a model minority, and defending Hindus from "anti-Hindu" sentiments. An example of this is the California textbook controversy: the HAF and other Hindu groups have demanded changes to the representation of Hindus and India

in public school textbooks, such as the removal of references to caste, and these changes have been challenged by left-wing Hindus and other South Asian organizers and academics (Bose 2008; George 2017). "Official" voices like HAF thus represent political and religious perspectives that are not shared by all Hindus.

10 The Multiculturalism Act affirms that "everyone has the freedom of conscience, religion, thought, belief, opinion, expression, peaceful assembly and association ... the Government of Canada recognizes the diversity of Canadians as regards race, national or ethnic origin, colour and religion as a fundamental characteristic of Canadian society and is committed to a policy of multiculturalism designed to preserve and enhance the multicultural heritage of Canadians while working to achieve the equality of all Canadians in the economic, social, cultural and political life of Canada" (Act, Preamble, 1988).

11 As Virdi shows in this volume, caste-based forms of social discrimination, particularly with regard to marriage, are also maintained among Sikhs in Canada.

12 I have assigned initials at random to each interview participant, rather than using pseudonyms. This is because the politics of Hindu names are complex; assigning a random pseudonym might imply particular positionalities in terms of caste or region that are unintended. Moreover, because the queer and social justice communities are quite small, a further degree of anonymity seemed desirable.

13 It is interesting to note that the women in the sample below the age of thirty-five were much more hesitant to claim an activist identity, and cited a feeling that they were not doing enough to legitimately claim it – though it seemed to very much characterize their work in the community.

14 For many Hindus, "cultural" and "religious" spaces often overlap significantly (Holtmann and Nason-Clark 2013).

15 An earlier term serving a similar function is "Desi." This term is still in use in some communities, but has been rejected in favour of "South Asian" because "Desi" is often seen as entrenched in Indian, Hindu, and Hindi-speaking identities.

16 Desh Pardesh was a South Asian arts festival in Toronto between 1988 and 2001 (Fernandez 2006). The festival has been recognized by activists and academics as a groundbreaking space of queer South Asian organizing, and many members of Toronto's South Asian arts and activist communities who came of age in the 1990s were connected with it. Although Desh ended in 2001 and no large-scale queer South Asian event has replaced it, other music, dance, and arts events in the city are linked to this history.

REFERENCES

Banerjee, Sikata, and Harold Coward. 2009. "Hindus in Canada: Negotiating Identity in a 'Different' Homeland." In *Religion and Ethnicity in Canada*, edited by Paul Bramadat and David Seljak, 30–51. Toronto: University of Toronto Press.

Bannerji, Himani. 2000. "The Paradox of Diversity: The Construction of a Multicultural Canada and 'Women of Color.'" *Women's Studies International Forum* 23, no. 5: 537–60. https://doi.org/10.1016/S0277-5395(00)00130-8.

Bascaramurty, Dakshana, and Caroline Alphonso. 2017. "A Community Divided: The Fight over Canadian Values Threatens to Boil over in Peel." *Globe and Mail*, 28 April 2017. https://www.theglobeandmail.com/news/toronto/a-community-divided-the-fight-over-canadian-values-threatens-to-boil-over-inpeel/article34852452/.

Beyer, Peter, and Rubina Ramji. 2013. *Growing up Canadian: Muslims, Hindus, Buddhists*. Montreal and Kingston: McGill-Queen's University Press.

Bose, Purnima. 2008. "Hindutva Abroad: The California Textbook Controversy." *The Global South* 2, no. 1: 11–34.

Braziel, Jana Evans, and Anita Mannur, eds. 2003. *Theorizing Diaspora: A Reader*. 1st edition. Malden, MA: Wiley-Blackwell.

"Caste in the United States: A Survey of Caste among South Asian Americans." 2018. Equality Labs. 2018. https://www.equalitylabs.org/caste-survey-read.

Dhruvarajan, Vanaja. 1993. "Ethnic Cultural Retention and Transmission among First Generation Hindu Asian Indians in a Canadian Prairie City." *Journal of Comparative Family Studies* 24, no. 1: 63–79.

Dua, Enakshi. 2007. "Exclusion through Inclusion: Female Asian Migration in the Making of Canada as a White Settler Nation." *Gender, Place and Culture* 14, no. 4: 445–66. https://doi.org/10.1080/09663690701439751.

George, Varghese K. 2017. "Controversial U.S. Textbooks Get Nod." *The Hindu*, 10 November 2017. https://www.thehindu.com/news/international/controversial-us-textbooks-get-nod/article20109769.ece.

Ghosh, Sutama. 2013. "'Am I a South Asian, Really?' Constructing 'South Asians' in Canada and Being South Asian in Toronto." *South Asian Diaspora* 5, no. 1: 35–55. https://doi.org/10.1080/19438192.2013.724913.

Gopinath, Gayatri. 2005. *Impossible Desires: Queer Diasporas and South Asian Public Cultures*. Durham, NC: Duke University Press.

Hasan, Nadia, Sailaja Krishnamurti, Omme-Salma Rahemtullah, Nayani Thiyagarajah, and Nishant Upadhyay. 2019. "Brown Bodies, Borders, and Boats: Reading Tamil 'Irregular Arrivals' through the History of the Komagata Maru." In *Unmooring The Komagata Maru: Charting Colonial Trajectories*, edited by Rita Dhamoon, Davina Bhandar, Renisa Mawani, and Satwinder Kaur Bains, 121–40. Vancouver: University of British Columbia Press.

Hausner, Sondra L., and Jane Garnett, eds. 2015. *Religion in Diaspora: Cultures of Citizenship*. London: Palgrave Macmillan.

Kazimi, Ali. 2012. *Undesirables: White Canada and the Komagata Maru: An Illustrated History*. Vancouver: Douglas and McIntyre.

Kim, Hanna. 2010. "Public Engagement and Personal Desires: BAPS Swaminarayan Temples and Their Contribution to the Discourses on Religion." *International Journal of Hindu Studies* 13, no. 3: 357–90. https://doi.org/10.1007/s11407-010-9081-4.

Kokot, Waltraud, Khachig Tölölyan, and Carolin Alfonso. 2004. *Diaspora, Identity, and Religion: New Directions in Theory and Research*. London: Routledge. http://www.loc.gov/catdir/toc/ecip049/2003021155.html.

Kurien, Prema. 2007. *A Place at the Multicultural Table: The Development of an American Hinduism*. New Brunswick, NJ: Rutgers University Press.

Lee, Becky R., and Terry Tak-ling Woo, eds. 2016. *Canadian Women Shaping Diasporic Religious Identities*. Studies in Women and Religion/Études sur les femmes et la religion 13. Waterloo, ON: Wilfrid Laurier University Press.

Lopez, Ian Haney. (1997) 2006. *White by Law: The Legal Construction of Race*. 10th anniversary edition. New York: NYU Press.

Narayan, Anjana, and Bandana Purkayastha. 2009. *Living Our Religions: Hindu and Muslim South Asian American Women Narrate Their Experiences*. Sterling, VA: Kumarian Press.

Narayanan, Vasudha. 2006. "Hinduism in North America: Including Emerging Issues." In *Encyclopedia of Women and Religion in North America*, edited by Rosemary Skinner Keller and Rosemary Radford Ruether. Indiana University Press. https://muse.jhu.edu/chapter/391608.

Pearson, Anne Mackenzie. 1996. *Because It Gives Me Peace of Mind: Ritual Fasts in the Religious Lives of Hindu Women*. McGill Studies in the History of Religions. Albany: State University of New York Press.

Pearson, Anne, and Preeti Nayak. 2016. "Being Hindu in Canada: Experiences of Women." In *Canadian Women Shaping Diasporic Religious Identities*, edited by Becky R. Lee and Terry Tak-ling Woo, reprint edition, 269–300. Waterloo, ON: Wilfrid Laurier University Press.

Puar, Jasbir K. 2012. "'I Would Rather Be a Cyborg than a Goddess': Becoming-Intersectional in Assemblage Theory." *PhiloSOPHIA* 2, no. 1: 49–66.

Rahemtullah, Omme-Salma. 2012. "Bollywood in Da Club: Social Space in Toronto's 'South Asian' Community." In *The Magic of Bollywood: At Home and Abroad*, edited by Anjali Gera Roy, 234–53. New Delhi: Sage Publications India.

Shah, Nayan. 2012. *Stranger Intimacy: Contesting Race, Sexuality and the Law in the North American West*. Berkeley: University of California Press.

Shakir, Uzma. 2008. "Demystifying Transnationalism: Canadian Immigration Policy and the Promise of Nation Building." In *Organizing the Transnational: Labour, Politics, and Social Change*, edited by Luin Goldring and Sailaja Krishnamurti, 67–82. Vancouver: University of British Columbia Press.

Spina, Nanette R. 2017. *Women's Authority and Leadership in a Hindu Goddess Tradition*. London: Palgrave Macmillan.

Sundar, Aparna. 2008. "South Asia Left Democratic Alliance: Dillemmas of a Transnational Left." In *Organizing the Transnational: Labour, Politics, and Social Change*, edited by Luin Goldring and Sailaja Krishnamurti, 206–14. Vancouver: University of British Columbia Press.

Thobani, Sunera. 2007. *Exalted Subjects: Studies in the Making of Race and Nation in Canada*. Toronto and Buffalo: University of Toronto Press.

Upadhyay, Nishant. 2016. "'We'll Sail Like Columbus': Race, Indigeneity, Settler Colonialism, and the Making of South Asian Diasporas in Canada." PhD dissertation, York University. https://yorkspace.library.yorku.ca/xmlui/handle/10315/32688.

Vertovec, Steven. 1994. "'Official' and 'Popular' Hinduism in Diaspora: Historical and Contemporary Trends in Surinam, Trinidad and Guyana." *Contributions to Indian Sociology* 28, no. 1: 123–47. https://doi.org/10.1177/006996694028001005.

– 2000. *The Hindu Diaspora: Comparative Patterns*. London: Routledge.

Walcott, Rinaldo. 2007. "Homopoetics: Queer Space and the Black Queer Diaspora." In *Black Geographies and the Politics of Place*, edited by Katherine McKittrick and Clyde Adrian Woods, 233–46. Toronto: Between the Lines.

– 2015. "Foreword." In *Disrupting Queer Inclusion: Canadian Homonationalisms and the Politics of Belonging*, edited by OmiSoore H. Dryden and Suzanne Lenon, vii–x. Vancouver: University of British Columbia Press.

Younger, Paul. 2012. "Hindus." In *The Religions of Canadians*, edited by Jamie S. Scott, 219–60. Toronto: University of Toronto Press.

3

Writing Home

Diaspora, Identity, and Religion in *Halfbreed* and *In Search of April Raintree*

Ken Derry

LITERATURE, IDENTITY, APPROACH

In this essay I consider questions of diaspora, identity, and religion in Maria Campbell's *Halfbreed* and Beatrice Mosionier's *In Search of April Raintree.*[1] More specifically, my aim is to show the ways in which I have come to see these texts by Métis women as implicating colonial religion in the diasporic situation of Indigenous people in Canada, and conversely pointing to Indigenous religions – and writings – as critical to the process of recovering a sense of home.

Together, the two books by Campbell and Mosionier comprise the foundation of modern Indigenous literature in Canada, and are critical to conversations about modern Indigenous *women* in Canada. In making this statement I do not mean at all to suggest that there are no critical differences between Métis and other Indigenous peoples, or between various Métis peoples themselves. There is, in fact, tremendous – and tremendously important – diversity among and between these various communities.[2] This diversity is evident when comparing *Halfbreed* and *In Search of April Raintree.* Maria Campbell is part of (and was raised among) the Red River Métis in Manitoba, and in her book she traces this ancestry through the history of her people, and her own repeated interactions with Métis communities (Adese 2016). On the other hand, Beatrice Mosionier, like her protagonist April, was separated from her parents and grew up in non-Indigenous foster homes, with no relation to other Métis people or family members. Nêhiyaw-Métis author and scholar Emma LaRocque asserts in this regard that April and her sister Cheryl "clearly do not have Red River Cree-Métis cultural identity," and so she has "found it troublesome that non-Métis critics use [Mosionier's] novel as a standard of defining the Métis" (2002, 222–3). When looking at Métis literature *as* Métis literature, then, it is crucial "to ask questions about *how* the authors are Métis" (Adese 2016, 59). Keeping this point in mind, my focus in this essay is not on *Halfbreed* and *April Raintree* as examples or representations of specifically Métis literature or identity. Instead I am concerned with these texts as they are critical in the development of "Indigenous literature" in Canada broadly, however that category might be understood.[3]

Campbell's text is generally considered to be centrally responsible for inspiring in 1973 the rapid proliferation of Indigenous writing that has been going on in Canada for over forty-five years (Acoose 1993b). *Halfbreed* has been called "the most important ... book authored by a Native person from Canada" (Lutz 1991, 41). It is in this respect that Chippewa author/storyteller Lenore Keeshig-Tobias and Delaware-Tuscarora poet/playwright Daniel David Moses refer to Campbell as "The Mother Of Us All" (Keeshig-Tobias 1991, 83). Published ten years after *Halfbreed*, *In Search of April Raintree* became similarly vital in the emergence of "a uniquely Aboriginal form of literature" (Young-Ing 1993, 183). It is also the first Indigenous literary work in Canada to have a critical edition (Suzack 1999, 2). According to Métis scholar Jo-Ann Episkenew, a significant number of Indigenous writers have said that Mosionier's text "influenced their literary development more than any other work of literature" – with the single exception, she notes, of *Halfbreed* (Thom [a.k.a. Episkenew] 1999, 295).

As influential as these texts have been for Indigenous writers and critics, however, they have typically been ignored by *non*-Indigenous academics. LaRocque (1990), for instance, explains that writers like her have generally felt "like they have been speaking into a vacuum ... The lonely echoes of our own words have been amplified by a strange but perhaps predictable colonial phenomenon: white intellectual judgement and shunning of Native intellectuals" (xxii–xxiii). This phenomenon is "predictable," of course, because as LaRocque also notes, "literature is political in that its linguistic and ideological transmission is defined and determined by those in power. This is why Shakespeare rather than Wisakehcha is classified as 'classical' in our school curriculums" (xvi). To put the matter bluntly: Indigenous literature is too often considered inferior, or even "primitive," by white scholars, and therefore unfit for serious study.[4] Such a view both results from, and perpetuates, the larger "colonial myth … of imagined White superiority" – a myth that is countered, as Episkenew argues, by Indigenous literature itself (2009, 2–3).

As someone whose background is Irish, Welsh, and English, and who was raised in the suburbs of Toronto, Canada, I grew up steeped in the colonial myth. Reading these books by Campbell and Culleton – recommended to me by the wonderfully insightful and humane Tamil Canadian literary scholar, Chelva Kanaganayakam – was a profoundly upsetting and destabilizing experience. I was confronted with the ways in which the culture that shaped and supported me committed unspeakable acts of violence against Indigenous people. But of course this violence is only "unspoken" by settler culture itself, and so it is crucial to listen to other voices. Thus Campbell declares at the start of *Halfbreed* that she is writing "for all of you, to tell you what it is like to be a Halfbreed woman in our country" (2).[5] She later told Mosionier that *In Search of April Raintree* will "help a dominant society understand and feel the lives of a people it almost destroyed" (Culleton [1983] 1992, 7). As LaRocque points out more generally, "both white and Native communities are implicated" in Indigenous literature, and so "both are invited to hear" (1990, xxix). In a similar spirit, Episkenew affirms: "Indigenous literature reaches out to settler communities to advance social justice, to heal the wounds of oppression, and to reconcile our communities" (2009, 194).

Métis-Salish author Lee Maracle recently asserted that, when considering a writer's works, the point should never be to try to get inside their head: "In the study of literature, Western instructors often pose the question, 'What was the author thinking, doing, intending?' Salish thinkers and philosophers (orators) regard such questions as invasive, and do not grant themselves the right to ask them, much less answer, in the absence of the author. Such questions are meaningless in terms of the function of story in our society. The point of hearing (and now reading) story is to study it in and of itself" (2007, 55). For Maracle, the invasively Western approach to literature is fundamentally colonial. It is connected to the fact that colonizers have historically "granted themselves the right to claim discovery, and then proceeded to define, delineate, and demarcate the cultural, intellectual, economic, spiritual, and physical being for the entire world" (55). In my discussions of *Halfbreed* and *In Search of April Raintree* below, I have done my best to follow Maracle's advice. Which is to say that I have attempted, as an outsider, to understand these books on their own terms, even while recognizing that there is likely much I will not see, much I may be wrong about. In this respect I have tried to minimize errors in my readings of two texts by Indigenous women in part by listening to scholars and writers who are themselves Indigenous women.[6] I have also tried to bear in mind Lenore Keeshig-Tobias's response to German scholar Hartmut Lutz's question about whether non-Indigenous scholars should write about Indigenous literature. Keeshig-Tobias, who has been a passionate critic of appropriation, makes it clear that she does not make a priori decisions about who should and should not speak about Indigenous people and cultures, but tries to judge on a case-by-case basis: "I think I always give people the benefit of a doubt, first. And if you prove yourself to be [laughs] an arsehole, I'll tell you" (1991, 82).

DIASPORA, COLONIALISM, RELIGION

Originally, "diaspora" referred to the Jewish people being removed from their homeland in Israel. The term has come to include (not without debate) many different groups who in various ways are separated from, and in certain respects look toward, home. Lily Cho observes that despite disagreements over what exactly this word means, "everyone seems to agree that diaspora, in its most basic sense, refers to a scattering of peoples who are nonetheless connected by a sense of a homeland, imaginary or otherwise" (2007, 12). Khachig Tölölyan similarly states that, for people identified as diasporic, "a homeland orientation is usually taken for granted" (2011, 9). In one sense Indigenous people in the Americas do not fit this definition, as broad as it is, because they continue to live on the continent they have always called home. They have, however, inarguably been physically and often violently separated from their original lands within the larger territory of the Americas. They have in fact been *relentlessly* dispossessed of their home by colonial settlers, governments, and militaries. Renate Eigenbrod argues that, for Indigenous people, their very proximity to their original homes enhances rather than diminishes their diasporic situation, as it "produces an acute, tangible, and re-traumatizing daily reminder of their displacement" (2012, 136). Thus many commenters have affirmed, along with Sophie McCall: "There is no doubt that Aboriginal people's experience in Canada has been and continues to be diasporic" (2012, 23; see also Boyarin and Boyarin 2002, 22–3; Clifford 2007; Eigenbrod 2012, 136–40; Fiola 2021; Harvey and Thompson 2005; Smithers 2014, 4–5; cf. Cho 2007, 13; Goeman 2013).[7]

Colonial efforts have also separated Indigenous people from their home traditions, cultures, and languages, creating a different type of diasporic situation. Thus Nêhiyaw scholar Neal McLeod states: "I define the removal of an Indigenous group, in this case the *Nêhiyawak*, from their land as *spatial diaspora* ... I call the alienation from one's stories *ideological diaspora*: this alienation, the removal from the voices and echoes of the ancestors, is the attempt to destroy collective consciousness" (2001, 19). In many ways the ideological diaspora for Indigenous people has been facilitated by the spatial diaspora, given the emphatically locative, place-centred nature of many Indigenous beliefs and practices.[8] Most notoriously, in Canada, Indigenous children were taken from their families by the Canadian government and placed into foster care and/or church-run residential schools. In these schools children were forced to speak only English or French, and to practise only Christianity. The explicit aim of the residential school system was famously articulated with awful clarity in 1920 by Duncan Campbell Scott, deputy superintendent of the Department of Indian Affairs from 1913 to 1932: "I want to get rid of the Indian problem ... Our object is to continue until there is not a single Indian in Canada that has not been absorbed into the body politic and there is no Indian question, and no Indian Department."[9]

The diasporic situation of Indigenous people has been promoted further by the fundamental racism that has supported colonial policies and practices. As Eigenbrod (2012) points out, "their alienation is perpetuated by stereotypes about them so that their spatial diaspora is heightened by an ideological diaspora that not only separates them from their own world views, but also marks them as inferior to the rest of society" (139). This point brings to mind Frantz Fanon's immensely influential 1952 examination of colonial race issues in the Antilles: *Peau noire, masques blancs* (*Black Skin, White Masks*). Fanon focuses on the ways in which colonists set out to refashion Indigenous identity by transforming colonized peoples into images of themselves, and how this effort in turn typically induces a desire *within* the colonized to become like those now in power; they create, that is, a situation in which "the black man wants to be white" ([1952] 1967, 9).

As Eigenbrod's comment intimates, though, there is a critical ambivalence at the heart of this colonial project: the belief that the colonized people are fundamentally inferior to the colonizers. Despite all attempts at assimilation, Indigenous people are always marked in various ways as *lesser than* (Fanon [1952] 1967, 10). Building on Fanon's work, Homi Bhabha (1984) argues that the colonial project is in fact one of transforming Indigenous people into *incomplete* imitations of the colonizers. Colonial desire, then, is "for a reformed, recognizable Other, as *a subject of difference that is almost the same, but not quite*" (126). Bhabha further reworks this understanding into the dictum, "*Almost the same but not white*" (130).[10]

So: the colonization of the Indigenous peoples of the Americas has created a diasporic situation with multiple aspects: they have been alienated from their homeland, from their traditions, and from being treated as equal members of the larger colonial society. In what ways do *Halfbreed* and *In Search of April Raintree* envision that it is possible to move forward from this situation?

In their accounts of various studies of diaspora and religion, both Steven Vertovec (2004) and Paul Johnson (2012) emphasize the importance of keeping the Jewish origins of the term "diaspora" in mind. Doing so impels us to remember that there is a critical difference between two very different historical reasons for the Jewish diaspora: "free movement" of people who chose to leave their homeland, and "involuntary movement due to a conquest of the territory that was/is considered home" (Vertovec 2004, 276). This second reason resonates in obvious ways with the situation of Indigenous people around the world, and it is the one that for Johnson is particularly important for studies of religion: "Revisiting the early theological meaning of diaspora as an inchoate alienation imposed from the beyond … is important since it underlines the origins of Diaspora as a thoroughly religious crisis. One approach to the relation between Religion and Diaspora, then, is to explore Diaspora as a problem that invites various possible religious solutions" (2012, 100). In my reading of *Halfbreed* and *In Search of April Raintree*, Campbell and Mosionier agree with Johnson on this point: religion does in fact offer the prospect of healing some of the wounds inflicted by their diasporic/ colonial situation.

I want to add a quick word of caution here regarding my focus on colonialism in relation to these texts. Commenters have been pointing out for over three decades now that such a focus when discussing Indigenous people can itself be inherently colonial. Cherokee-European author Thomas King, for example, points out that this perspective ends up implicitly defining Indigenous people in *terms* of colonialism, rather than on their own terms (1990; see also Cho 2007, 20; Miller 1991, 323; Trigger 1985, 105). That said, both *Halfbreed* and *In Search of April Raintree* are themselves explicitly concerned with issues of colonialism; bringing this focus to these texts therefore is meant to reflect their interests rather than impose my own. In taking this approach, however, I have tried at all times to recognize the agency of the people involved in these narratives, their existence as whole beings and not simply as colonial subjects. Finally, there is the critical point mentioned by Métis-Anishinaabe-Kwe scholar Chantal Fiola (2021) in her own chapter in this volume, that the communities with which both Campbell and Mosionier identify, the Métis, are themselves a "postcontact Indigenous people" (260). She adds: "The history of the Métis Nation is intricately tied to colonization, dispossession, forced dispersal and relocation, settlement, and policies of segregation, marginalization, and assimilation that continue to impact Métis people, including our relationships with spirituality" (264).

HALFBREED: "WE WHO OWN OURSELVES"

Maria Campbell begins *Halfbreed* with a picture of her old home, and an evocation of absence:

> The house where I grew up is tumbled down and overgrown with brush. The pine tree beside the east window is dried and withered …
>
> The store is still there, old and lonely, looking like the country around it, and, like the people it serves, merely exists. The French owners who came from Quebec are dead and their families are gone. It is as if they were never there.
>
> Grannie Campbell's house is gone. (1)

Campbell builds on this description in her first two chapters as she sketches a history of the Red River Métis, and similarly problematizes the notion of "home" for her people generally. She notes how they were pushed west by settlers, from Ontario and Manitoba to Saskatchewan. In the late 1800s the settlers arrived again and they were removed from the lands on which they had just started to take root, in a cycle that continued for decades. Every home they made was taken from them, until "they drifted back to the road lines and crown lands ... So began a miserable life of poverty which held no hope for the future" (8). Campbell's personal experience in many ways reflects that of her people: throughout *Halfbreed* she is continuously fighting against oppression, struggling with poverty, and searching for a home.

A great deal of Campbell's personal and communal dispossession is precipitated by white Christians who want Natives and "Halfbreeds" to be like them but draw clear lines that are not to be crossed. As Campbell points out, for example, "all our people were Roman Catholic" (28),[11] but when she and her mother try to attend a church for whites they are quickly asked to leave (28). The local priest refuses to perform funeral services for Campbell's mother, a very devout Catholic, because her father forgot to have the Last Sacrament administered before she died (78). And in what essentially amounts to a literal enactment of Homi Bhabha's "not quite/not white" paradigm, non-Native Christians donate their cast-off goods to Campbell's community at Christmas, but then taunt the Métis for wearing their old clothes (27).

Campbell in fact specifically identifies religion as one of the most powerful tools used by colonizers for the oppression and control of Indigenous people in Canada:

> Our people talked against the government, their white neighbours and each other, but never against the church or the priest regardless of how bad they were ... I used to wonder why my mother was not even critical, because surely if a little girl could see the fat priest for what he was, then she could. But she accepted it all as she did so many things because it was sacred and of God. (31–2)

As a child, Campbell hears a teacher point to Indigenous people as examples of those who are "poor in spirit" (61). "Big deal," she retorts in anger. "So us poor Halfbreeds and Indians are to inherit the Kingdom of Heaven, but not till we're dead" (61).[12]

Another key tool of colonialism is communal discord. When Campbell comes home from school after being teased by white kids for eating gophers, she kicks at her mother and says she hates her, and her father, and "all of you no-good Halfbreeds" (50). After this incident, her great-grandmother Cheechum tells her the story of a group of Métis who tried to escape colonial rule by leaving their homes to begin new, free lives:

> but because some of them said, "I want good clothes and horses and you no-good Halfbreeds are ruining it for me," they lost their dream. She continued: "They fought each other just as you are fighting your mother and father today. The white man saw that was a more powerful weapon than anything else with which to beat the Halfbreeds, and he used it and still does today. Already they are using it on you. They try to make you hate your people." (51)

At one point Campbell's father becomes involved in trying to create "a strong united voice that would demand justice for our people" (73). His efforts ultimately fail, Cheechum explains, because some of the (Indigenous) men working with him had been hired by the government, "and that this had caused much fighting among our people, and had divided them" (75).[13] During the early stages of her own political work, Campbell sees this pattern of colonialism-induced conflict repeated (178), and soon experiences it herself as she and her friend Marie are "manipulated and divided" by the government (180).

Campbell finds that one way in which her people are divided by colonialism is deeply gendered. She explains that when they were left to themselves, her community would have fun dancing and fighting in ways that were filled with joy and with women in control (56–7). When settlers were around, however, "one of the white men would bother the women. Our men would become angry, but instead of fighting the white men they beat their wives … Meanwhile the white men stood together in a group, laughing and drinking, sometimes dragging a woman away" (38). As an adult, Campbell encounters Indigenous men who are unable to accept women who voice their opinions, who take a strong stand (e.g., 168, 170). She sees this attitude as a key obstacle to realizing crucial goals, and one that is again rooted in church teachings: "The missionaries had impressed upon us the feeling that women were a source of evil. This belief … is still holding back the progress of our people today" (168).

Such division has a devastating effect on the course of Campbell's life, and documenting this effect is one of the key aims of *Halfbreed*. She is constantly torn between the love of her people, and shame and anger toward them and herself. For example, she declares: "I loved my people so much and missed them if I couldn't see them often. I felt alive when I went to their parties, and I overflowed with happiness when we would all sit down and share a meal, yet I hated all of it as much as I loved it" (117; see also 103, 139, 143, 159).[14] This shame leads her, even as a young girl, into dreams of escaping to "the big cities [she] had read about with good food and beautiful clothes" (87). She envies the possessions of her white friend, Karen: "my constant ambition was to finish school and take my family away to the city, giving them all Karen had and more" (94). It is only much later that she realizes that the objects of her desire, no matter how humble – "a toothbrush ... a bowl of fruit on the table ... a glass of milk and cookies" (133) – are nothing other than empty "symbols of white ideals and success" (134). Reaching desperately for these symbols, Campbell marries a white man who abandons her in Vancouver (133). She becomes a sex worker (133) and drug addict (136), living a life of squalor and depression that leads to an aborted suicide attempt (162). Finally, Campbell has a nervous breakdown, overdoses and blacks out, and is institutionalized in a psychiatric hospital (163).

At the lowest point in her life, Campbell is only able to recover when she goes home in a particular sense, when she returns to the teachings of her great-grandmother. From the beginning of *Halfbreed*, it is clear that Cheechum is not subject to the same colonial forces that Campbell sees undermining her people. In addition to her refusal to become a Christian (11), she also will not "sleep on a bed or eat off a table" (16), and does not comply with government demands to leave the cabin that she built on land later designated as part of Prince Albert National Park (she in fact fires shots over the heads of the men sent to remove her from her home, until they leave her alone [10]). As much as she is able to, she lives on her own terms: "Offers of relief from welfare were scorned and so was the old age pension. While she lived alone she hunted and trapped, planted a garden, and was completely self-sufficient" (11). Cheechum summarizes her perspective in a warning to her great-granddaughter: "when the government gives you something, they take all that you have in return – your pride, your dignity, all the things that make you a living soul. When they are sure they have everything, they give you a blanket to cover your shame" (159).

Cheechum also teaches Campbell "to see beauty in all things ... that inside each thing a spirit lived ... that heaven and hell were man-made and here on earth" (82). This is a lesson that stays with Campbell throughout her life:

> I have never found peace in a church or in prayer. Perhaps Cheechum had a lot to do with that. Her philosophy was much more practical, soothing and exciting, and in her way I found comfort. She told me not to worry about the Devil, or where God lived, or what would happen after death ... She said it was a pure waste of time that could be used more constructively. (81–2)

For years, however, the world that Cheechum offered was subsumed by Campbell's colonialism-induced desire for the trappings of middle-class white existence. It is not until she absorbs Cheechum's most important lesson that she is able to take control of her life and begin the long-term work of effecting real change. This teaching is composed of two elements. First, Cheechum tells Campbell to "go out there and find what you want and take it, but always remember who you are and why you want it" (98). This task is not easily accomplished, however, as "each of us has to find himself in his own way and no one can do it for us" (175). This idea, Campbell explains, "is expressed in our language *ka tip aim* meaning 'we who own ourselves.' That means *you have to own yourself*" (48; emphasis in the original).

The second element of Cheechum's teaching involves not just Campbell, but her community: "if our way of life were to improve I would have to find other people like myself, and together try to find an alternative" (167). This is exactly what she does. Campbell joins AA, becomes involved with Native political organizations, and works to establish a halfway house for young women living on the street. She becomes part of something larger than herself, an engaged community that enables her to live with dignity and genuine purpose: "I have brothers and sisters, all over the country. I no longer need my blanket to survive" (184).

IN SEARCH OF APRIL RAINTREE: "ALL LIFE DIES TO GIVE NEW LIFE"

As with *Halfbreed*, Beatrice Mosionier's *In Search of April Raintree* presents the first-person account of a Métis woman struggling with her identity and the difficulties of her life. Also similar to *Halfbreed*, this account is highly autobiographical in several respects. Most notably, the lives of April Raintree and her sister Cheryl, like those of Mosionier and her family, include experiences of foster care, rape, and suicide (Culleton 1991, 97–100; see also Damm 1993a, 108–9; Hoy 1994; Kelly 2002, 164, 167–8). Despite these similarities, however, Mosionier worked to distance her story from real people and events in several respects: "I didn't write about my own sisters because they had family, and I didn't want to write about and intrude on the privacy of other people. So, of course, that's why I wrote fiction. I didn't write about my family at all" (Culleton 1994, 312; see also Mosionier 1999, 248).

Unlike the happy and stable home life that Campbell recalls, the childhoods of April and her sister Cheryl involve alcoholism, violence, and infidelity (10–13). The two girls are eventually taken from their parents to a Catholic orphanage (17), and then placed in foster care (23). Cheryl is raised in two very loving homes, while April has a brief experience with a kind family (23–37) before being sent to another, very cruel one (38–87). April eventually finds a place of her own in Winnipeg, where Cheryl comes to stay with her for a while (93, 101). Eventually April marries into a rich white family and moves to Toronto (110). This family takes her in and teaches her how to be like them (113). However, April leaves when she not only discovers that her husband is having an affair, but also overhears her mother-in-law approving of the transgression because she "would simply dread being grandmother to a bunch of little half-breeds" (126). In this moment April experiences fully the state of being "almost the same, but not white."

Like Campbell's text, *In Search of April Raintree* foregrounds the destructive impact of colonialism on Indigenous people in Canada, but in a more wholly systemic way. At several points in her life, for example, April encounters people who assume that Indigenous women are sexually promiscuous, a point often underscored with the epithet "squaw" (e.g., 40, 72, 79, 107, 143). The sisters are also given an apparently well-intentioned warning about "native girl syndrome," meant to help them avoid becoming alcoholics, drug addicts, and sex workers, like "many other native girls" (66–7). In school, they receive continual instruction in "how the Indians scalped, tortured and massacred brave white explorers" (57). Mosionier's novel shows such colonial views to be both deeply entrenched and highly destructive;

Agnes Grant considers *In Search of April Raintree* to be "one of the most scathing indictments of Canadian society that has ever been written" (1990, 129; see also Hoy 1994, 162).[15]

The novel links this indictment of society in general to Christianity in particular. We learn early on that April's mother – who ultimately kills herself (219) – was raised in a Catholic residential school (11). Even still, April is taught that the church is infallible and is not to be questioned (25). The authoritarian nature of Christianity is also referenced indirectly: April's first boss is "Mr. Lord" (97), and she calls her controlling mother-in-law "Mother Superior" (113). The Christian view of history that the Raintree sisters learn presents Indigenous people as savages who tortured missionaries and deserved to be subjugated (44). Cheryl thus rages against "white churches sitting back in idle, rich comfort, preaching what ought to be, but making sure it isn't" (197).[16] Christian institutions and ideologies appear, in other words, as a vital part of the power structure that denies Indigenous people humanity and equality.

Having absorbed the colonial representations of Indigenous people, April is horrified of being Métis: "anything to do with Indians, I despised" (44–5). She thus declares that she is "ashamed," that she "can't accept being a Métis" (110–11). Cheryl, however, is deeply proud of her heritage and resentful of the treatment of Indigenous people by the dominant culture (e.g., 57, 75, 77, 85). April remains skeptical, convinced that their ancestors "should have stood up for their rights instead of letting themselves be walked on" (170); consequently, she argues, they suffer "because they allow it to happen to them" (120). April ultimately attempts to distance herself as much as possible from any connection with Indigenous people: she tells her friends that her parents died in a plane crash (90); she schemes to prevent anyone she knows from meeting her darker-skinned sister (92); and when talking with Cheryl about Métis families she has met, she declares: "*They* are a disgusting people" (120; emphasis added).[17]

April's extreme attempts to divorce herself from other Indigenous people are intertwined with an equally extreme form of colonial desire. Even as a very young girl in Winnipeg, she is drawn toward the local white children and repelled by the Indigenous ones: "they were dirty-looking and they dressed in real raggedy clothes. I didn't care to play with them at all. The other group was white-skinned and I used to envy them, especially the girls with blond hair and blue eyes" (15). As she grows older April realizes that, because of her relatively light skin colour, she in fact "could pass for a pure white person" (49). Like Campbell, she dreams of all the material things she associates with white culture – "a beautiful home, a big fancy car and the most gorgeous clothing ever" (100) – all the while "reading books on proper etiquette, preparing myself for my promising future in white society" (107). It is no surprise that Cheryl ultimately accuses April of seeing the world "through white man's eyes" (115).[18]

The eventual transformation of April's perspective is precipitated by three traumatic events in her life. The first is the end of her marriage, which leads her to return home to Winnipeg, and to move in with Cheryl. Here she begins to realize that the two of them are not as different as she once thought, and to recognize the deeper truth behind her casual observation about their appearance: "we could have been almost identical twins, except for our skin-coloring" (115). Their physical similarity, however, leads horrifically to the second traumatic event, when April is raped by a group of men who mistake her for Cheryl (139–45, 182–3). April almost does not bring the case to court, and even then tells the defense attorney that she barely, if at all, resisted her attackers (179). The implication of this assertion is that she could be seen as complying with the assault, that she was therefore responsible for what happened to her. In fact, however, April fought back passionately, elbowing, biting, and scratching the rapists (139–42). She also manages to see and remember the license plate number of the rapists' car after being dumped in the middle of nowhere (145), which leads to their arrest and prosecution. The parallel with April's own criticism of Indigenous people is clear, suggesting that they too did not simply "allow it to happen to them." The connection between April's rape and the colonization of Indigenous people is underlined by the fact that the rapists refer to her repeatedly as "Indian" (141), "savage" (142), and "squaw" (140, 143, 145).[19]

Slowly, after the trauma of her rape, April does at last start to listen to Cheryl and to look at the world through "Native eyes." She gives Cheryl a copy of Dee Brown's *Bury My Heart at Wounded Knee* (155); she tells her new (white) boyfriend that she is Métis (156); she connects with the local Indigenous community for the first time and has a transformative experience at a Pow Wow: "It went deeper than just hearing and seeing. I felt good. I felt alive. There were stirrings of pride, regret and even an inner peace. For the first time in my life, I felt as if all of that was part of me, as if I was a part of it" (166). At the Friendship Centre April meets White Thunderbird Woman, an Elder who helps her continue this journey:

> The old woman suddenly reached towards me and put her hand on mine … And I no longer found her touch distasteful … She had seen something in me that was special, that was deserving of her respect. (174–5)

Even as April begins to reclaim a sense of pride in her identity, however, and to establish connections to a community, she remains haunted by the same colonial perspective she has had since childhood. As she tells her sister: "It would take an awful lot for me to be able to change what I've felt for a lifetime. Shame doesn't dissolve overnight" (167–8).

The third trauma that catalyzes April's transformation is set in motion two years before she is raped, when Cheryl tracks down their father. She had idealized him, but discovers that he is a desiccated, selfish alcoholic, a "gutter-creature"; she is devastated by shame (217–8). Slowly Cheryl's life falls apart, as she becomes an alcoholic and a sex worker, and eventually kills herself (209). In her anger and grief over her sister's death, April rails against the forces that "had torn apart the lives of *our people*" (214; emphasis added). The next day the significance of this wording hits her: "The denial had been lifted from my spirit. It was tragic that it had taken Cheryl's death to bring me to accept my identity. But no, Cheryl had once said, 'All life dies to give new life'" (228). The novel ends with April's proud, impassioned vow to help create a better future: "I would strive for it. For my sister and her son. For my parents. For my people" (228).

CONCLUSION: WRITING HOME

In ways that are both similar to and very different from April Raintree, I grew up looking at the world "through white man's eyes." These are eyes taught to see through the lens of the colonial myth that Jo-Ann Episkenew critiques, the myth that affirms white superiority and Indigenous inferiority. *Halfbreed* and *In Search of April Raintree* challenge this lens in crucial but complex ways. As Métis scholar Aubrey Jean Hanson points out, "April's internalized views of what 'being a half-breed meant' lead to the fact that she is in many ways the primary voice of racism in the novel. As a result, inasmuch as April spends two hundred pages struggling to come to terms with her identity, the reader must spend those same two hundred pages struggling to maintain a vigilant and critical decolonizing analysis of April's perspective." In other words, "in order to read to decolonize … we as readers must constantly disagree with and challenge the novel's protagonist" (2012, 27–8). This point is true for Campbell's text as well as for Mosionier's, but in both cases, of course, it only holds when the protagonists are in fact seeing through white man's eyes. In various ways, at different points in each woman's life, their vision clears. Our responsibility as readers is to be able to see these shifts; but the books also *help* us to see them. Encountering them for the first time many years ago began to change my own vision, inviting and inciting me to engage the evolving perspectives of the women who tell their stories, and to begin trying to decolonize my ways of looking at the world. I cannot say how successful I have been, but in this conclusion I offer a few thoughts on what I have come to see.

In terms of the issues raised by the idea of "diaspora," it seems to me that *Halfbreed* and *In Search of April Raintree* share several key features. The narrators of the books engage with both spatial and ideological diasporas as they struggle to find a home, recounting incredibly painful personal and communal experiences of dislocation and dispossession, some of which are deeply gendered. These experiences are traumatic and inextricable from colonialism. They include profound feelings of shame at being Métis, leading to the desire for colonial identity – which in April's case means literally trying to pass as "white" – and to conflict with other Indigenous people. Shame, in other words, leads to further individual and collective dissolution. This shame is finally overcome after a great deal of suffering and loss, as the protagonists regain both their sense of self-worth and their sense of "home," their connection to a larger community.[20]

The sources of, and solutions to, the traumas experienced by Maria Campbell and April Raintree involve some understanding of "religion." Christian people, views, and institutions in Canada are identified in these texts as fuelling many of the narrators' most profound struggles, including those involving shame: the Christian message that Campbell and April repeatedly receive is that as Indigenous people – and more specifically as Indigenous women – they are fundamentally inferior. Significantly, in their critiques of Christianity neither Campbell nor Mosionier essentialize the tradition as being inherently or necessarily harmful/colonizing. They both pointedly include several Christians in their stories who are sincerely good people. Their concern, rather, is with the ways in which Christian teachings and power structures are mobilized in patriarchal, racist ways to dehumanize and disempower Indigenous people.

On the other hand, (re-)turning to Indigenous traditions helps the women in these books push back against the effects of colonization, and begin the process of healing.[21] With Cheechum as her teacher and inspiration Campbell finds new brothers and sisters, and no longer needs her shame-covering blanket; similarly, April sees in the Elder's eyes that she has value, and is spurred by Cheryl's life and death to identify *as* an Indigenous person, and *with* Indigenous people. Neither book actually goes into much detail about Indigenous traditions, though, which reflects the fact that both narrators are largely unfamiliar with these traditions: they are just beginning their discoveries by the end of their stories. But the glimpses we get accord with how others have understood what is often referred to as Métis and/or Anishinaabe spirituality (Fiola 2015; Gross 2014).

We do learn a few critical things about the Indigenous traditions in these two books, particularly as they are contrasted with Christianity. First, the teachings are passed along by women who are members of a community, rather than by men/priests who are institutionally appointed.[22] Second, they are not authoritarian: neither Cheechum nor White Thunderbird Woman tells the young women what to do or think, but instead they offer support and guidance. Cheryl's suicide note similarly pushes against human authority and arrogance: "Man thinks he can control nature. Man is wrong. The Great Spirit has made nature stronger than man by putting into each of us a part of Nature" (227). Third, these traditions are very much of this world. Whereas in *Halfbreed* the church uses the promise of a reward in heaven after death to encourage Indigenous people to accept their suffering/oppression (61), Cheechum teaches Campbell to focus on life here on earth (81–2). April's experience with the Elder similarly has the very material impact of helping her feel better about herself and her community (174–5).[23] This effect brings up the fourth and final point, which ties the others together: the Indigenous traditions we see are fundamentally about the importance of *relationships* – with oneself, with other women, with one's family and community, and with the larger human and other-than-human worlds.[24]

Relationships are of course critical to both narrators' transformations. These transformations suggest that identities, communities, and homes are not stable or fixed or independent of one another, but are instead interconnected processes of development. As Helen Hoy (1994) argues, for example, April Raintree's "final claim to have accepted her identity has less to do with some essence she discovers in herself (or other Métis or Native people) than with her mobilization of the relations, historic and present, in which she finds herself" (177). Similarly, Janice Acoose (1993a) sees Campbell in *Halfbreed* demonstrating "how her identity has been constructed for her" by colonial culture (139), an identity she is ultimately able to refashion in large measure due to her recollections of Cheechum. But by the end of these stories neither protagonist is finished becoming who they are, as they are only just starting out on their new paths of self-respect and community.[25] And so "home" is not a particular place at which either woman finally arrives, but a state of being in the world that is in flux, and is tied to these same questions of identity and community and relationship. This perspective is expressed in Sophie McCall's understanding of *I Knew Two Métis Women*, a collection of poetry by Métis author Gregory Scofield: "home in this text is a process of home-*making* that continually unfolds" (2012, 33).[26]

It is important to mention, finally, that this process of home-making is not simply *represented* by *Halfbreed* and *In Search of April Raintree*, but that the texts themselves participate in the process. In the preface to *Halfbreed*, after describing how the place where she grew up is no longer the same, Campbell states:

> Going home after so long a time, I thought that I might find again the happiness and beauty I had known as a child. But as I walked down the rough dirt road, poked through the broken old buildings and thought back over the years, I realized that I could never find that here. Like me the land had changed, my people were gone, and if I was to know peace I would have to search within myself. *That is when I decided to write about my life*. (2; emphasis added)

The way in which Campbell remembers who she is, and constructs her new home, involves telling her story. Similarly, in a letter to Mosionier, Campbell affirms that *In Search of April Raintree* "is the kind of writing that will begin the healing of our people" (Culleton [1983] 1992, 7).

In *Taking Back Our Spirits*, Jo-Ann Episkenew offers a detailed and powerful analysis of the ways in which Indigenous literature in Canada functions "as a healing implement" that "'treats' the minds, bodies, and hearts of individuals and repairs the rifts in communities" (2009, 194).[27] In this sense writing is itself religious, spiritual, ceremonial: in Anishinaabe author Basil Johnston's conception, "words are medicine that can heal or injure ... words possess an element of the manitou [spirit, mystery, potency, potential] that enabled them to conjure images and ideas out of nothing" (1990, 12).[28] Episkenew points to colonial stories – like the ones told to Maria Campbell and April Raintree about Indigenous people generally, and Indigenous women in particular – as clear examples of destructive medicine; this destruction calls out for Indigenous stories to overturn racist, patriarchal mythologies, to rebuild and reclaim identities, communities, and – crucially – *homes* (2009, 13–14). Such stories *must* be told, in Cherokee scholar Jace Weaver's phrase, "that the People might live" (1997, 161). Or as Episkenew herself affirms: "Indigenous literature is, indeed, powerful medicine with which contemporary Indigenous writers are taking back our spirits" (2009, 194).[29]

NOTES

1 *In Search of April Raintree* was originally published under Mosionier's (married) surname at the time, Culleton. I am using that original version and so I have listed the text in the reference list under "Culleton," but will refer to the author as "Mosionier" throughout my chapter since that is the name she now goes by.

2 For brief overviews of the diversity of the Métis in terms of history, geography, religion, and government policies, see Episkenew (2009, 53–67); Fiola (2015, 15–21). For a detailed discussion of the historical complexities of Métis identity specifically in relation to Métis literature, including both *Halfbreed* and *In Search of April Raintree*, see Adese (2016); Bidwell (2014).

3 For discussions by Indigenous scholars of the value of shared notions of Indigeneity, particularly regarding literature, see Heiss (2001, 207) and Weaver (1997, 26). For reflection on – and critique of – the practice of both writing and reading Indigenous literatures as generically "Indigenous" without consideration of the specific communities to which authors belong, see Acoose (2008) and Adese (2016).

4 For discussions of the disregard of Indigenous literature by non-Indigenous scholars see Allen ([1986] 1992, 54–66); Donovan (1998, 46–8); Fee (1999a, 142–7); Harjo and Bird (1997, 20, 28); Krupat (1989, 45–6); Weaver (1997, 20–2).

5 Given the high number of citations in this essay to *Halfbreed* and *In Search of April Raintree*, when referring to these two texts I will simply put the page numbers in brackets, and not include the years of publication.

6 In addition to Campbell and Mosionier, these women include Janice Acoose, Jennifer Adese, Paula Gunn Allen, Kateri Akiwenzie-Damm, Jeanette Armstrong, Kristina Fagan Bidwell, Gloria Bird, Jo-Ann Episkenew, Chantal Fiola, Mishuana Goeman, Aubrey Jean Hanson, Joy Harjo, Lenore Keeshig-Tobias, Emma LaRocque, and Lee Maracle.

7 Critically, not everyone agrees with categorizing Indigenous people's displacements as "diasporic." Lee Maracle (2007), for one, equates "the Diaspora" in North America and elsewhere with European colonizers, and therefore remarks, "invasiveness marks the nature of the Diaspora" (55; see also Cho 2007, 28n1; Eigenbrod 2012, 135–6). Celia Haig-Brown (2009) brings up a related point in her critique of theorists who (like Maracle) apply the term "diaspora" to those who arrived "here" from "there," but who (*unlike* Maracle) disregard those who were here in the first place. Thus, she argues, "a refusal by diaspora theorists to engage with indigeneity re-creates the invisibility of the peoples who first occupied the lands that now form these nations. The very construction of a diasporic discourse in the US holds a certain irony when it fails to see the oppression of Native Americans as integral to the formation of both the nation and inextricably related to the many Diasporas now there" (10). In other words, "to focus on the people of the Diasporas in North American (and other) contexts is too often to lose sight of the land and people of the place to which they are dispersed. In this blindness, the efforts at cultural genocide exemplified by residential schools and land grabs are reinscribed" (12).

8 For a discussion of the central, critical importance of *place* in Native American traditions – and how the colonial appropriation and destruction of sacred Indigenous places has been devastating to these traditions – see Vine Deloria Jr's classic 1973 text *God Is Red*, particularly chapter 16 ("Sacred Places and Moral Responsibility").

9 Quoted in Weis (1986, 32); see also the Truth and Reconciliation Commission of Canada (2015, 2–3, 57). Scott made these comments during his testimony before the Special Parliamentary Committee of the House of Commons, which was examining Scott's proposals to amend sections of the Indian Act involving Indigenous enfranchisement in Canada.

10 Italics in the original text.

11 "All our people" includes Campbell's mother and maternal grandmother, both of whom were educated in convents (15). As discussed below, however, this group critically does *not* include Cheechum, her great-grandmother on her father's side.

12 For discussions of colonialism and Christianity in relation to *Halfbreed* see Acoose (1993a, 143–4); Campbell (1991, 46–7); Donovan (1998, 31).

13 Campbell recounts that the government used the same tactic during the Riel Rebellion. The great Métis leader Louis Riel and his followers were demanding that the government address their grievances. The government refused until Riel's victory at Duck Lake, at which point they "issued land scripts to assure the Halfbreeds of their land claims. But these were issued purposely to a chosen few which caused a split within the Halfbreed ranks" (5). Soon after, government troops were able to overpower the divided force and capture, and hang, Riel (5–6).

14 For discussions of the links between shame and colonialism in *Halfbreed* see Damm (1993a, 106–7) and Episkenew (2002, 60–2).

15 For discussions of systemic colonial racism and abuse in *In Search of April Raintree* see Damm (1993a, 110–12); Donovan (1998, 28–30); Episkenew (2001, 62–5); Fee (1999b); Kelly (2002, 169–72); Lundgren (1995, 63–5).

16 In her interview with Makeda Silvera, Mosionier pointedly critiques such "paternalistic attitudes on the part of the Church" (Culleton 1994, 330).

17 For commentaries on the link between colonial constructions of Indigenous identity and April's shame and self-hatred see Damm (1993a, 96); Divya (2013, 73); Kelly (2002, 169, 172); LaRocque (2002, 216); Lundgren (1995, 64–5).

18 For detailed discussions of April's attempts to become "like a real white person," see Acoose (1999, 232–3); Culleton (1994, 317–18); Donovan (1998, 27–8); Fee (1990, 171, 175–6; 1999, 215–19); Lundgren (1995, 74–5).

19 Because of such epithets, Cumming (1999) notes that the assault on April "is more centrally about her rape as a Native person – and through her, I believe, about the 'rape' of all Native peoples" (314). Other commentators who have made this connection include Clarke (1986, 141); Damm (1993a, 110–11); Fee (1990, 176; 1999, 220–3).

20 Such a connection is also a common feature of stories by Indigenous authors more generally. Jace Weaver (1997) in fact asserts that "the single thing that most defines Indian literatures relates to this sense of community and commitment to it" (43).

21 The experience that Maria Campbell and April Raintree have of being raised in the Catholic Church, taught to see themselves and their communities as inferior, and finding support and healing in Indigenous traditions is one that Chantal Fiola (2015) has found repeated in the lives of many Métis people.

22 In terms of gender and the transmission of Indigenous teachings, there is an interesting link here with Native literature in Canada. The first Indigenous writer in this country to gain widespread recognition was Pauline Johnson (Mohawk), working in the late nineteenth and early

twentieth centuries. The next such writer to appear (several decades later) was Maria Campbell, whose *Halfbreed* was quickly followed by several critically important books by Indigenous women, including Beatrice (Culleton) Mosionier, Jeanette Armstrong, Lee Maracle, and Beth Brant.

23 In a reverse echo of the Catholic teaching in *Halfbreed*, Anishinaabe scholar Lawrence Gross points out that the central Anishinaabe concept of *bimaadiziwin*, of living a long and good life, "concentrates on this world, and not reward in an afterlife" (2014, 205; see also Johnston 1995, xvii).

24 Chantal Fiola similarly states: "Kinship relationships give our lives meaning; they teach us about who we are, our roles and responsibilities to our communities and beyond" (2021, 267–8; see also 2015, 9–10; Adese 2016; Gross 2014, 207–9; Johnston 1995, xix–xx). In her study of Indigenous women's literature in North America, Tonawanda Seneca scholar Mishuana Goeman (2013) considers the ways in which gender is involved in these critical relationships: "On a daily basis, *women* in all of our variously conceived communities strive to keep the connections among family, stories, histories, and the land alive and well" (206; emphasis added).

25 For other discussions of the fluid, constructed self in Indigenous literature in Canada see Damm (1993b), Fee (1999b), and Thompson (1995).

26 Mishuana Goeman (2013) similarly remarks that, in writings that respond to the displacements caused by heteropatriarchal settler colonialism, Indigenous women "produce places of their own making that are vital to Native communities" (208). Renate Eigenbrod (2012) points to this process of home-making in the work of Ojibwe author Richard Wagamese: "Wagamese's fictional work is written out of the diasporic experiences of an Anishinaabe person responding to his personal displacements, as well as those experienced by his people systemically; it expresses in various plots and through different literary devices a longing to return, not to a specific home or the past, but to a connectedness with values and beliefs that emanate from an ancestral homeland and a pre-colonial past. Instead of dwelling on experiences of dispossession, his work is about transformation as it adapts stories that carry Indigenous values to new situations and translates them into new contexts" (149–50). Lily Cho (2007) finds a comparable dynamic operating in diasporas more generally, noting, "the question of origins is not one of genesis for an established and fixed past, but of a dialectical emergence from a history that is both restorative and incomplete" (17).

27 Episkenew's study includes discussions of both *Halfbreed* (76–86) and *In Search of April Raintree* (110–25). For other considerations of Indigenous writing and/as healing see Acoose (1993a, 139); Cox and Justice (2014,

10–11); Weaver (1997). Reflecting on the meaning and power of stories in relation to colonialism and Indigenous people in Canada, Celia Haig-Brown highlights Pnina Werbner's comment regarding diasporas more generally: "Although the experience of exile is, in the first instance, personal and individual, long term diasporas create collective literary genres, symbolic representations, historical narratives of loss and redemption, and practical forms of political alliance and lobbying that are uniquely theirs. They are embodied and perpetuated through communal celebrations and transnational economic and political connections that are often invisible to the wider society" (Werbner 2000, 17; quoted in Haig-Brown 2009, 14–15). For similar thoughts on the ways in which writing helps to form individual and collective identities among diasporic people see Bhabha (1994, 18); Cho (2007, 19–20); Tölölyan (2011, 12).

28 Johnston offers these and other translations of "manitou" (1990, 11; see also Johnston 1995, 242). Johnston's comment about words and medicine is cited in Episkenew 2009, 13.

29 I want to thank the book's editors, Sailaja Krishnamurti and Becky Lee, for asking me to participate in this project. I like and respect both of them immensely, and I am deeply grateful for their invitation.

REFERENCES

Acoose, Janice. 1993a. "*Halfbreed*: A Revisiting of Maria Campbell's Text from an Indigenous Perspective." In *Looking at the Words of Our People: First Nations Analysis of Literature*, edited by Jeannette Armstrong, 137–50. Penticton, BC: Theytus.

– 1993b. "Post *Halfbreed*: Indigenous Writers as Authors of Their Own Realities." In *Looking at the Words of Our People: First Nations Analysis of Literature*, edited by Jeannette Armstrong, 27–44. Penticton, BC: Theytus.

– 1999. "The Problem of 'Searching' for April Raintree." In *In Search of April Raintree: Critical Edition*, by Beatrice Culleton Mosionier, edited by Cheryl Suzack, 227–36. Winnipeg: Portage and Main.

– 2008. "Honoring *Ni'Wahkomakanak*." In *Reasoning Together: The Native Critics Collective*, edited by Janice Acoose et al., 216–33. Norman, OK: University of Oklahoma Press.

Adese, Jennifer. 2016. "The New People: Reading for Peoplehood in Métis Literatures." *Studies in American Indian Literatures* 28, no. 4: 53–79.

Allen, Paula Gunn. (1986) 1992. *The Sacred Hoop: Recovering the Feminine in American Indian Traditions*. Boston: Beacon.

Armstrong, Jeannette. 1990. "Words." In *Telling It: Women and Language across Cultures*, edited by Sky Lee et al., 23–9. Vancouver: Press Gang.

Bhabha, Homi K. 1984. "Of Mimicry and Man: The Ambivalence of Colonial Discourse." *October* 28: 125–33.

– 1994. *The Location of Culture*. London: Routledge.

Bidwell, Kristina Fagan. 2014. "Metis Identity and Literature." In *The Oxford Handbook of Indigenous American Literature*, edited by James H. Cox and Daniel Heath Justice, 118–36. Oxford: Oxford University Press.

Boyarin, Jonathan, and Daniel Boyarin. 2002. *The Powers of Diaspora: Two Essays on the Relevance of Jewish Culture*. Minneapolis, MN: University of Minnesota Press.

Campbell, Maria. (1973) 1983. *Halfbreed*. Halifax: Goodread-Formac.

– 1991. Interview with Hartmut Lutz. In *Contemporary Challenges: Conversations with Canadian Native Authors*, by Hartmut Lutz, 41–65. Saskatoon, SK: Fifth House.

– 1994. "It's the Job of the Storyteller to Create Chaos." Interview with Beth Cuthand. In *The Other Woman: Women of Colour in Contemporary Canadian Literature*, edited by Makeda Silvera, 264–70. Toronto: Sister Vision.

Cho, Lily. 2007. "The Turn to Diaspora." *Topia: Canadian Journal of Cultural Studies* 17 (Spring): 11–30. http://topia.journals.yorku.ca/index.php/topia/article/viewFile/13229/22406.

Clarke, Margaret. 1986. "Revisioning *April Raintree*." *Prairie Fire* 7, no. 3: 136–42.

Clifford, James. 2007. "Varieties of Indigenous Experience: Diasporas, Homelands, Sovereignties." In *Indigenous Experience Today*, edited by Marisol de la Cadena and Orin Starn, 197–224. Oxford: Berg.

Cox, James H., and Daniel Heath Justice. 2014. "Introduction: Post-Renaissance Indigenous American Literary Studies." In *The Oxford Handbook of Indigenous American Literature*, edited by James H. Cox and Daniel Heath Justice, 1–11. Oxford: Oxford University Press.

Culleton, Beatrice. (1983) 1992. *In Search of April Raintree*. Winnipeg: Peguis.

– 1991. Interview with Hartmut Lutz. In *Contemporary Challenges: Conversations with Canadian Native Authors*, by Hartmut Lutz, 97–105. Saskatoon, SK: Fifth House.

– 1994. "I Decided to Go with Reality." Interview with Makeda Silvera. In *The Other Woman: Women of Colour in Contemporary Canadian Literature*, edited by Makeda Silvera, 311–31. Toronto: Sister Vision.

Cumming, Peter. 1999. "'The Only Dirty Book': The Rape of *April Raintree*." In *In Search of April Raintree: Critical Edition*, by Beatrice Culleton Mosionier, edited by Cheryl Suzack, 307–22. Winnipeg: Portage and Main.

Damm, Kateri. 1993a. "Dispelling and Telling: Speaking Native Realities in Maria Campbell's *Halfbreed* and Beatrice Culleton's *In Search of April Raintree*." In *Looking at the Words of Our People: First Nations Analysis of Literature*, edited by Jeannette Armstrong, 93–114. Penticton, BC: Theytus.

– 1993b. "Says Who: Colonialism, Identity and Defining Indigenous Discourse." In *Looking at the Words of Our People: First Nations Analysis of Literature*, edited by Jeannette Armstrong, 9–25. Penticton, BC: Theytus.

Deloria, Vine, Jr. 1973. *God Is Red: A Native View of Religion*. New York: Grosset and Dunlap.

Divya, K. Vishnu. 2013. "Healing through Imagination: A Study of Beatrice Culleton's *In Search Of April Raintree*." *Journal of Literature, Culture and Media Studies* 5, nos. 9–10: 71–8.

Donovan, Kathleen. 1998. *Coming to Voice: Feminist Readings of Native American Literature*. Tucson: University of Arizona Press.

Eigenbrod, Renate. 2005. *Travelling Knowledges: Positioning the Im/Migrant Reader of Aboriginal Literatures in Canada*. Winnipeg: University of Manitoba Press.

– 2012. "Diasporic Longings: (Re)Figurations of Home and Homelessness in Richard Wagamese's Work." In *Cultural Grammars of Nation, Diaspora, and Indigeneity in Canada*, edited by Christine Kim, Sophie McCall, and Melina Baum Singer, 135–51. Waterloo, ON: Wilfrid Laurier University Press.

Episkenew, Jo-Ann. 2002. "Socially Responsible Criticism: Aboriginal Literature, Ideology, and the Literary Canon." In *Creating Community: A Roundtable on Canadian Aboriginal Literature*, edited by Renate Eigenbrod and Jo-Ann Episkenew, 51–68. Penticton, BC: Theytus.

– 2009. *Taking Back Our Spirits: Indigenous Literature, Public Policy, and Healing*. Winnipeg: University of Manitoba Press.

Fanon, Frantz. (1952) 1967. *Black Skin, White Masks*. Translated by Charles Lam Markmann. New York: Grove.

Fee, Margery. 1990. "Upsetting Fake Ideas: Jeannette Armstrong's 'Slash' and Beatrice Culleton's 'April Raintree.'" In *Native Writers and Canadian Writing*, edited by W.H. New, 168–80. Vancouver: University of British Columbia Press.

– 1999a. "Aboriginal Writing in Canada and the Anthology as Commodity." In *Native North America: Critical and Cultural Perspectives*, edited by Renée Hulan, 135–55. Toronto: ECW.
– 1999b. "Deploying Identity in the Face of Racism." In *In Search of April Raintree: Critical Edition*, by Beatrice Culleton Mosionier, edited by Cheryl Suzack, 211–26. Winnipeg: Portage and Main.
Fiola, Chantal. 2015. *Rekindling the Sacred Fire: Métis Ancestry and Anishinaabe Spirituality*. Winnipeg: University of Manitoba Press.
– 2021. "Diaspora, Spirituality, Kinship, and Nationhood: A Métis Woman's Perspective." In *Relation and Resistance: Racialized Women, Religion, and Diaspora*, edited by Sailaja Krishnamurti and Becky R. Lee, 259–80. Montreal and Kingston: McGill-Queen's University Press.
Goeman, Mishuana. 2013. *Mark My Words: Native Women Mapping Our Nations*. Minneapolis: University of Minnesota Press.
Grant, Agnes. 1990. "Contemporary Native Women's Voices in Literature." In *Native Writers and Canadian Writing*, edited by W.H. New, 124–32. Vancouver: University of British Columbia Press.
Gross, Lawrence W. 2014. *Anishinaabe Ways of Knowing and Being*. New York: Routledge.
Haig-Brown, Celia. 2009. "Decolonizing Diaspora: Whose Traditional Land Are We On?" *Cultural and Pedagogical Inquiry* 1, no. 2: 4–21.
Hanson, Aubrey Jean. 2012. "'Through White Man's Eyes': Beatrice Culleton Mosionier's *In Search of April Raintree* and Reading for Decolonization." *Studies in American Indian Literatures* 24, no. 1: 15–30.
Harjo, Joy, and Gloria Bird. 1997. Introduction to *Reinventing the Enemy's Language: Contemporary Women's Writings of North America*, edited by Joy Harjo and Gloria Bird, 19–31. New York: W.W. Norton.
Harvey, Graham, and Charles D. Thompson Jr. 2005. *Indigenous Diasporas and Dislocations*. Aldershot, UK: Ashgate.
Heiss, Anita. 2001. "Aboriginal Identity and Its Effects on Writing." In *(Ad)dressing Our Words: Aboriginal Perspectives on Aboriginal Literatures*, edited by Armand Garnet Ruffo, 205–32. Penticton, BC: Theytus.
Hoy, Helen. 1994. "'Nothing but the Truth': Discursive Transparency in Beatrice Culleton." *Ariel* 25, no. 1: 155–84.
– 2001. *How Should I Read These? Native Women Writers in Canada*. Toronto: University of Toronto Press.
Johnson, Paul Christopher. 2012. "Religion and Diaspora." *Religion and Society: Advances in Research* 3: 95–114.

Johnston, Basil. 1990. "One Generation from Extinction." In *Native Writers and Canadian Writing*, edited by W.H. New, 10–15. Vancouver: University of British Columbia Press.
– 1995. *The Manitous: The Spiritual World of the Ojibway*. Toronto: Key Porter.
Keeshig-Tobias, Lenore. 1991. Interview with Hartmut Lutz. In *Contemporary Challenges: Conversations with Canadian Native Authors*, by Hartmut Lutz, 79–88. Saskatoon, SK: Fifth House.
Kelly, Jennifer. 2002. "'You Can't Get Angry with a Person's Life': Negotiating Aboriginal Women's Writing, Whiteness, and Multicultural Nationalism in a University Classroom." In *Creating Community: A Roundtable on Canadian Aboriginal Literature*, edited by Renate Eigenbrod and Jo-Ann Episkenew, 147–86. Penticton, BC: Theytus.
King, Thomas. 1990. "Godzilla vs. Post-Colonial." *World Literature Written in English* 30, no. 2: 10–16.
Krupat, Arnold. 1989. *The Voice in the Margin: Native American Literature and the Canon*. Berkeley: University of California Press.
LaRocque, Emma. 1990. "Preface, or Here Are Our Voices: Who Will Hear?" In *Writing the Circle: Native Women of Western Canada*, edited by Jeanne Perreault and Sylvia Vance, xv–xxx. Edmonton: NeWest.
– 2002. "Teaching Aboriginal Literature: The Discourse of Margins and Mainstream." *Creating Community: A Roundtable on Canadian Aboriginal Literature*, edited by Renate Eigenbrod and Jo-Ann Episkenew, 209–34. Penticton, BC: Theytus.
Lundgren, Jodi. 1995. "'Being a Halfbreed': Discourses of Race and Cultural Syncreticity in the Works of Three Métis Women Writers." *Canadian Literature* 144: 62–77.
Lutz, Hartmut. 1991. *Contemporary Challenges: Conversations with Canadian Native Authors*. Saskatoon, SK: Fifth House.
Maracle, Lee. 2007. "Oratory on Oratory." In *Trans.Can.Lit: Resituating the Study of Canadian Literature*, edited by Smaro Kamboureli and Roy Miki, 55–70. Waterloo, ON: Wilfrid Laurier University Press.
McCall, Sophie. 2012. "Diaspora and Nation in Métis Writing." In *Cultural Grammars of Nation, Diaspora, and Indigeneity in Canada*, edited by Christine Kim, Sophie McCall, and Melina Baum Singer, 21–41. Waterloo, ON: Wilfrid Laurier University Press.
McLeod, Neal. 2001. "Coming Home through Stories." In *(Ad)dressing Our Words: Aboriginal Perspectives on Aboriginal Literatures*, edited by Armand Garnet Ruffo, 17–36. Penticton, BC: Theytus.
Miller, J.R. 1991. "Owen Glendower, Hotspur, and Canadian Indian Policy." In *Sweet Promises: A Reader on Indian-White Relations*

in Canada, edited by J.R. Miller, 323–52. Toronto: University of Toronto Press.

Mosionier, Beatrice Culleton. 1999. "The Special Time." In *In Search of April Raintree: Critical Edition*, by Beatrice Culleton Mosionier, edited by Cheryl Suzack, 247–50. Winnipeg: Portage and Main.

Smithers, Gregory D. 2014. "'What Is an Indian?' – The Enduring Question of American Indian Identity." In *Native Diasporas: Indigenous Identities and Settler Colonialism in the Americas*, edited by Gregory D. Smithers and Brooke N. Newman, 1–27. Lincoln: University of Nebraska Press.

Suzack, Cheryl. 1999. Introduction to *In Search of April Raintree: Critical Edition*, by Beatrice Culleton Mosionier, edited by Cheryl Suzack, 1–7. Winnipeg: Portage and Main.

Thom, Jo-Ann. 1999. "The Effect of Readers' Responses on the Development of Aboriginal Literature in Canada: A Study of Maria Campbell's *Halfbreed*, Beatrice Culleton's *In Search of April Raintree*, and Richard Wagamese's *Keeper'n Me*." In *In Search of April Raintree: Critical Edition*, by Beatrice Culleton Mosionier, edited by Cheryl Suzack, 295–305. Winnipeg: Portage and Main.

Thompson, Dawn. 1995. "Technologies of Ethnicity." *Essays on Canadian Writing* 57: 51–69.

Tölölyan, Khachig. 2011. "Diaspora Studies: Past, Present and Promise." *IMI Working Papers Series* 55. https://www.imi.ox.ac.uk/publications/wp-55-12.

Trigger, Bruce G. 1985. *Natives and Newcomers: Canada's "Heroic Age" Reconsidered*. Montreal and Kingston: McGill-Queen's University Press.

Truth and Reconciliation Commission of Canada. 2015. *Honouring the Truth, Reconciling for the Future: Summary of the Final Report of the Truth and Reconciliation Commission of Canada*. Winnipeg: Truth and Reconciliation Commission of Canada. http://publications.gc.ca/collections/collection_2015/trc/IR4-7-2015-eng.pdf.

Vertovec, Steven. 2004. "Religion and Diaspora." In *Textual, Comparative, Sociological, and Cognitive Approaches*, edited by Peter Antes, Armin W. Geertz, and Randi Warne, 275–303. Vol. 2 of *New Approaches to the Study of Religion*. Berlin: de Gruyter.

Weaver, Jace. 1997. *That the People Might Live: Native American Literatures and Native American Community*. New York: Oxford University Press.

Weis, L.P. 1986. "D.C. Scott's View of History and the Indians." *Canadian Literature* 111: 27–40. http://canlit.ca/canlitmedia/canlit.ca/pdfs/articles/canlit111-Scott(Weis).pdf.

Werbner, Pnina. 2000. "The Materiality of Diaspora – Between Aesthetic and 'Real' Politics." *Diaspora: A Journal of Transnational Studies* 1: 5–19.

Young-Ing, Greg. 1993. "Aboriginal Peoples' Estrangement: Marginalization in the Publishing Industry." In *Looking at the Words of Our People: First Nations Analysis of Literature*, edited by Jeannette Armstrong, 177–87. Penticton, BC: Theytus.

4

The Role of Women in the Pre-Second World War Japanese Diaspora in Canada

Cary Takagaki

In the late nineteenth and early twentieth centuries, women in Japan were excluded from leadership roles in most organizations. They were also unable to join political parties or attend political meetings (Ichikawa 1977, 131–4), and although the ban on the latter was abolished in 1922, women still could not join political groups until after the Pacific War in 1945.[1] On top of such bans, as many researchers have noted, women generally were neither socialized nor encouraged to participate in political activities or occupy positions of power and authority. They lacked both role models and opportunities in the realm of politics (Bokemeier and Tait 1980, 240). It would seem to follow that this would be the case for women in the Japanese diaspora as well. Nevertheless, many studies have claimed that women did have an influence on the direction of religious practice and religious institutions when they emigrated – although those studies fail to attend to the social, political, and religious contexts within which women exercised their influence. This sort of general insistence on the influence of Japanese women in the diaspora is evident, for instance, in Brian Hayashi's 1995 study of Japanese Christians in California, wherein he states, "Issei women, though they held few positions of authority in the three local churches, nevertheless exerted a good deal of influence through the *fujinkai* or women's societies … they cooked meals, organized entertainment, and, to some extent, took part in American-style charitable work, previously unknown among Japanese immigrants" (95). Similarly, Michihiro Ama (2011) cites Aya Honda's work on the Buddhist Women's Association's activities in Seattle in the 1930s, which notes that the BWA designed the kitchen facilities for a new church, and at "major services delivered congratulatory messages to the congregation. Their proficiency in raising funds was reflected in their ability to collect and donate $6,000 for new construction. The BWA skilfully coordinated gatherings of the congregation and hosted various cultural festivals. For instance, Honda writes, 'The bon odori could not have functioned without the Fujinkai's involvement'" (82–3). And, writing more broadly about Buddhist women in the United States, Ama notes that "in 1933, BMNA [the Buddhist Mission of North America] officials discussed the possibility of setting up a ministerial training program for women, but because of budget limitations and other priorities, adoption of the proposal was postponed" (83).

The difficulty in understanding the role of women in the early diaspora, much like the challenge in studying the role of women generally in the prewar era, is that there is very little written about them other than in such wide terms. Moreover, the few documents we do have about Japanese women from before the war were written by men and from a male perspective.[2] As Hayashi (1995) notes with respect to records of the Methodist Church in California, "not a great deal is known about the fujinkai of the Holiness and Union churches because the records no longer exist; the main source of information is church bulletins, which occasionally mention fujinkai activities. Fujinkai records for the Methodist Church are at times very detailed, but because the speakers from whom the women took notes were often males, the records tend to reflect what many males thought was best for women rather than what women themselves thought" (178n1). Similarly for the Canadian context, Michiko Midge Ayukawa (2008) notes in her book on Hiroshima immigrants in Canada that "the [Japanese immigrant] women described here, and others like them, have not been celebrated by chronicles of the early twentieth-century Japanese-Canadian community" (56). As Anne Walthall (1994) has observed, literature concerning the role of women in rice riots and peasant uprisings in early modern Japan "leaves the reader with the impression that women did nothing but offer support in the shadows" (131). And although there is a chapter on the "Great Power of Women" in Nakayama Jinshirō's *Kanada dōhō hatten taikan furoku* (Encyclopedia of Japanese in Canada) (1921, 1683–702), and his *Kanada dōhō hatten shi* (History of the

Japanese in Canada) (1917, 591–612) includes short biographies of female Japanese immigrants that note their devotion to duty and their activities in various women's associations, these women are usually, as Ayakawa writes, "presented as means to enhance the social position of their husbands" (2008, 57).

Thus, there is no doubt that the role of Japanese immigrant women in Canada was not far removed from the role of women in Japan. But, as caregivers in the diaspora, they would have played a part in maintaining and passing on their religious traditions. Religion was not a determining factor in the emigration of Japanese to Canada in the late nineteenth century, but it often became a major connection to their cultural identity and the social norms of their homeland. However, living in a new environment and strategizing for acceptance meant adapting to new customs and transforming their traditions. Women were also inevitably swept up in trends and political events over which they had no control, and this had an effect on their religious practices as well. But the question arises as to whether women actually had any real degree of empowerment and agency with respect to their religious traditions. Any conclusions reached with regard to this question are complicated by the nature of religious practice in Japan, the changing role of women in Japan, and the meaning of empowerment and agency.

DISTINGUISHING JAPANESE IMMIGRANTS FROM CHINESE IMMIGRANTS

Following Britain's humiliating treatment of China after the Opium Wars, the influential intellectual and educator Fukuzawa Yukichi argued that Japan had to distinguish itself from its neighbours China and Korea, as they were hopelessly mired in conservative traditions and therefore doomed to perpetual backwardness. If Japan aspired to make progress, it had to forsake Asia and become part of the Western world – in effect, it had to "globalize" (Fukuzawa 1885). Imperialism was part of that process, and this, combined with Japan's economic strides, brought international recognition to the country. With the abolition of various unequal treaties and recognition of tariff autonomy, Japan had achieved almost complete equalization in its relations with Western powers by 1911. To ensure its status on the international scene, the Japanese felt it important that the West see their country in a positive light. Thus, Meiji leaders were at pains to emphasize that Japanese emigrants differed from others, in order to avoid discriminatory policies such as the 1882 Chinese Exclusion Act in the United States and the Chinese head tax in Canada. But this presented a problem: since the Japanese and Chinese were both Asian, distinctions between them could not be made on the basis of "race," and so Japanese officials "sought to explain anti-Asian prejudice not on the basis of race but on the basis of 'backwardness' or the failure to modernize, whether on the part of individuals or on the part of entire nations" (Geiger 2007/2008, 47).

In a consular dispatch to the minister of foreign affairs dated 10 May 1892, Japanese consul Chinda Sutemi argued that the "Japanese who come to this city [San Francisco] must be the true representatives of the Japanese people who can indeed maintain Japan's national honor ... I beg your excellency to pay immediate and particular attention to this matter and instruct the respective government officials to adopt appropriate measures so as to prevent the departure of ... undesirable Japanese to this country in the future" (quoted in Wilson and Hosokawa 1980, 114–15). Who were these "undesirable" Japanese? They were the "lower classes," who, it was felt, were not yet "modern" and so could damage the reputation of the more sophisticated "upper" classes. As Baron Rempei Kondo, a member of the House of Peers, noted in 1914, "the Japanese who go to America generally belong to the lower classes. When they suddenly make their appearance in America, it is no wonder that they do things the Americans do not like" (quoted in Masaoka 1914, 36). Thus Japanese leaders did not see white racism as the cause of anti-Asian policies; rather, they characterized these policies as the result of the appearance and behaviour of Japanese immigrants, who often lived in squalid ghettos and did not adapt to Western customs. To this point, Japanese magazines such as *Amerika tobei zasshi* and *Tobei shinpō*, aimed at Japanese readers considering emigration, stressed that only the "right kind of people" should go; their behaviour should not be like previous "animal-like" emigrants who "picked their teeth, picked their noses, scratched their heads, and undress in public" (quoted in Sawada 1991, 344). As a result, historian Mitziko Sawada notes, Japan created emigration policies in order to be treated as an equal by the West (1991, 339–40). That is, to the Japanese, it was important that they initiate their own restrictions on emigration so as not to have restrictions imposed on them by a foreign power.

This attitude was not unique to Japanese leaders; Japanese immigrants were also concerned with distinguishing themselves from Chinese immigrants. "Beginning with the first student-laborers in the late nineteenth century," Yuji Ichioka writes, "Japanese immigrants [to the United States] always differentiated themselves from Chinese immigrants. From the student-laborer's point of view, Americans had excluded the Chinese, understandably and justifiably, because the Chinese were lower class laborers who had not adapted themselves to American society" (1988, 191). As Tabata Kisaburō noted in 1908 in his *Zaibeisha seikō no tomo* (The friend of success for Japanese in America), "We must seek to avoid clashes with customs. By striving to assimilate with white people, social relationships can be moderated. If our compatriots desire individual success, they must forget that they are Japanese ... If not, we will be treated as the Hawaiian Japanese immigrant and have to endure the shame of being called 'Jap' from morning to night" (quoted in Sawada 1991, 344).

RELIGION AS ASSIMILATION

This concern with assimilation was reflected in the religious traditions of the Japanese diaspora in North America. Many early immigrants converted to Christianity. The inroads made by Christianity among early Japanese immigrants were largely due to practical concerns. Christian ministers administered to more than just the spiritual needs of these immigrants, acting as interpreters, establishing night classes to teach them English, and acculturating them to Canadian customs. During the Spanish Flu epidemic of 1918, when the regular hospitals were full or would not attend to the needs of Asians, Methodist ministers established a hospital in Vancouver to care for Japanese immigrants (Kawano 1998, 13).

In many cases, immigrants converted to Christianity because they were grateful to the ministers and were repaying debts to them, acting on a strong social value informed by the traditional Japanese sense of obligation (*on*). This would have been especially true of many early immigrant mothers who were isolated while raising children. Ken Adachi imagines this sense of obligation for us in the following way: "The missionary comes to the door and in very polite Japanese invites the *Issei* mother to a tea at the church. There she sits around and talks to some of her neighbours. As she is leaving, the missionary politely expresses the wish to see her again. And the

Issei mother, having accepted his hospitality, feels obligated to attend the church" (1991, 112).

Of course, there were those who were drawn to Christianity for its spiritual benefits, but even the Christian organizations that came to the aid of the early Japanese immigrants seem to have made the assumption that conversion was not only a spiritual matter, but a practical one. Survival in Canada entailed understanding Canadian culture and the North American way of life, and immigrants saw conversion to Christianity as an integral step in this process. As a result, by the 1930s there were 4,789 Japanese members of the United Church, representing about 20 per cent of the Japanese in Canada. But practically speaking, any "assimilation" was only superficial and limited. Japanese Christian converts attended segregated churches apart from the white population and services were given in Japanese. Any social events associated with the churches were conducted and attended only by Japanese. Contact with the white community remained limited and was usually restricted to interactions with white Christian ministers. At that time, assimilation was not really possible (Adachi 1991, 112).

What really seems to have been going on is that the willingness to accept Canadian norms was seen as a characteristic that differentiated the Japanese from the Chinese immigrant. It was this willingness, rather than the conversion itself, that was important. The Japanese consul in Canada, T. Nosse, stated: "we all know that the Chinese who come from Canton are the lowest in the scale. They smoke opium; they start gambling dens; they are unclean; they never assimilate with the population. The Japanese, on the contrary," he continued, "are a highly civilized people. They are clean and frugal; they set up a family; they open churches. There are fifteen thousand Chinese in British Columbia; and about eight hundred Japanese, all told. The latter are Christians, or the majority of them" (*Victoria Daily Colonist* 1897, 2).

Conversion to Christianity, then, came to be seen as a symbol of the progressive nature of the Japanese: "Christian Japanese liked to claim that Christianity was a liberating factor facilitating their adjustment to Canadian life. As it was looked upon as an integral part of Western civilization, many Japanese underwent conversion so that they might identify themselves more closely with white society and then claimed that they were more 'Canadianized' and 'progressive' than the Buddhists" (Adachi 1991, 111).

Conversion also reinforced the Japanese immigrant's feelings of superiority over Chinese immigrants, and women, even though they did not take a leadership role in the conversion process, were explicitly utilized to promote accommodation as a sign of Japanese cultural identity. This can be seen in Brian Hayashi's (1995) account of the minutes of a 1920 lecture given by a male speaker at a fujinkai at the Los Angeles Japanese Methodist Episcopal Church: "'The shortcoming of modern Japanese women ... is that they never show their [true] nature' but submerge it under other peoples' customs. That should not be, he argued, 'because the Japanese women's [true] nature is to be preferred over [the] white [woman's true nature] and is to our credit ... We need to work to display this beautiful nature [so that we] can itemize our beautiful traits without being inferior to whites'" (99).

Hayashi notes that the speaker argued that women could adopt the language and customs of Americans without losing their cultural heritage: "We really have to assimilate ... We must do this in all situations without losing confidence in one's self, which is not inferior to whites and is said to be the [true nature of] the Yamato maiden" (99). Being able to assimilate thusly was seen as an intrinsically *Japanese* trait, and Japanese women, as holders of the Japanese spirit, should display that spirit by adapting to North American society. Assimilation, then, came to symbolize the superiority of the Japanese.[3]

The willingness of Japanese immigrants to embrace Canadian customs is also evident in the acceptance of Sunday schools by Japanese mothers. In Japan, there was no tradition of local Buddhist temples being utilized as a source of moral instruction, either through regular sermons or through any equivalent to Sunday school. Sending children to Christian Sunday schools may have been a concession to Canadian concepts of moral education, but perhaps more importantly, it was also a recognition that some sort of moral and ethical training was better than none. In Japan, it was not only the family that instilled a sense of ethics and morality; there were also social institutions (i.e., schools, employers, the government) that constantly imposed values on the public. Thus, the practice of sending children to religious institutions, initially to Christian churches and later to Buddhist temples, can be seen as stemming from a culturally derived sense of the importance of institutions for instilling discipline and a sense of order. While immigrant mothers may not have had any role in the leadership of religious institutions, they did have agency with respect to the upbringing of their children. As Midge Ayukawa argues, "while most Japanese women may have been obedient to their husbands, they were certainly not passive individuals. They actively sought to improve their lives, and more particularly, the lives of their children" (1995, 112).

Questions as to the "pragmatism" of sending children to Christian churches for moral training did not present a problem to the Japanese immigrant because the Japanese did not feel the need to identify with a single creed and traditionally utilized more than one religious tradition. As is often noted, the Japanese turn to Shintō for life events and to Buddhism for death rituals. Once Buddhist temples were established in Canada, however, they came to be the preferred institution to send their children to because they also provided cultural ties to Japan. The first Buddhist Sunday school was established at the Vancouver Buddhist Church in 1921. In the beginning there was opposition by some members of the Japanese community because of its association with Christian churches, but it became popular and Sunday schools were eventually incorporated into all Buddhist churches in Canada. Women not only supported them but were also active as teachers.

The Japanese diaspora likewise came to accept the introduction of kindergartens even though they were run by Christian churches. It was initially felt that literacy in the Japanese language was essential because the ultimate goal of early immigrants was to return to Japan; in fact, many families sent their children to Japan to stay with grandparents and attend Japanese schools. Later, however, more of the diaspora came to see Canada as a permanent home, and many whose children could only speak Japanese when they started public school realized the importance of preparing their children for the Canadian education system. Methodist and Anglican churches offered kindergartens to these immigrant children to prepare them with some English instruction, and these were supported by various fujinkai.[4] Again, the issue of instruction by a Christian organization did not present an obstacle to non-Christian immigrant women.

This willingness to adopt Canadian traditions and thus be "good immigrants" (in putative contrast to the Chinese) was also seen in the architecture of the Buddhist temples the community built. In 1911, the first Buddhist temple was built in Vancouver in the style of a Western church, complete with a steeple and arched windows. As Gail Lee Dubrow notes in her study of the Japanese American immigrant experience, "the design and construction of key community institutions were occasions when collective decisions had to be made about how much to stand out as Japanese immigrants or blend in as potential Americans" (2005, 121). The Buddhist temple in Vancouver is an example of an attempt to blend in.

The architecture of institutions became manifestations of the Japanese proverb, *Deru kugi wa utareru* (the nail that sticks up gets hit down), and assimilation through architectural conformity may again be perceived as evidence of a feeling of superiority, rather than inferiority, on the part of the Japanese community:

> The adaptive nature of Japanese social forms has played a role in facilitating the current high level of structured assimilation of Japanese Americans. There is no inherent contradiction in Japanese culture between maintaining a sense of distinctive "peoplehood" while adopting a variety of cultural elements from a host country. Indeed, as Reischauer points out, in traditional Japanese culture "ethics blends off into politeness and good manners" ... To be a "good Japanese" is to "fit in" and "not to make trouble." Within this context, then, it is not surprising to find that the Japanese in America have seen being a good American as an expression of being a good Japanese. (Fujita and O'Brien 1991, 41)

FUJINKAI (WOMEN'S ASSOCIATIONS): AGENCY THROUGH ORGANIZATIONS

Through the acceptance and support of Sunday schools and kindergartens run by Christian instructors, women came to have a role in the direction of religious practice in their new environment. However, women also seem to have had agency through the development of associations or clubs, of which there were many within the Japanese diaspora. As noted above, Japan had been undergoing a rapid change from a feudal society to a modern nation-state in order to meet the challenges of imperialism. The resulting acceptance of Western culture, development of new urban occupations, and loosening of traditional family obligations meant that the youth of Japan had more opportunities for advancement and self-expression than ever before. They started to gather in various organizations and associations that represented new ideals of democracy and citizenship for males (Cook 2005, 260). Of course, there had been groups for youth in the former Tokugawa era as well, but they were based on traditional family values and had an internal hierarchy that was replaced by more horizontal democratic relations in the new organizations (Pyle 1969, 9–15).

The ideals of democracy and citizenship also extended to women, and many women's associations were established in the late nineteenth century. As Mara Patessio notes, some of these groups differed little from informal gatherings of a few friends discussing books or fashion, but "the fact that they were publicized in newspapers and magazines that did not criticize their existence shows that they were in line with the 'enlightened and progressive' policy supported by Meiji society" (2011, 108–9).

The first women's association in Vancouver, the Nihon Fujinkai (the Japanese Women's Association), was established in 1904, followed by the Aikoku Fujinkai (Women's Patriotic Association) in 1905. Although these were started by the wives of Japanese consuls, other groups were established by ordinary immigrants.[5] Once Buddhist churches were established in British Columbia, they all developed Buddhist Women's Associations, providing social and economic support to the Japanese community as well as being involved in recreational and educational activities. These fujinkai were counted among the many associations for members of both sexes and for all ages in the diaspora, and, although subordinate to the adult male associations and unions, they were still popular and attracted many members (Young and Reid 1938, 113, 115; Nakayama 1921, 1607–701).

Fujinkai were mainly involved in social activities in the Christian and Buddhist churches, providing refreshments and raising funds through bazaars. Although these activities reinforced traditional gender roles, they did give women venues to express creativity and allowed them some say in the activities of these institutions. Moreover, although men had almost exclusive access to positions of authority and decision making, the number of men who held those positions was limited, and so most men, even in their associations and clubs, were unable to interact in public and in their community in the way women were able to in their traditional gender roles. That is, socialized as caregivers and nurturers, women could find fulfillment and satisfaction in these roles, whereas men outside positions of power and authority in the community had far less potential for interaction in the public sphere. As Naomi Tsunematsu has observed with respect to contemporary fujinkai, since they involve activities that men traditionally do not imitate, they "have given women a place to exhibit their power and agency in a local community in forms which challenge the dichotomous power relations between men and women in the contrast of the public and the domestic." She goes on to say, "Of course this public performance of domestic roles (e.g., preparing foods for church social events) can reinforce stereotypical gender roles" (2004, 105). But her argument is that, since cooking could be seen as a skill that men did not normally possess in the prewar years, it represented a strength, as women could determine what foods to prepare and how they were to be presented (103).

But women performed more than domestic roles in those groups. Women's associations could react quickly to local issues in a way that more prestigious male organizations could not. In both the United States and Canada, various women's associations launched relief funds to send clothing, food, or money in response to such disasters as the Great Kantō Earthquake of 1923. As Tsunematsu (2004) goes on to say, "the small scale negotiations of power in the everyday lives of women suggests the existence of a significant arena of power exertion which has often been overlooked" (101).

However, fujinkai in the Japanese diaspora differed in some respects from fujinkai in Japan, and this allowed further empowerment for women.

> The construction of volunteerism as benign, if somewhat useless work, has veiled the way in which upper-class women are power brokers in their communities ... upper-class volunteers influence the allocation of resources and the promotion of values in their communities ... Upper-class volunteers recreate class in three ways: They justify their own privilege through their ethic of "giving back" to the community, they impose conservative perspectives on professionals and clients within the organizations they serve, and they have access to large sums of money that they tap for fund-raising efforts ... The discourse surrounding "volunteer" masks the power relations achieved through it as well as women's actual experiences as volunteers ... Volunteering is thus ideological. (Abrahams 1996, 793–4n1)

In Meiji Japan, organizations and associations represented new ideals of democracy and citizenship, and class distinctions were particularly deemphasized in Japan's nation-state building endeavours, as in the Russo-Japanese War of 1904–05. With respect to this, Mrs Sadazuchi Uchida, the wife of a Foreign Ministry official, wrote, "Even as all class distinction is put aside by the men in the army, which is composed of noblemen, merchants, students, and common laborers, so it is with women who do their part at home [i.e., through various 'women's' organizations]" (Uchida 1904, 403). Even though peasant women were traditionally supposed to work hard, "Now even the wives of the wealthy," note Sharon Nolte and Sally Ann Hastings, "could not justify sitting by the brazier reading novels" (1991, 172). Thus fujinkai represented a sense of egalitarianism and so a certain degree of empowerment for women of lower social status in Japan. Although the first fujinkai in Canada were established by the wives of Japanese consuls or Buddhist ministers, the later ones were more horizontal in terms of their power structure. The vertical power relations implicit in Japan were mitigated by the fact that these women were all immigrants and generally from the same socio-economic background. The executives of the fujinkai were elected among their members, and although power relations still existed (often based on the status of the husband), they were far less pronounced than in Japan.

Moreover, these fujinkai were ideological; as was the case with those in Japan, they represented empowering venues for issues that women had not considered before. One issue was the role of the mother itself. By the mid-Meiji period, the Japanese government had universalized the ideal samurai wife to apply to all members of Japanese society (Uno 1991, 38); "'Good Wife, Wise Mother' became the guiding aphorism for government policy on women and the phrase resonates in Japanese society still today. The term evokes visions of women hovering over their children, providing tutoring and snacks with equal zeal" (Nolte and Hastings 1991, 158).[6]

But women's associations also offered the "good wife, wise mother" opportunities to learn new and modern ways to care for her family, and so the domestic role of women, traditionally seen as a private issue, increasingly came into the public sphere (Patessio 2006, 167).[7] Thus in the Meiji period Japanese women had acceptable venues to express themselves, and certain women's issues were allowed to become public. Moreover, an idealized Western model of the household also came to be appropriated by these associations. In the West, the Christian and Victorian role of women was to take care of the home and the children. However, "in predominantly Protestant nineteenth-century America," according to Rumi Yasutake, "middle-class women gained moral authority by claiming that they were innately more pious and pure than men. Emboldened by their moral authority, they participated in evangelical, benevolent, and reform activities outside their homes and expanded their domestic roles as mothers and guardians of the home into the public sphere" (2002, 93).

In a country in the process of Westernizing, this role for women fit in well with the concept of "good wife, wise mother":

> Japanese state policy with regard to women promoted such views, and women were depicted in public discourse as being naturally disposed to serve as the leaders of a harmonious household ... In mainstream journals with a general readership, the household was often likened to a miniature society with the wife playing the role of the domestic minister while the husband went out in the world as the foreign minister ... The sense that these nuclear family units, led by women, were the building blocks of a strong public society lent an increasingly public significance to women's fulfillment of the role of good wife and wise mother. (Starling 2013, 283)

This view was actively promoted in the fujinkai of the Jōdo Shinshū sect of Buddhism. "In the Shin Buddhist world," argues Jessica Starling, "the push for women's education and the emerging concept that women as good wives and wise mothers were to be the moral back-bone of public society led to a new prominence for women, particularly laywomen, within the sect, as *Bukkyō fujinkai* began to proliferate in the 1890s" (284). This is the school of Buddhism that was brought over to North America, and as noted above, it was the wives of Jōdo Shinshū Buddhist ministers who started the first Buddhist church fujinkai.

Thus, women's associations and the new "public" role that Japanese women now had gave them agency and a profile that had not existed in the previous Tokugawa period. However, though the founders of the first fujinkai in Canada were married to Japanese consuls or Buddhist ministers, since the majority of members would have been women from small rural villages, it is not unreasonable to question whether they would have comprehended concepts such as gaining "moral authority" due to their nature as "innately more pious and pure than men." What could they have made of the argument that they were playing the role of the domestic minister and functioning as the "building blocks of a strong public society"? Could they have appreciated that the rhetoric of the role of women as "good wife, wise mother" and as domestic ministers did not conflict with the ban on women partaking in political activity – but rather enhanced their new role?[8] Could this have resonated with women who came from poor villages in Japan in the early twentieth century?

But Mara Patessio argues that, with respect to the Women's Temperance Society in Japan in the late nineteenth century, "although the *ryōsai kenbo* [good wife, wise mother] ideal, Christianity, and the Victorian understanding of womanhood are not normally considered to have supported feminism, we shall see how the women of the Kyōfūkai [the Women's Temperance Union] did indeed find in them not only the basis for a new assertion of women's potential power within the home, but also a new confidence outside it" (2006, 168).

That is, the recognition and acceptance of fujinkai by government authorities and male intellectuals gave credibility to these associations as more than informal gatherings of women with common interests. The roles women played in supporting and participating in Christian traditions such as Sunday schools and the ability to support kindergartens run by Christian instructors gave women a sense of agency and confidence that would not have been available to them before the Meiji Restoration. As Naomi Abrahams notes, these are, again, "small scale negotiations of power. Even among relatively visible political activists … work to affect what they view as positive change was often done 'behind-the-scenes' … [C]ommunity participation reveals an important dynamic in the operation of power relations through collective identities … Women are 'the bricks that hold the building up'" (1996, 793).

CONCLUSION

The issue of the role of women in the religious life of the early Japanese diaspora in Canada is complicated by several factors. One is the role that religion played in the assimilation process; another is the fact that these immigrants came from a country that was itself undergoing a process of rapid Westernization, which included values and perceptions profoundly influenced by Protestantism. Religious values and modern Western values were often conflated by the Japanese, who were anxious to distinguish themselves from Chinese neighbours whom they perceived as stubbornly unwilling to change and thus rightfully subject to discriminatory policies. Yet, although there is no doubt that women had a limited role in the administration of religious institutions in Canada, they nonetheless had some sway over the acceptance or rejection of religious practices stemming from their role as their children's primary caregivers. This agency was empowered by a confidence gained through the formation of women's associations.

One other point must be considered with respect to the question of agency: the model of the "association" that had developed in Japan represented a Western sense of democracy and modernization, but that "democracy" was limited to males (by 1925 in Japan, all males over the age of twenty-five were granted the franchise). Women in Japan did not have the franchise, nor were they allowed to participate in politics. However, in Canada, no Japanese, male or female, could vote (except for a small number of war veterans who had fought for Canada during World War I). Did the disenfranchisement of Japanese males in Canada impact positions of power and authority within the Japanese diaspora? That is, did it level the playing field between Japanese men and women in Canada? Undoubtedly not; the patriarchal system remained intact. Traditional gender roles were preserved despite the fact that both sexes were equally excluded from voting, and from entering or advancing within certain professions. Thus, just as in Japan, the rhetoric of modernization afforded women little political advantage, since that rhetoric positioned women as transcending rather than participating in politics. The fact that men in the diaspora were denied the political and social advantages that they would have had in Japan did little to destabilize traditional gender roles in their new home.

NOTES

1 The issue, according to Nolte and Hastings, seems to have been "that political meetings were disreputable affairs that might compromise women's virtue or entice youth to take a wrong turn" (1991, 156).

2 "The universe of ideas, images, and themes – the symbolic modes that are the general currency of thought – have been either produced by men or controlled by them. In so far as women's work and experience have been entered into it, it has been on terms decided by men and because it had been approved by men. This is why women have had no written history until very recently, no share in making religious thoughts, no political philosophy, no representation of society from their view" (Smith 1987, 19).

3 Kiyoshi K. Kawakami (1914), who studied political science in the United States and eventually worked as an unofficial publicist for the Japanese

Foreign Ministry, promoted the idea that the Japanese, because they were not originally a homogeneous peoples but an amalgamation of various races, were able to adopt elements of Chinese culture and later Western culture. Thus, they had an inherent capacity to assimilate when circumstances required (62–4).

4 An example of this can be seen in Steveston, a fishing community to the south of Vancouver. Mitsuo Yesaki writes, "The Methodist Mission was too small for an enrollment of 92 pupils, so the *Fujinkai* (Japanese Women's Association) initiated a fund-raising campaign for a new school. Their campaign was so successful that they raised $3,000, well above their target of $800 … The *Fujinkai* operated and maintained the building, and the Women's Missionary Society provided the staff for the kindergarten" (2003, 66).

5 For example, Toyo Takata writes about Jirō Inouye's wife, Kane, who "had hardly settled in Canada when she gathered the few *Issei* women in Haney in 1910 to form a women's club, the first Japanese organization in the [Fraser] Valley to discuss mutual problems and to learn English and Canadian customs" (1983, 72). For more on Kane, see her biography in Nakayama (1917, 574).

6 According to the *Meiroku Zasshi*, the phrase "good wife, wise mother" was created by Nakamura Masanao (1832–1891) in the early 1870s as part of the goal of creating a strong, powerful nation (*fukoku kyōhei*) (1995, 401).

7 Patessio also writes that "even when lacking the political power to change their lives, a larger number of Meiji women were nevertheless able to organize and to voice their demands in society, making public topics that were considered private, or unworthy of attention, by male society, such as the abolition of concubinage and women's property rights" (2006, 156).

8 Nolte and Hastings write that "the ban [on joining political organizations] placed women in the same category as public figures, including military men, public and private school teachers and students, and shrine and temple officers. The grouping implied that women were like civil servants whose political activity would be inappropriate or whose responsibilities were so weighty as to preclude their participation … wives were public figures, veritable officers of the state in microcosm, the home. Their mission was a noble one that transcended petty partisan politics. Thus, the justification of women's political exclusion was primarily in terms of their home and family duties, and not of their physical, mental, or moral incapacity" (1991, 157).

REFERENCES

Abrahams, Naomi. 1996. "Negotiating Power, Identity, Family, and Community: Women's Community Participation." *Gender and Society* 10, no. 6: 768–96.

Adachi, Ken. 1991. *The Enemy That Never Was*. Toronto: McClelland and Stewart.

Ama, Michihiro. 2011. *Immigrants to the Pure Land*. Honolulu: University of Hawai'i Press.

Ayukawa, Midge. 1995. "Good Wives and Wise Mothers: Japanese Picture Brides in Early Twentieth-Century British Columbia." *BC Studies*, nos. 105–106: 103–18.

– 2008. *Hiroshima Immigrants in Canada, 1891–1941*. Vancouver: University of British Columbia Press.

Bokemeier, Janet L., and John L. Tait. 1980. "Women as Power Actors: A Comparative Study of Rural Communities." *Rural Sociology* 45, no. 2: 238–55.

Cook, Theodore F. 2005. "Making 'Soldiers': The Imperial Army and the Japanese Man in Meiji Society." In *Gendering Modern Japanese History*, edited by Barbara Molony and Kathleen Uno, 259–94. Cambridge, MA: Harvard University Asia Center.

Dubrow, Gail Lee. 2005. "The Nail That Sticks Up Gets Hit." In *Nikkei in the Pacific Northwest*, edited by Louis Fiset and Gail M. Nomura, 120–45. Seattle: Center for the Study of the Pacific Northwest.

Fujita, Stephen S., and David J. O'Brien. 1991. *Japanese American Ethnicity: The Persistence of Community*. Seattle: University of Washington Press.

Fukuzawa, Yukichi. 1885. "Datsu-a ron" [The Argument for abandoning Asia], *Jiji shinpō*, 16 March.

Geiger, Andrea. 2007/2008. "Negotiating the Boundaries of Race and Class Meiji Diplomatic Responses to North American Categories of Exclusion." *BC Studies*, no. 156: 37–51.

Hayashi, Brian Masaru. 1995. *'For the Sake of Our Japanese Brethren': Assimilation, Nationalism, and Protestantism among the Japanese of Los Angeles, 1895–1942*. Stanford, CA: Stanford University Press.

Ichikawa, Fusae, ed. 1977. *Nihon fujin mondai shiryō shūsei*, vol. 2, *Seiji*. Tokyo: Domesu shuppan.

Ichioka, Yuji. 1988. *The Issei: The World of the First Generation Japanese Immigrants, 1885–1924*. New York: Free Press.

Kawakami, Kiyoshi K. 1914. *Asia at the Door*. New York: F.H. Revell Co.

Kawano, Ronald M., ed. 1998. *A History of the Japanese Congregations in the United Church of Canada (1892–1959)*. Scarborough, ON: Japanese Canadian Christian Church Historical Project.

Kondo, Baron Rempei. 1914. "Japan Harbors No Ill Feeling toward America." In *Japan to America: A Symposium of Papers by Political Leaders and Representative Citizens of Japan on Conditions in Japan and on the Relations between Japan and the United States*, edited by Naoichi Masaoka, 34–8. New York: G.P. Putnam's Sons.

Meiroku Zasshi: Journal of the Japanese Enlightenment. 1976. Translated by William R. Braisted. Cambridge, MA: Harvard University Press.

Nakayama Jinshirō. 1917 *Kanada dōhō hatten shi* (History of the Japanese in Canada), vol. 2. Vancouver: Tairiku Nippōsha.

– 1921. *Kanada dōhō hatten taikan, furoku* [Encyclopedia of Japanese in Canada]. Tokyo: Nakayama Jinshirō.

Nolte, Sharon H., and Sally Ann Hastings. 1991. "The Meiji State's Policy toward Women, 1890–1910. In *Recreating Japanese Women, 1600–1945*, edited by Gail Lee Bernstein, 151–74. Berkeley: University of California Press.

"Nosse in Montreal." 1897. *Victoria Daily Colonist*, 28 March.

Patessio, Mara. 2006. "The Creation of Public Spaces by Women in the Early Meiji Period and the Tōkyō Fujin Kyōfūkai." *International Journal of Asian Studies* 3, no. 2: 155–82.

– 2011. *Women and Public Life in Early Meiji Japan*. Ann Arbor: University of Michigan Press.

Pyle, Kenneth B. 1969. *The New Generation in Meiji Japan*. Stanford, CA: Stanford University Press.

Sawada, Mitziko. 1991. "Culprits and Gentlemen: Meiji Japan's Restrictions of Emigrants to the United States, 1891–1909." *Pacific Historical Review* 60, no. 3: 339–59.

Smith, Dorothy. 1987. *The Everyday World as Problematic: A Feminist Sociology*. Boston: Northeastern University Press.

Starling, Jessica. 2013. "Neither Nun nor Laywoman: The Good Wives and Wise Mothers of Jodo Shinshu Temples." *Japanese Journal of Religious Studies* 40, no. 2: 277–301.

Takata, Toyo. 1983. *Nikkei Legacy: The Story of Japanese Canadians from Settlement to Today*. Toronto: NC Press.

Tsunematsu, Naomi. 2004. "Gender Power under Female Leadership: A Local Women's Association in Japan." *Japanese Studies* 24, no. 1: 97–114.

Uchida, Mrs. Sadazuchi. 1904. "What the Women of Japan Are Doing." *Harper's Weekly*, 12 March.

Uno, Kathleen S. 1991. "Women and Changes in the Household Division of Labor." In *Recreating Japanese Women, 1600–1945*, edited by Gail Lee Bernstein, 17–41. Berkeley: University of California Press.

Walthall, Anne. 1994. "Devoted Wives/Unruly Women: Invisible Presence in the History of Japanese Social Protest." *Signs* 20, no. 1: 106–36.

Wilson, Robert A., and Bill Hosokawa. *East to America: A History of the Japanese in the United States*. New York: Morrow.

Yasutake, Rumi. 2002. "Transnational Women's Activism: The Woman's Christian Temperance Union in Japan and the United States." In *Women and Twentieth-Century Protestantism*, edited by Margaret Lamberts Bendroth and Virginia Lieson Brereton, 93–112. Urbana: University of Illinois University Press.

Yesaki, Mitsuo. 2003. *Sutebusuton: A Japanese Village on the British Columbia Coast*. Vancouver: Peninsula Publishing Company.

Young, Charles H., and Helen R.Y. Reid. 1938. *The Japanese Canadians*. Toronto: University of Toronto Press.

5

Diasporic Sikh Women

Negotiating Gender Equality in Montreal

Julie Vig

In the past two decades, Quebec Sikhs have been at the centre of a range of public debates around secularism. The Multani case (better known as the "kirpan case") which took place between 2001 and 2006 has revived discussions about the place of religious symbols in public spaces (*Multani v. Commission scolaire Marguerite-Bourgeoys* 2006; Stoker 2007). This case, as well as others involving different religious groups, led to the creation of the Consultation Commission on Accommodation Practices Related to Cultural Differences (commonly referred to as the Bouchard-Taylor Commission, named after the two public intellectuals who led it, Gérard Bouchard and Charles Taylor). Between 2007 and 2008, the commission investigated issues of reasonable accommodation and shaped ongoing discussions about interculturalism as the best model of cultural integration (Bouchard and Taylor 2008; Tremblay 2010). In 2011 and 2013, Montreal Sikhs had to renegotiate their place in the public arena as two successive provincial governments – le Parti Libéral and le Parti Québécois – proposed bills (Bill 94 and Bill 60, respectively) that argued for prohibiting public employees from wearing religious symbols in the workplace in the name of promoting state secularism and religious neutrality. More recently, in June 2019,[1] the new government formed by the Coalition Avenir Québec passed a secularism law, Bill 21, prohibiting certain groups of employees in the public sector from wearing religious symbols.

The Bouchard-Taylor Commission and the proposed bills prompted representatives of the Quebec Sikh community to publish two briefs providing an overview of the Sikh tradition to promote a better understanding of Sikh identity in Québécois society (Sikh Community of Montréal 2007; Sikh Community of Quebec 2013). Although the briefs present a general portrait of the Sikh tradition, they focus significantly on the issue of gender equality within Sikhism, deploying this equality to legitimize Sikh beliefs and values to the wider Québécois society. It is in this broader context that the present chapter examines how Sikh women in Quebec position themselves in relation to discourses on gender equality fostered by their tradition and by their community. How do Sikh women relate to the representations of gender equality promoted by generally male religious elites? How do they perceive their role within the Sikh temple or *gurdwara* in relation to discourses on gender equality? Based on eight semi-structured interviews conducted in 2008 with first- and second-generation Sikh women, as well as participant observation within Quebec's largest gurdwara, the Gurdwara Nanak Darbar of Lasalle, I argue that not only are discourses on women and gender equality transformed in the Quebec context, but also that these discourses have an impact on Sikh women's representations of their role within the gurdwara.

As I will show, all those who participated in this study perceive the teachings of the Sikh gurus as empowering women and promoting gender equality, but most of them perceive inequalities within the gurdwara, especially between initiated (*amritdhari*) and noninitiated Sikhs. According to the interviewees and based on my observations, women who have taken *amrit* and who have become *amritdhari* (a status attained after undergoing an initiation ceremony) seem to have access to positions of greater power within the gurdwara at Lasalle. The women I interviewed – who ranged in age from eighteen to thirty-one years old and included four first-generation and four second-generation women, born, respectively, in the Indian Punjab and in Quebec[2] – expressed themselves on a variety of themes and topics, but I focus here on their representations of gender equality in relation to their tradition, and on their understandings of their roles within the gurdwara. It is important to note that while my research took place in a gurdwara whose administration values a way of being Sikh based on the Khalsa identity – an identity that refers to the community of initiated or "pure" that follow an orthopraxic definition of Sikh identity – the data collected represents a small window into the many ways of being Sikh, since the women interviewed represent a range of relationships with the Khalsa tradition.

SIKHS IN QUEBEC: HISTORY AND REPRESENTATION

The first Sikhs established themselves in Quebec in the early 1950s (Sikh Community of Montreal 2007; Sikh Community of Quebec 2013). However, according to Manjit Singh, president of the Gurdwara Sahib Greater Montreal, Montreal Sikhs only began to gather for the organization of religious services in the early 1960s. In 1971, Sikhism in Montreal became further institutionalized when a hundred-year-old neo-Gothic Baptist church was transformed and inaugurated as the first gurdwara (Castel 2007; Stoker 2013). Over the next three decades, four other gurdwaras were built on the island of Montreal and one in Brossard. However, following two successive waves of migration in the 1980s and 2000s, the community became significantly larger (Castel 2010, 446). In the 1980s, Sikhs experienced marginalization and violence in the Punjab, Haryana, and Delhi following Operation Blue Star and the assassination of Indian prime minister Indira Gandhi in 1984 (Castel 2007; Jakobsh and Walton-Roberts 2016; Tatla 1999). Many Sikhs migrated to English-speaking Canada, while others chose Quebec as their home. Newcomers in Ontario and British Columbia were able to integrate into already-established communities, but Sikhs who migrated to Quebec joined a much smaller community, composed of only 1,785 Sikhs (Castel 2007; 2010). Through the 1990s, the Sikh population rapidly doubled to reach 8,225 in the province of Quebec in 2001, out of which nearly 96 per cent lived in Quebec (Castel 2007). In this context, newcomers not only had to adapt to the specific sociocultural context of Quebec, but also had to build institutions to ensure the preservation and transmission of their identity. Today, the number of Sikhs in Quebec is estimated at 11,000.[3]

Since the early 1950s, the Quebec Sikh community went from having a few isolated members to being relatively large. These seven decades have also been marked by important transformations for Quebec. Sikhs, in turn, responded by submitting a brief during the public consultation in the context of the Bouchard-Taylor Commission in 2007. That brief presents a general portrait of the values and foundations of the Sikh religion and argues that Sikhs in Quebec live in complete harmony with Québécois values (Sikh Community of Montreal 2007, 5; see also Sikh Community of Quebec 2013, 7). The brief makes a case for more acceptance of Sikhs and Sikh traditions within Québécois society based on the assertion that women and men are equal within the Sikh tradition. This argument is based on a particular interpretation of the Sikh scripture, as well as of Sikh history and the roles played by women and men since the beginnings of Sikhism in the sixteenth century (Sikh Community of Montreal 2007, 3). The brief also argues that equality between women and men is at the core of the teachings of the ten Sikh gurus and that this principle of equality is enacted within both the social and religious dimensions of today's Sikh community in Quebec (Sikh Community of Montreal 2007, 7).

It is not uncommon in modern Sikh historiography to describe the beginning of Sikhism as revolutionary in its view of women and gender equality (see, for example, Aneja 1979; Gill 1995; H. Singh 1978; S. Singh 1979). This view is well reflected in both the 2007 and 2013 briefs. For instance, the ten Sikh gurus, from Guru Nanak (1469–1539) to Guru Gobind Singh (1666–1708), are represented as having worked toward improving the condition of women by condemning such practices as *sati* (widow immolation on her husband's funeral pyre), and by promoting remarriage of widows and access to liberation (*mukti*) for everyone regardless of caste, religion, or gender. The ten gurus are also remembered as having given more power to women in the religious and social spheres by welcoming them into the congregation (*sangat*) and allowing them to attend as well as lead religious ceremonies. Such representations are echoed throughout the two briefs presented by the Sikh community in Quebec. According to both, "Sikh women have enjoyed rights similar to men through the centuries" (since the beginning of Sikhism), and "Sikh women play an equal role in our religious and social spheres" (Sikh Community of Montreal 2007, 3; Sikh Community of Quebec 2013, 8).

WOMEN'S VOICES: REPRESENTATIONS OF GENDER EQUALITY

In keeping with the representations presented in the briefs, many of the women I interviewed perceive the teachings of the gurus as empowering. For all interviewees, the teachings of the gurus are unequivocal on the question of gender equality. Daljit, born in Quebec, reports that the hymns of the gurus about women and gender equality are well known to all women and men in her community. According to her, the most valuable passage for women, which she finds inspiring, is an integral part of several religious ceremonies at the gurdwara:

> But you know in our religion, boys and girls are equals. [And] there's a line in Asa di Var that says *so kiu mandā ākhīai jitu jamahi rājāna*, "why would you call a woman inferior if she's the one who gives birth to the kings of the world?" So if the king is kingly then the woman who brought the king on earth is also, kingly or queenly or however you want to express it. That is the line which is always used by the poetry analysts to come and talk on stage: women are equals and that women are very important in the Sikh life. This is definitely inspiring how we ... it's probably something that every Sikh person, man and woman knows that line by heart.

For many, this passage (*Asa di Var*) reflects the central position of women inherent in the foundations of Sikh doctrine. All the women interviewed mentioned (on or off the record) the importance of this passage. Nikky-Guninder Kaur Singh (1993; 2006; 2008) argues that the passage is one of many examples of the pervasive feminine imagery within the Guru Granth Sahib that is empowering for women. However, in her study of Sikh women in Vancouver, Nayar observes that this passage can "reinforce feelings of alienation among Canadian-born Sikh women" (2010, 268–9) because the values it fosters are not generally realized within their community.

For Simran, also Quebec-born, not only are the teachings of the gurus more progressive than other religious traditions, but she perceives them to be more progressive than norms in several countries where the introduction of equal political and legal rights has only recently occurred: "Even before the equality appeared in the world, it was already there in our religion! It is something of pride." Daljit's mother, Pawan,[4] expresses the view that although the teachings of the gurus are egalitarian, inequalities between women and men still persist within the community because people are blinded by their cultural prejudices:

> The gurus, in our scriptures, have always respected women. There is no saying that will put women down. Women have never been put down but ... this exists culturally, that women are put down, just like the caste system they abolished, but

> people are still following it … it's a shame for women! The gurus respected women a lot, Guru Nanak Dev ji respected women a lot, he guided them, he taught them, he considered them as his children, his daughters so the women were never looked down by our gurus but culturally, people do! Our guru tried to change people, he tried to change the thinking of people five hundred years ago, he tried, but people don't learn! They are stuck with their comfortable way of thinking … a man will feel superior to his wife and he [will do] it openly. I have seen *granthis* coming and disrespecting their wives. On stage. So when I hear something like that I walk out! This guy is putting his wife down! It's all been carried by people … it's very sad and ironic that a woman will put down another woman too.

Pawan's words illustrate the discrepancy Sikh women experience between what they know about the teachings of the gurus and what they observe within the gurdwara. In all the interviews, women attributed the cause of gender inequalities not to religion but to norms of Punjabi culture that they perceive as sexist. This view is evident in statements by Parvinder (born in the Indian Punjab) and Joti (born in Quebec):

> Our Sikhism, our holy book says that both men and women are equal, but in our culture they (are not). You have to do! It happens when (my husband) is coming from outside, we have to give him a glass of water. Why when I'm coming from outside, why he's not standing to give me glass of water? You understand what I'm saying? So how can we say both are equal? (Parvinder)

> If I can add something very quickly, that … even though we're talking about Sikhism … Punjabi culture and Sikhism they kind of like … they clash! But the funny thing is that most Sikhs are Punjabis but … Punjabi culture and Sikh culture are completely different … it's just … interesting. You get confuse? (laughter) (Joti)

Mahmood and Brady argue that, for second-generation Sikh women growing up in North America, concepts such as "gender" and "choice" significantly shape their discourse (2000, 30). And Nayar also observes a desire among second-generation Sikh women in Vancouver to distinguish between the religious and the cultural (2010, 264). Daljit was concerned with this distinction throughout her interview. According to her, the religious does not prescribe any role based on someone's gender. When one actually observes an unequal division of labour, this can be exclusively attributed to Punjabi culture, whose norms and values regarding gender roles are still strongly internalized by Sikhs in the Punjab and the diaspora. Daljit also expressed that as a wife she is well aware that she fulfills certain roles shaped by Punjabi culture, but she feels that gender equality is not an issue with her husband because the roles she plays are personal choices. In Vancouver, this tension between fulfilling traditional roles as a wife, daughter, and mother is mostly experienced by second-generation women (260). According to Nayar, it is the third generation that questions cultural and gender norms more openly, and uses the Guru Granth Sahib as a tool to empower themselves as women (269–70).

For Ramina, also second generation, certain aspects of Punjabi culture clash with the foundations of Sikhism, especially on the question of relationships between women and men. Although gender equality is a central value conveyed by the teachings of the gurus, in reality women often take full responsibility for the household: "No, no, no!! [My husband and I] we're gonna help each other! We are going to clean together, we are going to cook together, you know, I'm gonna work! And I'm not gonna quit my work to clean! You know, I had not studied in my books like this for eighteen hours a day to make *chapatis* and be told 'well ... you've put too much salt.' Hey!" For Ramina, gender inequality is also a matter of culture. However, according to her, Sikh women are favoured twice as much as other women. Not only can they rely on the Charter of Rights and Freedoms in the civil sphere, but they can also rely on the Guru Granth Sahib in the religious sphere to denounce all forms of discrimination:

> No, no, no, no, it's not religion! It's the thoughts, the culture, the society! You know [there are] stupid men, who get together and they sit down and they talk their shit together – "oh, women shouldn't do this, women shouldn't do that," you know, it's just a small faction. But I ... I'm not able to tolerate that even though it's maybe 1 or 2 per cent of the whole community, I'm not able to tolerate because me, I want equality for all men, all women, that's it! End of story. We have a constitution? Canadian Constitution, the Charter of Rights and Freedom and the Guru

> Granth Sahib telling … you know, men and women are equals and the Guru Granth Sahib is even saying women should be put on a pedestal and worshiped! That's what the Guru Granth Sahib says. And I don't see that happening.

Ramina's parallel between the Charter of Rights and Freedoms and the Guru Granth Sahib illustrates that the Sikh scripture itself can be used as a tool to criticize patriarchal culture and inequality. The same way that Sikh women can rely on the Charter to claim legal and social rights within society, they can rely on their religious texts to criticize cultural inequalities within their community, strengthening the role of religion in their lives.

Some first-generation women express being closer to their religion since they arrived in Quebec, which is not uncommon among migrants who feel the need to assert certain values and aspects of their identities (Levitt 2009, 1236). Indeed, as Harpreet points out, it is not unusual to observe Sikhs in Quebec having a more intimate relationship to religion than in their country of origin. According to her, while in India the religious was intrinsically linked to the cultural, in Quebec Sikhs are closer to their religion, since they are distant from their referent cultural identity: "[Here] your parents absolutely want to give you all the values of religion because they do not want to lose something because they are so far away. You end up being closer to religion, more conservative than you would have been in India." This is a reality that Manmeet, born in the Indian Punjab, also expresses: "I'm really changed, I don't know why in India I was maybe blind or something like that, I didn't know anything, but now, I think I'm very near God. I've found I'm very very near more. Because every day, every weekend, I go to the temple, [sing a] lot of *kirtan* and everything. I've changed!" Relocation in a migratory context, which involves a distancing from the home context, generates an increased rapprochement with the religious, which becomes an important pole of identification. While religion is not the only site for the articulation of a diasporic identity, many have argued that religion plays an important role in migrants' reaffirmation of identities and values (Boisvert 2006; Levitt 2009, 1236; Meintel 2014; Rousseau 2006). As Harpreet expresses above, some parents feel the anxiety of seeing their children grow up in an environment where their cultural and religious values are not shared by the larger society. The gurdwara can become a site where first-generation Sikhs and their children engage with their religion, and where they can create relationships with other members of the community who share similar values.

WOMEN IN THE CODE OF CONDUCT: THE STATUS OF AMRITDHARI

Whereas the Quebec briefs present an interpretation by the leadership of three important gurdwaras in Quebec of how the Sikh gurus viewed women, the Sikh Code of Conduct (the Rahit Maryada) represents the authoritative view on Sikh identity promoted by the SGPC (Sikh Gurdwara Parbandhak Committee). In addition to managing the religious organization of all gurdwaras in the Punjab, Haryana, and Himachal Pradesh, this institution is influential within diasporic Sikh communities, and Quebec is no exception (McLeod 2007; Nayar 2008). This code, which is used in Quebec in the Gurdwara Nanak Darbar to regulate rituals and practices, has a significant influence on women's roles within the gurdwara; it also shapes behaviour within other Sikh centres (Rahit Maryada 1950). Completed in 1950, it represents a centralized and normative vision of Sikh regulatory practices. Directly derived from the words of the tenth guru, Guru Gobind Singh, the Rahit Maryada defines who is a Sikh based on the Khalsa identity (McLeod 2007, 105–14). In addition, the Rahit Maryada – which significantly modernizes and homogenizes earlier orthopraxic definitions of being a Sikh (Murphy 2007; Murphy 2012; Dhavan 2011) – also codifies rituals and practices that take place in the gurdwara, as well as the daily discipline to which all initiated or amritdhari Sikhs must subscribe. The Rahit Maryada also sets rules regarding birth rituals, initiation (*amrit sanskar*), marriage (*anand karaj*), and death. For all these rituals, and for the conduct of daily religious ceremonies and the public reading of religious texts, the code insists particularly on the fact that all initiated women (amritdhari) can, like initiated men, not only participate but lead.

At the Gurdwara Nanak Darbar, copies of the Rahit Maryada are freely distributed to members of the congregation and visitors during important festivals and celebrations. Informal interviews with official representatives of the Gurdwara Nanak Darbar and the president of the Gurdwara Sahib of Greater Montreal, Manjit Singh, also confirm that the organization of religious life is based on the Rahit Maryada. Yet, although the Rahit Maryada prescribes equality between women and men in regards to the amritdhari religious discipline, this discourse is not always enacted within the Gurdwara Nanak Darbar, where there remains a sexual division of labour.[5]

For example, several passages of the Rahit Maryada talk about women in relation to their religious practice at home and within the community.[6] Women and men are invited to the same daily religious discipline based on the reading of religious texts, meditation on the name of God (*nam simran*), fulfillment of service (*seva*), the same religious practice within the gurdwara, and access to the same functions. Nothing in the code prohibits initiated women (amritdhari) from being responsible for important tasks such as leading religious services or fulfilling administrative duties. The code also prohibits women from wearing the veil within the gurdwara,[7] which, it is argued, would contradict the principle of equality promoted by the Guru Granth Sahib. The remarriage of widows is allowed, and polygamy is explicitly proscribed along with the system of dowry (*daj*): "No Sikh should accept a match for his son or daughter for monetary consideration" (Rahit Maryada 1950, Article XVIII-I). It is stated that both women and men must learn the Gurmukhi script in order to be able to read the Guru Granth Sahib in its original language. Even though the Rahit Maryada emphasizes equality between women and men within the gurdwara, this principle of equality is not generally enacted in the organization of religious life at the Gurdwara Nanak Darbar.

I observed five interviewees in their religious practice at the gurdwara: Satwant, Parvinder, Manmeet, Simran, and Daljit. Although I cannot generalize about the differences observed between the three first-generation interviewees (Satwant, Parvinder, Manmeet) and the two second-generation interviewees (Simran, Daljit) regarding their relationships to the community as a whole, I can say that Simran and Daljit were more active within the gurdwara. Daljit, for example, took part in activities related to religious practice (reading scriptures in front of the congregation, teaching music), while Satwant, Parvinder, and Manmeet took part in activities belonging to the community sphere (community kitchen, cleaning). Even if I cannot establish a causal relationship between being first- and second-generation and the types of roles fulfilled at the gurdwara, it can nevertheless be suggested that Daljit's and Simran's status as amritdhari women allows them more freedom and greater mobility between the community sphere where women are usually assigned, and the sphere of religion that is usually managed by men.

At the Gurdwara Nanak Darbar, it is common to observe women being responsible for the community space, whereas men are commonly responsible for the religious sphere. This division of labour is well reflected in the two institutions that are central to Sikh ethics: the community kitchen (*langar*) and service (*seva*).[8] Although *seva* does not prescribe any particular role on the basis of gender, I observed at the Gurdwara Nanak Darbar that there exists a discrepancy between discourse and reality and that there exists an unequal distribution of roles based on a sexual division of labour. According to Nikky-Guninder Kaur Singh (2006), this division of labour is common within Sikh communities in the Punjab and in the diaspora, and is reflected mainly through *seva*:

> The principle of *seva* of the first Sikh community established by Guru Nanak in Kartarpur pervades all Sikh shrines as men and women together clean the precincts, cook *langar*, recite poetry, and give Punjabi instruction. The exception is that there are no women *granthi* (official reader) affiliated with any of the Sikh Gurdwaras, and so the men lead worship by taking *vak* (reading out the divine command for the congregation), reciting *ardas* (prayer that begins and concludes every ceremony), and distributing *karah prashad* (the Sikh sacrament). Daily ceremonies like *prakash* (opening of the Guru Granth) and *sukhasan* (putting it to rest in the evening) in Gurdwaras, the annual celebrations of Baiskahi and Gurpurabs (birthday or death anniversaries of the gurus), and all rites of passage for Sikh men and women are conducted and administered almost exclusively by men. The sexism and subjugation they directly experience in public spaces resonate deeply in the inner psyches of Sikh men and women, legitimizing women's deference and subordination to their fathers, brothers, uncles and husbands. (694)

Despite these observed discrepancies, women who have undergone the initiation ceremony appear to be more integrated within the religious sphere: they occupy positions of power in the administrative committee, and they perform religious functions such as the public reading of texts and (more rarely) the interpretation of the scripture before the community. Indeed, as Anne Murphy argues, *seva* has provided an ethical "field of action that allows for the participation of female actors as women" (2009, 166). However, according to some interviewees, non-amritdhari Sikhs are not allowed to touch the Guru Granth Sahib within the gurdwara at Lasalle, which excludes them from leading important rituals of passage and from publicly interpreting texts before the congregation. Instead of allowing women to perform these religious functions, the status of amritdhari seems rather to open the door to positions of influence (administration, *granthi*) within the gurdwara.[9]

THE STATUS OF AMRITDHARI: TOWARD A REAPPROPRIATION OF THE RELIGIOUS SPHERE

My observations at the Gurdwara Nanak Darbar are consistent with Jakobsh and Walton-Roberts's (2016, 177) and Kaur Singh's (2006, 694) contention that women in Canada and North America still play secondary roles in gurdwaras. While some attribute this distribution of roles to having less formal education and financial independence than men, others will argue that in the religious sphere, it is the amritdhari status that contributes to the relegation of non-initiated women to secondary roles.

During my observation within the gurdwara, it appeared to me that some amritdhari women were more integrated into the religious sphere than non-amritdhari women. As discussed above, the Rahit Maryada explicitly prescribes that both amritdhari women and men are authorized to lead rituals, daily religious ceremonies, and the public reading of the Guru Granth Sahib. While my observations led me to believe that amritdhari women were more involved in the religious sphere, it emerges from my interviews that the status of amritdhari is not only an ideal promoted by the community; it also seems to create a hierarchy between amritdhari and non-amritdhari Sikhs. According to Joti, who is second generation, the status of amritdhari is the institutionally sanctioned means of achieving spiritual liberation or *mukti*, but it is possible to grow spiritually by not taking *amrit*, and respecting the principles of Sikhism:

> Eh … I think that a lot of people would say that it is mandatory [to become amritdhari] but personally, and this is based on my own interpretation which is maybe more … liberal [laugh], I know that it's an optimal situation that we're expected to take amrit eventually and become amritdhari, we strive toward that so we can finally reach mukti but at the same time, I don't

> believe that God loves me any less if I don't reach that way ... as long as I'm growing and ... I'm taking the principles of Sikhism and try to follow in my everyday life.

Satwant, who is first generation, discusses the status of amritdhari in the same sense as Joti. She recognizes the institutional ideal of amritdhari, but also the fact that it establishes a hierarchy between Sikhs who decided not to take amrit and Sikhs who decided to take it: "In our gurdwara, yes, there is [a hierarchy] because they have a committee who takes the gurdwara functions like ... they participate, they have group meetings and they are the ones who organize different event [and] yes, they consider [that] the members should be amritdhari so there is a difference, they consider that there is a difference. Only the amritdhari, they say, can read the holy book in the gurdwara but we have the holy book at our home and we can read it anytime [laugh] so ... we prefer to read it at home yeah." If non-amritdhari Sikhs cannot touch the Guru Granth Sahib within the gurdwara at LaSalle, it excludes them from fulfilling religious functions. That said, the role of granthi, which is probably one of the most valued positions within the community, is accessible only to a minority of amritdhari. The granthi holds the power to produce religious knowledge since the granthi interprets scripture and transmits that interpretation to the congregation. Thus, in practice, non-amritdhari women can find themselves twice disadvantaged within the gurdwara in LaSalle: as a woman and as a non-amritdhari. In this sense, some non-amritdhari women avoid taking part in the activities of the gurdwara. This is what Manmeet, who was born in the Punjab, expresses when she claims to visit her gurdwara for the sole purpose of listening to religious songs (*kirtan*). Manmeet also claims to not be involved in the gurdwara because of the monopoly exerted by some amritdhari Sikhs who are fighting for power: "Yeah they say we have to be amritdhari, we have to, you know? We have to put *kirpan* [short sword], we have to [keep] our hair long, we have to never cut our blah blah blah, sorry for the blah blah blah but no, I don't think so I can take amrit. [And] in the gurdwara, [there are] two parties fighting, one party says 'I want to [be a] member!' and [the] other party says 'I want to be member' and then [they] fight! It's not good! They have to respect the religion, they have to understand everything!" While the status of amritdhari excludes in some way non-amritdhari from the religious sphere, it nevertheless seems to constitute an opening for amritdhari women that paves the way for positions of influence and power within the gurdwara (administration, granthi). According to Daljit, at the Gurdwara Nanak Darbar, about 10 to 15 per cent of women are amritdhari. She says that amritdhari women from different generations may look different based on the clothes they choose to wear. For example, I observed that many first-generation Sikh women chose to cover their head with a long scarf (*dupatta*), whereas many second-generation amritdhari women adopt the turban.

I also observed at the gurdwara that among young people of the second generation, although some were already amritdhari, several others follow the Rahit Maryada with the intention of becoming one, as Simran notes: "Now girls are more religious. They are really religious, the youngest, between eight and thirteen, are really religious now because they see older girls (and) they see them [doing] well." In the group of young people taking music and singing classes, Daljit is a teacher and Simran is the oldest student. Daljit is conscious of her position: "I think I'm a role model." Simran expresses that her choice to follow the Rahit and to take amrit was directly inspired by Daljit, who is nine years her senior. According to Simran, both now act as models for younger generations and parents: "Parents will also use us as example sometimes. They will say 'oh! It's good that you're doing this because she is also doing this, look how a good daughter she is.' Like me, when I was young, I was always with [Daljit], it was like … 'yes, she is older than me but check the way she is!'" Simran adds that some young Sikhs of her generation no longer practise their religion because they cannot identify with their parents. According to her, because they do not wish to self-represent as culturally Punjabi, they eliminate religion from their life: "everyone of my age … want to be too like the others!" She adds that she saw in Daljit a model for believing that being a Sikh and feeling a sense of belonging in Québécois society was possible: "Thanks to Daljit, I knew that I could be Sikh and have a normal life! Because she played hockey and all that! She influenced me! Because of her, I started playing football at my school and I finished captain! I was happy, I was like, I can!" This is what Daljit attests, and insists that being Sikh does not imply being culturally Punjabi: "I think being a young baptized Sikh, going to school, playing sports, eh … I think that is role model life for the other young kids that we *should* do these things, we *can* do these things, you don't have to choose between two kinds of life to be a good Sikh, you can do both." The recomposition of the religious experience is a phenomenon that appears to be taking shape among these young amritdhari Sikhs, or among those on the path of becoming one. Indeed, many of them distance themselves from what they perceive to be Punjabi culture; at the same time, they reappropriate the Sikh religion by studying it from its sources. Harpreet told me, "what I learned from religion and even through reading, I learned it much faster in a course than there (in India) where they learn a lot more gradually you know." In the same sense, Joti states that she probably knows more about her religion than the Sikhs in the Punjab because of her distance from the traditional cultural context: "What I found in India is that ... it's funny that I probably know more about Sikhism than people in India! It's just because it's so diverse in general and there's the predominance of one culture and everyone is just intertwined and so ... because of that, I find that maybe a new culture is being created here." By distancing themselves from Punjabi culture, young Sikhs who go the Gurdwara Nanak Darbar generate new representations of their religion and of themselves that can transform social relations. More precisely, within this group of young people, I observed that women take up the religious discourse on gender equality and appropriate the religious space generally occupied by men.

TRANSFORMATIONS OF WOMEN-MEN RELATIONSHIPS WITHIN THE GURDWARA

In my field observations at the Gurdwara Nanak Darbar, three situations illustrated the appropriation of the religious space by women: Daljit's music and religious singing classes; summer camps for young people; and the public reading of religious texts by women.

Music Education and Youth Summer Camps

Every Friday, Daljit goes to the gurdwara to teach traditional music and singing to a group of young people. Her role is not only to teach the technical side of music and singing, but also to explain how to read and understand the passages from the Guru Granth Sahib that they are singing. Simran discussed with me the relationship between music and prayer: "On Fridays and on Sunday mornings, we have music and language classes and [we learn] how to read the prayers because you know, prayers are religious songs and it's hard to read! It takes someone to help us understand and interpret them and all."

As she points out, Daljit's role also consists of guiding young people in their interpretation of the religious hymns recited. This interpretive function is significant. Indeed, it goes beyond the strict reproduction of the religious and allows for the transmission of a renewed reading of the texts by a woman. And Daljit is not shy about giving central importance to the principle of equality between women and men prescribed by her religion, in her life and in her teaching. It is a principle that she does not hesitate to pass on to her students. Simran once again testifies to Daljit's influence in this way: "We learn that everything a man can do, a woman can do because they are 100 per cent equal, there is nothing that stops us!"

As in the case of traditional music and songs, the summer camps for young people also illustrate that openings for women in the religious space exist in the Gurdwara Nanak Darbar. Daljit's mother is responsible for organizing the camps, and, working in collaboration with her daughter Daljit, she decides the content of the classes and teaches them. Like Daljit, her mother does not hesitate to pass on to the students the values of equality between women and men prescribed by the gurus. Daljit and Pawan's roles in the production of religion suggest that the Gurdwara Nanak Darbar is not resistant to the integration of women – at least, amritdhari women – in spheres of influence and power.

Function of Granthi

As mentioned above, the role of granthi occupies a central place in the organization of the religious life of the gurdwara. Whereas in India granthis are mainly responsible for leading religious services, according to the Rahit Maryada, their role in the diaspora sometimes involves much more:

> *Granthis* serving *gurdwaras* outside India perform additional educational functions, teaching children to play the instruments used in worship or to read Punjabi … Their effectiveness varies. Some are highly competent, fluent in English … Others possess only the basic skills required to conduct worship and ceremonies, which were the functions for which they were trained, and they speak only Punjabi … So far all *granthis* are Punjabi educated. There is no sign yet of a college for *granthis* being set up in the west though the need will increase as the cultural distance

between Punjab and the dispersion increases. (Cole and Sambhi 2006, 193)

Moreover, because there is no granthi training school in North America, diaspora communities now rely on granthis trained and established in the Punjab. These granthis usually travel from one gurdwara to another and the Sikh communities of the diaspora are rarely able to keep a permanent granthi at their disposal. That said, diasporic Sikh institutions are putting in place solutions to ensure the production and reproduction of religious life. In the Gurdwara Nanak Darbar there are two types of granthi. Granthis of the first type, exclusively men from the Punjab and trained in Punjab schools, stay at the gurdwara on a temporary basis. Their role is mainly to conduct religious services and to convey an interpretation of the scripture to the congregation. Simran describes these granthis as follows: "The granthi is the man sitting on the stage. [He is] going to interpret the scripture as necessary when there are congregations in the *darbar*, if there are many people here, [and] it is filled, you know, it is not easy to manage. So many people! It takes someone who knows, who can control the ceremonies … you know he graduated there, he'll be able to control. Also, he studied in India to do that … there are degrees in that." However, when there is no "professional" granthi in the gurdwara, any initiated woman or man at the gurdwara can perform the functions of the granthi. Daljit explains that she has already acted as this second type of granthi a few times.

Public Reading of the Scripture by Women

Every afternoon, a group of women occupies the hall to sing religious hymns from the Guru Granth Sahib. These women, usually elderly, sit on the ground to the left of the Guru Granth Sahib and carry their booklets, reciting passages from the book for approximately one hour.

Unlike the two preceding examples that concern the production of religious knowledge, the public reading of texts by women is more akin to the reproduction and maintenance of religion. When women take part in the collective singing of religious hymns (*kirtan*), they do not occupy the space to voice a public interpretation of those hymns. Women speak out when the gurdwara is rather empty, while the granthi, for example, speaks when more members of the congregation are gathered. The daily reading of religious texts by women in the

Gurdwara Nanak Darbar does indicate an openness on the part of the institution to give more space to women in the religious sphere. However, since they do not have the space to publicly voice their interpretations of the scripture like granthis do, their relegation to the reading rather than the interpretation can also be seen as a form of marginalization.

CONCLUSION

The Sikh community of Quebec is rather young in comparison to Sikh communities elsewhere in Canada. Since its beginnings in the 1950s, the community has grown in both membership and visibility within the broader Québécois society. Today, Sikh women play an important part within the community but still perceive discrepancies between the teachings of the Sikh gurus on gender equality and the lack of access by non-initiated women to the religious sphere that includes the interpretation of the scripture. Nonetheless, as is the case with other diasporic Sikh communities, and as Mahmood and Brady have observed, women from younger generations have the double advantage "of holding both 'the symbolic capital' of Sikhism … as well as the 'cultural capital' of the larger North American society through their education and associations with non-Sikhs" to foster changes (2000, 200). This foreshadows potential transformations of not only gender roles within the Gurdwara Nanak Darbar at LaSalle, but also of relationships between amritdhari and non-amritdhari Sikhs.[10]

NOTES

1 Bill 21 was passed right before the final edits of this chapter. How members of the Sikh community will respond to this law remains to be seen.

2 The first group of interviewees is composed of four first-generation women born in the Punjab, aged between twenty-six and thirty-one years old, and established in Quebec for less than twenty years: Satwant, Parvinder, Manmeet, and Harpreet. The second group of interviewees is composed of four women born in Quebec and aged between eighteen and twenty-nine years old: Ramina, Simran, Joti, and Daljit. The interviews took place in French and English. For the purpose of this chapter, I translated the

interviews conducted in French into English. For a more detailed analysis of the fieldwork, see Vig (2009).

3 This is an estimate calculated by Dr Frédéric Castel (Département de sciences des religions de l'Université du Québec à Montréal) based on statistics collected by Statistics Canada. Castel, personal communication, 26 March 2017.

4 Although Pawan was not included as an interviewee in my data set, we had a few informal conversations that are meaningful to mention here.

5 Danièle Kergoat (2007) defines sexual division of labour as a form of social division of labour that arises from gender relations and is a product of history and society. According to her, two organizing principles are at the basis of this form of social division of labour: the principle of separation and the principle of hierarchization. According to the principle of separation, there are roles naturally attributed to women and to men, respectively. The principle of hierarchization means that the roles of men have an added social value in relation to those of women (35–44).

6 Other scholars (for instance, Jakobsh 2003; 2015; Kaur Singh 2008; Mahmood and Brady 2000; Shanker 2002) have discussed the Rahit Maryada in relation to women.

7 To be distinguished from the rule that all Sikhs must cover their heads before entering a gurdwara as a sign of respect and humility toward the Guru Granth Sahib.

8 "Seva (Voluntary Service) is a prominent part of Sikh religion. Illustrative models of voluntary service are organised for imparting training, in the Gurdwaras. Its simple forms are: sweeping and plastering the floors … of the Gurdwara, serving water to or fanning the congregation, offering provisions to and rendering any kind of service in the common kitchen-cum-eating house, dusting the shoes of the people visiting the Gurdwara, etc." (Rahit Maryada 1950, Article XXI).

9 For a detailed ethnography of amritdhari women in North America, see Mahmood and Brady (2000).

10 Thank you to Sailaja Krishnamurti, Becky R. Lee, Preet K. Virdi, Anne Murphy, and Timothy Bellefleur for their comments and suggestions.

REFERENCES

Aneja, Gagan. 2007. *Great Sikh Women*. Chandigarh: Unistar Books.

Boisvert, Mathieu. 2006. "Incidence du facteur religieux dans la reconstruction de l'identité du migrant: le cas de la communauté tamoule hindoue d'origine sri lankaise." Paper presented at the Congrès annuel de la société canadienne pour l'étude de la religion, Ottawa, 1–4 June.

Bouchard Gérard, and Charles Taylor. 2008. "Building the Future: A Time for Reconciliation." *Commission de Consultation sur les Pratiques d'Accommodement Reliées aux Différences Culturelles*, mce.gouv.qc.ca/publications/CCPARDC/rapport-final-integral-en.pdf.

Castel, Frédéric. 2007. "Les Sikhs du Québec." *Revue Relations* 714, February. cjf.qc.ca/revue-relations/publication/article/les-sikhs-du-quebec/.

– 2010. "Dynamique de l'équation ethnoconfessionnelle dans l'évolution récente de la structure du paysage religieux québécois: Les cas du façonnement des communautés bouddhistes et musulmanes (1941–2001)." PhD dissertation, Université du Québec à Montréal.

Cole, Owen W., and P.S. Sambhi. 2006. *The Sikhs: Their Religious Beliefs and Practices*. Brighton and Portland: Sussez Academic Press.

Dhavan, Purnima. 2011. *When Sparrows Became Hawks: The Making of the Sikh Warrior Tradition, 1699–1799*. New York: Oxford University Press.

Gill, Mahindar Kaur. 1995. *The Role and Status of Women in Sikhism*. Delhi: National Book Shop.

Jakobsh, Doris R. 2003. *Relocating Gender in Sikh History: Transformation Meaning and Identity*. New Delhi: Oxford University Press.

– 2015. "Seeking the Image of 'Unmarked' Sikh Women: Text, Sacred Stitches, Turban." *Religion and Gender* 5, no. 1: 35–51.

Jakobsh, Doris, and Margaret Walton-Roberts. 2016. "A Century of Miri Piri: Securing Sikh Belonging in Canada." *South Asian Diaspora* 8, no. 2: 167–83.

Kergoat, Danièle. 2007. "Division sexuelle du travail et rapports sociaux de sexe." In *Dictionnaire critique du féminisme*, 2nd edition, edited by Helena Hirata, Françoise Laborie, Hélène Le Doaré, and Danièle Senotier, 35–44. Paris: Presses universitaires de France.

Levitt, Peggy. 2009. "Roots and Routes: Understanding the Lives of the Second Generation Transnationally." *Journal of Ethnic and Migration Studies* 35, no. 7: 1225–42.

Mahmood, Cynthia, and Stacy Brady. 2000. *The Guru's Gift: An Ethnography Exploring Gender Equality with North America Sikh Women*. Mountain View, CA: Mayfield Publications.

McLeod, W.H. 2007. "The Evolution of the Sikh Code of Conduct." In *Essays in Sikh History, Tradition, and Society*, 105–14. New Delhi: Oxford University Press.

Meintel, Deirdre. 2014. "Religious Collectivities in the Era of Individualization." *Social Compass* 61, no. 2: 195–206.

Multani v. Commission scolaire Marguerite-Bourgeoys, 2006 SCC 6, [2006] 1 SCR 256.

Murphy, Anne. 2007. "History in the Sikh Past." *History and Theory* 46, no. 3: 345–65.

– 2009. "Objects, Ethics, and the Gendering of Sikh Memory." *Early Modern Women: An Interdisciplinary Journal* 4: 161–6.

Nayar, Kamala Elizabeth. 2008. "Misunderstood in the Diaspora: The Experience of Orthodox Sikhs in Vancouver." *Sikh Formations* 4, no. 1: 17–32.

– 2010. "Sikh Women in Vancouver: An Analysis of Their Psychosocial Issues." In *Sikhism and Women: History, Texts, and Experience*, edited by Doris R. Jakobsh, 252–75. New Delhi: Oxford University Press.

Rousseau, Louis. 2006. "Comprendre le jeu de la dimension religieuse dans l'élaboration d'une conscience ethnique: discussion d'un modèle heuristique." *Cahiers de recherche du GRIMER* 5: 1–9.

Shanker, Rajkumari. 2002. "Women in Sikhism." In *Women in Indian Religions*, edited by Arvind Sharma, 108–33. New Delhi: Oxford University Press.

Sikh Community of Montreal. 2007. *Brief Presented to the Consultation Commission on Accommodation Practices Related to Cultural Differences*, October.

Sikh Community of Quebec. 2013. *Brief Presented to the Committee on Institutions on Bill 60 (Charter of Values)*, December.

Sikh Rahit Maryādā. 1950. Amritsar: SGPC (Shiromani Gurdwara Parbandhak Committee). www.sgpc.net.

Singh, Harbans. 1978. *Place of Women in Sikhism: The Message of Sikhism*. Delhi: Gurdwara Management Committee.

Singh, Nikky-Guninder Kaur. 1993. *The Feminine Principle in the Sikh Vision of the Transcendent*. Cambridge: Cambridge University Press.

– 2006. "Sikh Women in North America." In *Encyclopedia of Women and Religion in North America*, vol. 2, edited by Rosemary Skinner Keller and Rosemary Radford Ruether, 693–703. Bloomington: Indiana University Press.

– 2008. "Re-imagining the Divine in Sikhism." *Feminist Theology* 16, no. 3: 332–49.

Singh, Sundarshan. 1979. "Woman and the Sikh Gurus." In *Sikh Religion: Democratic, Ideals and Institutions*, 109–28. New Delhi: Oriental Publishers.

Stoker, Valerie. 2007. "Zero Tolerance? Sikh Swords, School Safety, and Secularism in Québec." *Journal of the American Academy of Religion* 75, no. 4: 814–39.

– 2013. "Other Accommodations: Sikh Advocacy, Religious Architecture, and Cultural Preservation in Québec." In *Sikh Diaspora: Theory, Agency, and Experience*, edited by Michael Hawley, 193–216. Leiden: Brill.

Tatla, Darshan Singh. 1999. *The Sikh Diaspora: The Search for Statehood.* London: UCL Press.

Tremblay, Luc. 2010. "The Bouchard-Taylor Report on Cultural and Religious Accommodation: Multiculturalism by Any Other Name?" *Review of Constitutional Studies* 15, no. 1: 35–75.

Vig, Julie. 2009. "Femmes et sikhisme à Montréal: Le cas des représentations des femmes et des rapports homme-femme." MA thesis, Université du Québec à Montréal.

PART II

Women in Transnational Religious Communities

6

Diaspora as a Spectrum

Punjabi-Sikh Subjects and the Gendered Context of Diaspora Membership

Preet Kaur Virdi

Migration within or as a result of marriage is often the most efficient socially acceptable means available to disadvantaged women to achieve some measure of social and economic mobility (Palriwala and Uberoi 2008, 23–4; Calavita 2006). Yet marriage migration, a social formation built on more than a century of transnational migration and a global network of diaspora communities, is vastly overlooked in the existing literature on the Punjabi-Sikh diaspora. Perhaps this omission in the existing literature is indicative of women's migration being seen as dependent on the actions of the men they travel with, to, or from. This chapter explores marriage migration, which is better understood, at least in part, as the result of a contractual relationship between individuals with differing national or residency statuses, which necessarily creates differences in the relational power of each spouse (Ballard 2001). Inherently gendered, this relational power contributes to a spectrum of variegated memberships in the diaspora community.

The concept of diaspora has been mobilized across a number of disciplines since the mid-twentieth century to describe a "scattering of peoples who are nonetheless connected by a sense of homeland, imaginary or otherwise" (Cho 2007, 12). The primacy of "homeland," of a place of origin, is challenged by Brian Keith Axel, who insists that the anthropological task of defining diaspora and context unwittingly perpetuates the project of genealogy, where the researcher may conceive of such terms ahead of time, thereby imputing to them a basic sense of *spatiality* (Axel 2004, 30; Lefebvre 1991). The concepts of diaspora and context demand a rejoining of what has already been sundered by history (i.e., the diaspora and the homeland); this would give the researcher impetus to generate an archive of information on the subject group, thus creating a repository of authoritative knowledge of the past. It is the very articulation of context, archive, and diaspora that foregrounds a broader inquiry into the histories of colonialism and anthropological knowledge production (Axel 2004, 29; Said 1978). The challenge for diaspora studies, therefore, lies in making claims about a given population group called "diaspora" without essentializing either its internal differences or its homogeneity (Axel 2004, 32).

This chapter begins with recognition of the complexities of settler colonialism in the nation-building project of Canada, its displacement of (First Nations) peoples and communities, and the legacies of colonialism and displacement in the present. The shift away from population groups (i.e., South Asian) and toward subjects (i.e., the model immigrant) is the prism through which the context of diaspora can be observed. In this chapter, I argue that the context of the Punjabi-Sikh diaspora in the Greater Toronto Area (GTA) is a spectrum of variegated memberships and self-perceptions of belonging that are inherently gendered. In my ethnographic research on transnational marriages and their breakdown, I discern three discrete yet overlapping subjectivities: the model immigrant and the multicultural citizen; the transnational competitive migrant; and, finally, the trans-local and sovereign subject. Through this spectrum of diaspora membership, I conduct a close analysis of gendered subjectivities in relation to their corresponding configurations of power in marriage and its breakdown. First, I provide overviews of the fieldwork, data, and subject groups the chapter is based on, and proceed to discuss local and transnational understandings of marriage and marriage breakdown. Then I discuss the spectrum of diaspora membership, addressing marriage and its breakdown in relation to each of the three above-mentioned groupings.

As a transnational migrant who pursued graduate education and marriage in a manner characteristic of my Punjabi-Sikh ancestors, I approach this chapter as a Sikh feminist studying "transnationalism from below" (Gardner and Grillo 2002) from a position of relative privilege (specifically of class and citizenship). I reside in New York City and as such extend my family's history of over one century of transmigration, from Punjab to East Africa, the United Kingdom, Canada, and now the United States.

This chapter emerges from a larger legal ethnography (Abu-Lughod 1991; Kotiswaran 2008; Merry 1993) that utilized legal case analysis (Fournier 2010), coding (Bryman and Burgess 1994), critical discourse analysis (Fairclough 2005; Ferguson 1996; Umphrey 1999) and semi-structured interviews (Mason 2002; Razack 1991, 1993). Primary data include fourteen Ontario family law cases from the province of Ontario and twenty-seven interviews with Punjabi-Sikhs in the GTA, the geographical area surrounding Canada's most diverse city, conducted between 2011 and 2016. All interview subjects are referred to by pseudonyms; legal cases are referred to by surnames, though without other identifying information.

The overwhelming majority of the twenty-seven interview participants in the larger study are first- or second-generation Canadians; with the exception of one white convert, the interview participants' parents are foreign-born. The majority of legal parties in the larger study were born outside Canada (table 1), reflecting the centrality of immigration in securing individual legal claims.

In this chapter, I draw on eight interviews, conducted with both female and male interview participants of varying ages, marital statuses, castes, socioeconomic backgrounds, and religious adherence. The female participants Jaspreet and Sunpreet are married, Isha and Paramjeet are divorced, and Deepa is remarried. Jaspreet is a Gursikh (a pious, observant Sikh), whereas Sunpreet, Isha, Paramjeet, and Deepa have differing personal understandings and connections to their faith. The male participants – Jatinder, Naindeep, and Sukhwinder – are all married Gursikhs. The three legal cases I draw upon in this chapter are *Kaur v. Brar* [2005] OJ 475, *Burmi v. Dhiman* [2001] OJ 2010, and *Sidhu v. Chahal* [2010] OJ 11. The interviewees and legal parties in family law cases use narrative to present their "side of the story." However, the law regulates the narration of these stories through the operation of various rules. The law attempts to discipline both the form and the substance of narrative in order to produce particular kinds of stories (Umphrey 1999, 40). Critical discourse analysis is a key methodology utilized to assess how narratives are co-constructed in the family law context.

Table 6.1
Type of migrant

	Primary	*Family-class*	*Professional*	*Student*	*Refugee*
Wife	0	6	2	1	0
Husband	2	9	2	1	0
Total	**2**	**15**	**4**	**2**	**0**

PUNJABI-SIKH SUBJECTS

The specification "Punjabi-Sikh" is not intended to simply weave together two autonomous formations, but rather involves the recognition of their mutual enmeshing and imbrications (Brah 2005). An important analytical distinction must be clarified between Sikh as a religious category and Sikh as a form of ethnicity. While the two aspects are entwined, the lived experiences of interview participants demonstrate that their individual connection to the Sikh tradition is varied. As Brah suggests, what makes Sikh ethnicities distinctively Sikh concerns their relationship to and embeddedness within a genealogy of ethics, values, institutions, and practices associated with Sikh history and the Sikh scriptures (159). I attribute the term Punjabi-Sikh to people, whether Canadian-born or otherwise, who could be identified through a matrix of keywords in my legal case search or self-identified in fieldwork as persons with origins or ties to the Punjab region and/or the Sikh tradition.

The Sikh tradition is informed by a unique inner revelation of its founder, Guru Nanak (1469–1539), who declared his independence from other traditions and thought forms prevalent in the religiously and customarily diverse Punjab (Pashaura Singh 2004, 79). Nanak was succeeded by nine gurus who oversaw the development of the community during the period of Mughal rule in the Indian subcontinent. The ten Sikh gurus can be considered early modern Punjabi reformers who introduced radical changes (Brah 2005, 160).

Punjab is a region located in the northwest of the Indian subcontinent. If dispersion is understood as applicable to any and every nameable population category that is to some extent displaced in space (Brubaker 2006), then Punjab has a modern history of dispersions: millions of people were displaced by the 1947 partition of India and Pakistan and the violence that followed, and then again by the 1966 reorganization of Punjab along linguistic and religious lines. Although agricultural production in Punjab is lauded as a success of the Green Revolution, the region's growth and productivity have not improved social development (Purewal 2010, 64), and inconsistencies between economic and social development are behind more than a hundred years of emigration (Pritam Singh 2008) – a trend that continues unabated.

The histories of Sikhs inside and outside of Punjab are typically framed as separate narratives; however, the mass movement of Sikhs was a product of new labour and economic networks created through the colonial project of empire (Ballantyne 2006, 69; Dusenbery 1997, 740). Transnational migration was and is intrinsically tied to caste inequality; only the relatively powerful and wealthy classes and caste groups from across South Asia have been able to mobilize the resources needed for western migration (Taylor, M. Singh, and Booth 2007, 329; Ballard 1994). There are approximately 5 million (East) Punjabis worldwide; over one quarter of Indian migrants are from a region that constitutes a mere 2 per cent of the national population (Taylor, M. Singh, and Booth 2007, 329–30; Walton-Roberts 2003). In the early twenty-first century, others estimate that there are over twenty-five million Sikhs worldwide and roughly one-third live outside Punjab (McLeod 2020; Pew Research 2012).

Punjabi-Sikhs have been successful in setting up local and transnational networks (Werbner 1993). Diaspora communities exist in Australasia (Bhatti and Dusenbery 2001; McLeod 1986), East Africa (Bhachu 1985; Herzig 2010), North America (Leonard 1996; Mongia 2003), Southeast Asia (Sandhu 1970), and the United Kingdom (UK) (Ballard 1982; Bhachu 1991a; Bhachu 1991b; Singh and Tatla 2006). Seldom, however, are the gendered dimensions of these diaspora communities discussed (Barrier and Dusenbery 1989; Dusenbery 1997; Nayar 2004; Singh and Tatla 2006; Tatla 2005; but see Ballard 1972; 1982; 1994; Bhachu 1985; Mand 2002; 2005).[1]

(UN)WELCOME TO CANADA

The origins and formation of South Asian communities in Canada are inseparable from Canada's elevated position in the British Empire as a white-European-settler colony, where South Asians were subalterns economically (as labouring classes), politically (as disenfranchised), and culturally (as representatives of "lower races") (Chilvers and Walton-Roberts 2014; Spivak 1988). The complexities of living in the wake of colonialism present urgent questions about the intersection of South Asian communities with evolving immigration and citizenship policies (Cho 2007).

Ontario is reportedly home to 61 per cent of Canadians of South Asian origin (Statistics Canada 2017a). In 2011, 454,965 Canadians reported they were Sikh, which makes Sikhs approximately 38 per cent of the South Asian population (Statistics Canada 2016, 39). The bulk of the migration from South Asia to Canada occurred after the mid-1960s, when Canadian immigration policies were liberalized (Dusenbery 1997). Before this period, a panic that "non-preferred," non-white immigrants would outnumber white settlers informed a number of restrictive policies that limited family migration to Canada until 1919.[2] The gendered impact of discriminatory immigration citizenship policies constructed immigrant Asian women in particular as a threat to white dominance since they were the reproducers of unwanted racial and cultural difference (Bannerji 2000; Thobani 2000). Consequently, early migration of Punjabi-Sikhs to Canada was predominantly a male preserve.

The popular use of the term "newcomer" therefore refers to non-European ethnic groups that have migrated to Canada after immigration and citizenship policies were liberalized (Goldring and Krishnamurti 2007). Indeed, the Immigration Act (1953), which granted preferential support to white immigrants, was replaced with the points system (1967), designed to classify immigrants based on various qualifications. The Immigration Act (1976–77) worked in tandem with a national policy of multiculturalism to reconstitute national identity after more than one hundred years of racist and sexist immigration policies.[3] The former policy managed immigration, whilst the latter managed citizenship, in order to reformulate national identity in a manner that remained racist and sexist, but systematically so, and couched in a language of "class" preference.

South Asians were no longer blatantly discriminated against on the basis of national origin, race, ethnicity, or religion; however, gender discrimination persisted because patriarchal ideologies continuously constructed immigrant women as wives of immigrant husbands, ignoring any qualifications or work experience from the source country (Ralston 2000). From 1980 to 2016, 45 per cent of sponsored family members entering Canada came from South Asia, with India and Pakistan among the top source countries (Statistics Canada 2017b;

Merali 2009). India has been a top source country for spouses and partners since 2008 (Mendicino 2020; CIC 2012).

Marriage migration is conventionally portrayed in the existing literature as primarily family related, where female marriage migrants are passive, dependent movers from one spatial location (regional, national or international) to another (Chant and Radcliffe 1992). This view of the individual migrant is a reflection of the dominant economic focus in migration studies, which obscures family-related migration and maintains the dichotomy of male producer/female reproducer (Kofman 2004). This view also to fails take account of the ways in which men and women migrants appear in varying concentrations in different migratory flows (Piper 2006), and the fact that men and women migrate through contrasting channels to take advantage of gender-specific labour markets (Williams 2010).

DIASPORA AS A SPECTRUM OF MEMBERSHIP

Marriage and its breakdown are apt phenomena for understanding diaspora as a globally mobile category of identification, due to the involvement of norms and practices variously located in Punjabi kinship traditions and customs, the Sikh tradition, Punjab, Canada, and/or the global network of diaspora communities.

In Punjab and the global Punjabi-Sikh diaspora, marriage plays a crucial role in the kinship structure of the community. Marriage is a pivotal event that consciously and unconsciously perpetuates the dominant values of a tradition. On a social level, the Sikh marriage rite, *anand karaj*, affirms the monogamous conjugal relationship created between bride and groom. On a spiritual level, the performance of marriage rites signifies the central place of the Sikh scriptures in the individual's/couple's entrance into householder life (*gristijiwan*), witnessed by the community (*Guru Panth*).

An analysis of marriage and its breakdown equally permits a gendered analysis of choices, challenges, forums, and actors pursued by the spouses and their respective families. Marriage represents much more than a union of two people; it simultaneously represents the joining of two extended families and therefore has the capacity to further propagate those same kinship networks, customs, and traditions, as well as Sikh values and ethics. Marriage breakdown therefore represents not only the separation of two spouses, but also the detachment of two extended families and a rupturing of traditional Punjabi kinship values. In this section, I demonstrate how this undercurrent to marital unions differently informs the three groupings. Various local and transnational experiences of marriage and its breakdown create variegated memberships in the diaspora community.

MULTICULTURAL CITIZENS AND MODEL IMMIGRANTS

The multicultural citizen/model immigrant group refers to the legal and political belonging of some subjects to the nation-state. It refers to both Punjabi-Sikhs born in Canada (multicultural citizens) and newcomers who have grown up in Canada (model immigrants). This group is characterized by class privilege, indicated through university education and profession, which makes the consciousness of Sikh identity and gender among this group distinct, particularly in comparison to transnational migrants originating from Punjab. Evolving understandings of arranged marriage demonstrate that there are observable shifts in cultural baggage and kinship norms within this group.

Arranged marriage is the predominant form of marriage practised in Punjab and its wide network of diaspora communities (Thandi 2013). The matrimonial match is arranged on the basis of kinship and corporate interest rather than romantic affect between two consenting adults. Matrimonial matches are subject to various factors, such as family needs, the family's standing (*izzat*), and the suitability for matrimony (Walton-Roberts 2003). This last category comprises a range of considerations, such as caste, *got* (exogamous clan or subcaste group), and region, as well as physique, geographic location, and education (Mand 2008).

Interview participants oftentimes clarified what they considered arranged marriage to be. In its current form in the GTA, it typically refers to marriage via an arranged introduction but with explicit individual assent. This is markedly different from how their parents' generation understand it, which is typically as marriage via parental or kin approval, often without explicit individual assent. Software developer Naindeep, a thirty-eight-year-old Gursikh and married father of two, explains arranged marriage in the following way:

> It depends on what your definition of arranged marriage is. I guess because from a Western perspective – a non-Indian

> perspective – arranged marriage is when you get married to someone and that's it. But if you look at it in the context of what most people go through, it's more of a setup, where someone is suggested to you and the formal introductions go through the parents …
>
> For myself, during the entire process of looking, there were a couple of times where the arranged aspect came into play: someone was suggested and it began with the idea that the parents should meet etc., etc. I always pushed away from that because I didn't want to go through that process. I wanted to agree to the person myself.

Naindeep was able to navigate the terms upon which he was introduced to women through his family. He was open to an introduction to the woman, but not her family; he implicitly knew that involving parents would take away his personal agency. Naindeep clearly articulates that autonomous consent is central to his acceptance of an introduction, a concept that older, Indian-born interviewees benignly admitted not considering; marriage was for their parents to determine, not them.

Another multicultural citizen, Jatinder, a thirty-eight-year-old banker with two children, takes Naindeep's point a step further: in his view, Canadian-born Punjabi-Sikhs do not have arranged marriages. "I don't know anybody our age in Canada who's had what you would call an arranged marriage. Most of the people I know – they either met because they knew each other or they went to school together or they met online. My mom calls it 'assisted marriages' which is the same thing as a referral. So it's, 'Hey, you guys should meet! If things work out, great! If not, no big deal' … I don't know anybody who's married [that would fit into] what I consider the definition of arranged marriage." The legal cases I examined explore marriages that were predominantly transnational arranged marriages through parents or kinship networks, while Canadian-born or brought-up Punjabi-Sikhs such as Jatinder disrupt any simple understanding of arranged marriages. Instead, people might be introduced, as Naindeep indicated. While arranged marriage remains a dominant form of marriage among Sikhs today, both in Punjab and the diaspora, such marriages "are better described as a complex and varied social trend than as traditional practice" (Thandi 2013, 234).

Punjabi-Sikhs in the diaspora continue to utilize arranged marriage as a tool to "assist" women and men to meet a spouse who meets the family's needs or expectations. This method continues to be preferred by some because arranging marriages through referrals is like an insurance policy in case things go awry. If there are discrepancies in reported bio-data, education, career, or family reputation, for example, the kin of each party traditionally act as advocates in a complex and protracted negotiation process (Thandi 2013, 236). Model migrant Deepa, a remarried beautician from India who came to Canada as a marriage migrant, has had her unfair share of personal hardship. She offers the following advice on marriage: "Honestly, what I noticed is that if your parents are strong, arranged marriage is very good – but, the boy should be good. First you have to check the background, don't just trust what somebody says ... In my [first marriage], they introduced and accepted the marriage proposal [*rishta*]. They didn't even ask [me]." Deepa's experience in the Indian context is comparable to the accounts provided by legal parties. She makes the critical point that the extent to which a traditional arranged marriage might work is dependent upon the parents' diligence in cross-checking all the details about the potential spouse and his or her family.

The region of Punjab is historically characterized by a social liberalism that gives caste a distinctly different character than in other parts of the subcontinent (Juergensmeyer 2009, 5–6; Ibbetson 1883). Caste is embedded in the Punjabi kinship system, and its primary function is to organize society into groups of endogamous inter-marrying clans (Hershman 1981). Caste and class are correlated, since *Jats* are the "dominant caste" and own over 80 per cent of available agricultural land (Taylor, M. Singh, and Booth 2007, 331; Jodhka 2002; Puri 2003).[4] Jat dominance has been noted in the British and Canadian contexts (Judge 2003; Verma 2002).

Arranged marriage is particularly significant for Punjabi-Sikhs who wish to adhere to traditional kinship understandings of caste endogamy. Among the twenty-seven interview participants, seven (26 per cent) noted that caste was important to them individually, and fifteen (56 per cent) noted that caste was important to their families. In the former group, it was almost evenly split between those over the age of forty (four participants) and those under forty (three participants). Within the latter group, while caste might have been important to participants' families, this did not stop six participants (22 per cent) from choosing their spouses from other caste groups.

For Isha, a thirty-year-old Canadian-born pharmacist, arranged marriage was her "choice," but she faced formidable pressure to consent:

> I would say it was an arranged marriage, but I had a choice at the end of the day. So, the way it worked was, my parents wanted me to meet my ex because he is also a pharmacist. He had all the credentials: Punjabi, Sikh, caste was the same; he was a pharmacist, professional, whatever. All this stuff, so they made me meet him.
>
> When I met him, I didn't like him. After the first date, I said that I didn't want to see him again and then, I had an intervention with my family. My aunts [*massis*] and my mom told me that I need to give him a chance because he checks all the boxes. They said that I would be happy.
>
> But I was telling them that there are [other] things that are important to me and their response was that those things would come. So at age twenty-three, twenty-four, I believed my family … Within four months, we had an engagement [*rokh*].

Sanctioned by both of their families, Isha and her ex-husband got to know each other to some extent. Isha's experience adheres to Punjabi marriage norms because her family facilitated the whole process and she entrusted her family to choose a suitable husband.

The preference for endogamous marriage according to caste affiliation is evident in Isha's story. Isha's mother's reasoning hinged on certain qualities and bio-data that she felt made it a "perfect" match: he came from a "good family" that was "well off"; he was "a professional," "Punjabi," "Jat," and "Sikh." Indeed, the lay understanding of caste preference is about much more. As Paramjeet told me, "There is a hierarchy within our community – well, first of all, within Sikhs and Punjabis, the caste system created the hierarchy – and then how much money, land and education you have." Though land is a commodity that has belonged to Jats in the modern period, the above quote exemplifies that caste preference is not just about affiliation, it is a multilayered concept that accounts for status-enhancing qualities (izzat) that are intrinsically bound with class (Bhachu 1991a).

Isha's family is not alone in their caste preferences. Sunpreet, an Indian-born, married dental assistant and mother of two who grew up in Singapore, had the following to say about caste and marriage: "My parents were 'typical Indian' in their mentality. The reason why my dad wanted to move away from Singapore was because there were a lot of Jats there and he was afraid that his two daughters would find some Jat guys. Since he was the only family member outside of

India, it would disgrace his family, and give him a bad name. So, we moved to Canada because we had a couple of relatives here and there were more *Ramgharias* here. He thought it would be better for his daughters as we approached marriageable age." Noting Sunpreet's double diaspora experience in Singapore and Canada, her remarks expose the ease with which some Sikhs migrate through transnational kinship networks. Sunpreet's father protected his own status and reputation (izzat) by relocating his family to the other side of the world to facilitate endogamous marriages for his daughters. Unlike Isha, Sunpreet was not so trusting of her parents' judgement:

> I was afraid he promised me to someone in India and I remember asking my parents. I told them they could not force me to marry anyone I didn't want to. They were shocked.
>
> But it worked out great that we moved to Canada because I saw Inderpal a couple of times on the subway, out of the blue, going to school. And a couple of weeks later, I saw him at the *Ramgarhia gurdwara* [place of worship] and one of our relatives knew his family, so the families got introduced.

Though she asserted her right to consent to marriage autonomously, Sunpreet was careful to work within the caste preferences her father so strongly adhered to. It was serendipitous that her path crossed with Inderpal's, a turbaned Sikh man from the same Ramgarhia caste.

Multicultural citizens such as Naindeep, Jatinder, and Isha, and model migrants such as marriage migrants Deepa and Sunpreet, discussed their personal experiences with arranged marriage practices in the Punjabi-Sikh diaspora community. Naindeep and Jatinder articulated a nascent Canadian diasporic understanding of "assisted" marriage, characterized by individual agency and autonomy that is distinct from arranged marriage. The remarks of Sunpreet and Isha, on the other hand, affirm that caste and class are entwined values that continue to underpin arranged marriage alliances.

TRANSNATIONAL COMPETITIVE MIGRANT

In countries located in the West, immigrants are no longer characterized as "persons who uproot themselves, leave behind home and country, and face the painful process of incorporation into a different society and culture." Rather, immigrants are increasingly characterized as transnational migrants, "whose daily lives depend on multiple constant interconnections across international borders and whose public identities are configured in relationship to more than one nation state" (Glick Schiller, Basch, and Szanton Blanc 1995, 48). The transition from immigrant to transnational migrant denotes a change to the type of migrant who moves back and forth between the West and the rest (ibid.). The second group I identify in my legal ethnography is composed of those subjects who seek to obtain immigration status in Canada. I characterize this group as "competitive" because of the manner in which Ontario family law courts portray and assess the credibility of transnational migrants and arranged marriage alliances. A woman's status as a marriage migrant connotes a dependent relationship (both legal and socioeconomic) to migrant men, and consequently denigrates their economic roles and endorses their assumed passivity as secondary migrants (Palriwala and Uberoi 2008). Implicit in this analysis are not only the power imbalances between spouses but also between legal parties with precarious or questionable statuses and the official legal actors empowered to decide their fate.

Female migration is typically paired with arranged marriage, where "the marital connection itself may be a more strategic entrepreneurial activity, but one that may later facilitate the reconstitution of family in a reconfigured form abroad" (Charsley and Shaw 2006, 339). Applications for spousal immigration to Canada amount to approximately one-quarter of all Canadian immigration from India; notably, more than 60 per cent of applicants are female (Walton-Roberts 2003). Of the fourteen Ontario family law cases concerning marriage breakdown among Punjabi-Sikhs between 1990 and 2010, arranged marriage occurred in ten legal cases (71 per cent). A remaining two cases (14 per cent) appear to be "love" marriages and the last two cases are uncategorized.

In *Kaur v. Brar* [2005] OJ 475, the justice appears skeptical of arranged marriage norms because the petitioner-wife, Kaur, had a disreputable history of failed transnational marriages entangled with immigration repercussions.

Kaur was born in Punjab; she had a high school education, and her first language is Punjabi. After two failed transnational marriages, Kaur was living in Brampton, Ontario. Kaur's deposition to the court states that in 1998 a man named Cheema contacted Kaur after landing in Canada, obtaining her information via their shared kinship network. Some time after he landed – and in contravention of conservative Punjabi kinship norms governing gender relations – Cheema cohabited with Kaur despite being married to someone else. In 1999, Kaur accompanied Cheema to India and they married according to Sikh rites; however, at the behest of Cheema, Kaur was "forced" to civilly register her marriage to Brar, the respondent in this case and a friend of Cheema's whom Kaur seemingly had no relation with. The sham marriage was meant to facilitate Brar's immigration to Canada. After the religious and civil marriages were complete, Kaur and Cheema returned to Canada while Brar stayed in Punjab to await his Canadian visa.

In her affidavit, Kaur states that she went along with the sham marriage to Brar because she was afraid that Cheema would desert her, and as a marriage migrant with no kin nearby, this frightened her. Mand's (2008) ethnographic study of transnational Sikh women in East Africa affirms that the question of "where would I go?" is highly pertinent. Female marriage migrants who confront difficulties in their marriages can be profoundly influenced by their immigration status as spouse or (economic) dependent. This is especially likely when a family is subject to external pressures related to migration, sponsorship, financial remittances, or otherwise. A review of Kaur's case proceedings indicates there were indeed ulterior motives behind her complicated marital history. Usually, the family members with the least effective bargaining power bear the brunt of these difficulties, and often (though not inevitably), it is the woman (Ballard 1982, 10).

Before the Brampton court, Kaur sought a divorce from Brar, the sham marriage spouse, on an urgent basis in order to legitimately and honourably marry her current boyfriend (who was in Canada on an expired visitor's visa). Brar was not in attendance because he resided in Punjab. Kaur's explanation to the court was that she was an unwilling partner in the sham marriage to Brar. However, clear evidence that the parties colluded to defraud the immigration authorities resulted in the court refusing to grant a divorce to Kaur, and the matter was referred to Citizenship and Immigration Canada. Though Kaur may have been aware she was doing something illegal, she naively underestimated the severity of her multiple marriages.

While the judge astutely saw through the legal strategizing in *Kaur v. Brar*, in the case of *Burmi v. Dhiman* [2001] OJ 2010, the presiding Justice Mesbur did not accept nor appreciate the arguments provided by the respondent-wife Dhiman that she was unfairly disadvantaged by a unilateral divorce. The petitioner-husband, Burmi, initiated proceedings to end a marriage solemnized in Punjab where the parties cohabited for a total of seven weeks. He also accused Dhiman of immigration fraud.

The parties were both of Punjabi descent, university educated, and in their mid-twenties when they were married. Burmi is a Sikh who worked at his father's business in Toronto, and Dhiman is a Hindu who shared the same Ramgharia caste affiliation as Burmi. She was a university student at the time of the parties' marriage.

Burmi and his parents travelled to Punjab in November 1998 to find him a suitable wife. They placed the following advert in the *Tribune*:

> Tall match for Ramgharia clean-shaven, Canadian Citizen 26/6'2" educated, well settled business family. Early marriage. Girl main consideration.

The advertisement indicated the Burmis were a business family that had Canadian citizenship. Their reference to caste affiliation indicated their preference for an endogamous match, and "clean-shaven" indicated that the suitor was not a Gursikh. The Dhiman family responded to the ad. The parties and their families agreed to the marriage and a formal engagement (*roka*) took place, followed by marriage according to Sikh rites in December 1998. They cohabited for the month of December and then again in March 1999. Burmi called Dhiman in May 1999 and unilaterally ended the marriage.

Having resolved to mend the relationship, Dhiman flew to Toronto in the autumn, but in retaliation Burmi petitioned for divorce in October 1999. Dhiman counter-petitioned in February 2001 for interim spousal support, claims for general and punitive damages for deceit, misrepresentation, assault, and a breach of fiduciary duty. Dhiman also motioned to add Burmi's parents and paternal aunt as respondents and claimed similar relief. The thrust of her counter-petition was that Burmi deserted her and she consequently faced social ostracism from her kin.

Burmi appealed to the court that Dhiman's motions were disingenuous because they were brought nearly two years after the parties separated. Dhiman's conduct and timing, he argued, were a means to bolster her immigration application and to punish him and his family. Burmi also pointed out that Dhiman speciously entered Canada on a student visa and was now applying for refugee status. Dhiman admitted to the court that she deceived Canadian immigration authorities upon entry, and remarkably admitted that she was claiming refugee status because of her tarnished izzat (personal honour). Specifically, she stated that she would face social ostracism for being a divorcée because she was no longer a virgin. In response to Dhiman's claims, Justice Mesbur commented:

> Though it may be untenable for someone in her position to remain in her community as a divorced woman that does not necessarily involve economic consequences, or hardship. The Respondent is young and educated and she concedes she could work in India if she chose. She has suffered no economic loss as defined by the Divorce Act as result of the marital breakdown. The Respondent's ability to support herself has been unchanged by the marriage or its breakdown. She maintains that she is now perceived as "damaged goods" in her religious community which will make it difficult for her to re-marry and the difficulty will also be experienced by her siblings. This type of consequence is not accommodated under the Divorce Act. (*Burmi v. Dhiman* [2001] OJ 2010, at 12)

While Ontario family law courts are obligated "to encourage and strengthen the role of the family" through their recognition of the "equal position of spouses as individuals within marriage" (Family Laws Act 1990, c.F.3), marriage breakdown is characterized by no-fault divorce and the principle of equal partnership (Abella 1981; Fineman 2013). It is clear, then, that Justice Mesbur's views, which are based on a formal equality approach, do not coincide with Dhiman's views, which are based on a gendered understanding of corporate family membership embedded in Punjabi (and South Asian) law and society. As a result, Dhiman was unsuccessful in arguing that the parties' arranged marriage entailed moral and fiduciary responsibilities for both families, which entitled her to spousal support. In denying Dhiman's petition, the justice went on to explain: "Wife's counsel urged me to find that the religious marriage ceremony in India carries with it a notion that it is some kind of agreement related to the support of the wife. There is no cogent evidence to persuade me of this, other than the wife's statements that she expected the marriage to continue, as a traditional marriage, forever. That expectation is no doubt shared by many spouses at the outset of their marriages, regardless of their religious affiliation" (*Burmi v. Dhiman* [2001] OJ 2010, at 13).

In this interim proceeding, Justice Mesbur allowed the parents and aunt to be added as parties to the legal case; however, he opined that under section 15 of the Divorce Act, Dhiman's claims were not a compensable reason for support. The judge also declined Dhiman's claim for interim spousal support. In the Indian context, where the welfare state is unable to support the practical demands of divorce and separation (Subramanian 2014), Dhiman's argument may have been considered legally viable. In the Ontario family law context, however, this normative understanding of marriage was amiss.

In a different take on transnational competitive migrants, the third and final case, *Sidhu v. Chahal* [2010] OJ 11, involved parties who did not have a transnational arranged marriage; rather, these two transnational migrants met and began a romantic relationship while studying at York University in Toronto. The students jointly approached the court to request an annulment.

On the date of the marriage in October 2007, Sidhu explained that the parties went to a friend's home and met a man who claimed to be a Christian priest. The man requested that the parties sign the marriage register. Chahal signed without reading and Sidhu signed when the man claimed that the parties needed to sign for roka, a form of engagement in the Sikh tradition. Each party testified that they were neither told they were getting married nor that the signed legal document meant that they were entering into a Canadian civil marriage. In her petition to the court, Sidhu stated: "It is very important to me that this marriage be annulled as I am afraid that other members of the [Punjabi-Sikh] community will find out and it would be very difficult for me to find a groom in our community, as I would be labeled as a divorced woman if my marriage was considered valid when I actually never got married" (*Sidhu v. Chahal* [2010] OJ 11, at 21). The parties jointly requested an annulment, which they preferred because it would be difficult and embarrassing to marry in the Sikh community if they were divorced. Marital disharmony and dissolution was believed by most respondents in an early Canadian study of Sikhs in British Columbia to be frequent yet highly undesirable (Ames and Inglis 1973/74). Divorce continues to be generally observed as a social taboo due to the disgrace it would bring upon an individual and her/his family (Jhutti 1998), but this understanding is shifting in the diaspora context (Virdi 2016).

Sidhu and Chahal explained to the presiding justice that neither of them told their parents about the marriage, lived together, or consummated the civil marriage. These details were important to both parties as it confirmed their status as chaste unmarried persons abiding by conservative Punjabi kinship values. Sidhu also explained to the court that she did not think signing papers counted as marriage: "I didn't believe that I was getting married by signing the registration. I believed that I could only get married in the temple in the presence of my family and with all the rituals" (*Sidhu v. Chahal* [2010] OJ 11, at 8–9). Sidhu's explanation coincides with earlier observations by Menski (1987, 1988), who asserted that British South Asians do not attach much importance to the legal consequences of a registered document; they are more concerned with the performance of marriage rites and rituals that affirm to their community they are recognized as married. Sidhu and Chahal did attach importance to legal consequences, however, since both parties explained to the court they did not want the marital status of divorced. Decades after Menski's observations, Sidhu explained plausibly that she thought the registration process was synonymous with the Punjabi-Sikh custom of roka.

In his judgement, the presiding Justice Wein understood that Sidhu's capacity to understand the nature of the marriage was absent since she thought it was equivalent to a Sikh engagement (albeit performed by a Christian). Both Sidhu and Chahal explained the significant differences between Sikh marriage rites and what they now understood to be a Canadian civil marriage. Though the evidence they submitted countered common sense to some degree, Justice Wein accepted that the civil marriage was not a fraud but a mistake as to the nature of the ceremony, and he granted an annulment.

It is poignant to note that before the justice granted the annulment, he carefully reviewed the parties' legal status in Canada and whether either Sidhu or Chahal misrepresented their legal statuses due to an ulterior motive. The routine request for an annulment therefore stands alongside the close surveillance of immigration status in this case. Once Sidhu and Chahal were determined to not have committed any fraud, Justice Wein relaxed his suspicions regarding the parties' explanation of Punjabi-Sikh cultural norms about marriage and izzat (personal honour), but not before making clear that "cultural" justifications are inappropriate in an Ontario courtroom. The judge's decision to grant an annulment instead of a divorce addressed the factual misunderstandings of the parties, but the annulment also permitted both Sidhu and Chahal to escape the social taboo of being a divorcé(e). Justice Wein makes it clear, however, that arguments or explanations about one's culture or religion would not be accommodated in Ontario family law.

The law's governance of the boundaries of marriage is strict, particularly when addressing the transnational nature of Punjabi-Sikh marriage and marriage breakdown. This brief snapshot of three family law cases shows how marriage migration involves much more than the marriage itself. It hinges on an official legal actor's assessment of credibility and sincerity in light of immigration considerations. This treatment of transnational migrants, keeping in mind certain characteristics of Punjabi-Sikh marriage migration, has distinct gendered implications. Some of the common factors in Punjab that perpetuate transnational arranged marriage include growing economic hardship due to decreasing land holdings and increased indebtedness, limited employment opportunities for women, and heightened economic and materialist aspirations. The last motive in particular precipitates the perception of daughters as "mere commodities" who not only contribute to the family's prestige (izzat), but serve a strategic function to further the strategy of chain migration (Thandi 2013). Because transnational marriage customs and traditions are often illegible in Canadian family law courts, the result is that female transnational migrants often bear a disproportionate burden for the marriage breakdown. Moreover, immigration surveillance is present in all three legal cases, signalling that the family law court plays a dual role in adjudicating marriage breakdown while protecting Canadian citizenship. On the one hand, it governs marriage norms and practices of newcomer Canadians; on the other, it acts as a gatekeeper to diaspora membership.

TRANS-LOCAL AND SOVEREIGN SUBJECT

The trans-local and sovereign subject transcends certain Punjabi cultural practices, such as caste adherence, and even kinship in some instances (recognizing that kinship is how cultural norms are passed down and enforced). In accordance with Axel's study of diaspora "Khalistani" Sikhs – who are initiated (*amritdhari*) Sikhs and members of the Khalsa ("the pure"), a martial order of loyal Sikhs inaugurated by the tenth Sikh guru in 1699 – I use "trans-local" to refer to the dialectic of displacement and "place" (i.e., temporality), where displacement itself constitutes the condition of possibility for the diasporic individual, the local, and the present (2004, 45). Axel's analysis is directly relevant here because a number of female and male interview participants were Gursikhs – specifically, amritdhari Sikhs. The turban, in particular, is the marker of individual sovereignty traditionally worn by amritdhari men. However, as Mahmood and Brady (2000) found, an increasing number of amritdhari women in Canada and the United States have donned the turban. The concept of sovereignty is more than just physical, it is also psychological, and simultaneously the two constitute a social practice and serve as a means of intensifying social relations (N. Singh 2004). The act of a woman donning a turban warrants consideration because it challenges gendered identities, relational power, as well as public/private roles within the family and the Sikh diaspora community.

Diaspora communities can sometimes "fossilize" norms and practices from their home countries (Uberoi 1998), and as this chapter has shown, continued caste preference exposes these static ideas. Caste was not found to be important to all participants, however. It is within this third group, trans-local sovereign subjects, that I deciphered how some participants were able to transcend sociocultural norms regarding caste and kinship because they were enabled by their amritdhari identity.

Sukhwinder and Jaspreet, a married amritdhari couple who have been together for three years and belong to different caste affiliations, met while volunteering at a Sikh youth camp. When they finally broached the subject of getting married with their parents, both Sukhwinder and Jaspreet encountered resistance. Jaspreet explains: "Yeah … for my mom it was kind of like 'He's not Jat,' whatever. But I think she got over it when she started to get to know him. Then she said he is such an amazing guy, how can I say no just because of that one little thing. But my dad, from day one, was okay [with Sukhwinder]." Jaspreet explained that between her mom and dad's kinship networks, she was the first one who was not marrying a Jat. It therefore required the buy-in of Jaspreet's mother's natal kin; their acceptance of Sukhwinder helped Jaspreet's mother overcome her caste prejudice and accept Sukhwinder into the family.

Sukhwinder's parents had a different reaction. He told me, "My parents were a bit more subtle, I think. They were beating around the bush a little bit, asking questions about her level of education, and I said that's not important. And then they would ask something else like, would the families get along? And I said, 'That's up to you!' [laugh]." Jaspreet and Sukhwinder each took a different tack, but both were able to reason with their parents on the basis of their Sikh values and principles. Marriage is indeed a union of both individuals and their respective families. Both Sukhwinder and Jaspreet noted that their parents are cordial with each other, but aside from their Sikhi,[5] their parents do not share any commonalities: Jaspreet's parents do not speak English fluently like Sukhwinder's, and whilst her parents prefer home-cooked Punjabi meals, Sukhwinder's parents often go out to restaurants. The social differences between the families are not only caste-based, but also class-based. However, these differences have not stopped Sukhwinder and Jaspreet from establishing firm roots in each other's families, which has also facilitated their efforts to influence their siblings and cousins to overcome caste prejudice in courtship.

This is merely one example of overcoming the strong currents of caste and kinship norms in the Punjabi-Sikh community. However, Sukhwinder and Jaspreet were not alone in dealing with various acts of resistance and strategic bargaining. Men and women of varying marital statuses used their Gursikh identity to contest and challenge entrenched and unfair gender biases in marriage, and marriage breakdown seemed to occur among Punjabi-Sikhs whose membership in the diaspora community was not in question. This is perhaps related to varying religious identifications in the transnational space of diaspora. In Canada, the United States, and the United Kingdom, for example, the subject of gender relations is increasingly incorporated into community and academic conversations. None of the legal parties examined in my fieldwork fell into this final grouping; rather, it was among interview participants, explicitly those with Canadian citizenship or immigration status, where I saw this type of strategic bargaining.

CONCLUSION

The marriage norms and practices of my Punjabi-Sikh interview participants demonstrate how and to what extent the diaspora context in Canada might have its own distinct patterns. Marriage norms and practices ensure that the diaspora community persists for another generation. The terms upon which Canadian-born or brought-up Punjabi-Sikhs are willing to adhere to these expectations, however, are not prevalent in the legal cases involving transnational Punjabi-Sikh migrants. Integral to the establishment of diaspora communities, marriage migration constitutes a large proportion of total migration and the overwhelming bulk of female migration among Punjabi-Sikhs (Palriwala and Uberoi 2008, 28–9). The assignment of multicultural citizen versus transnational migrant corresponds with the possibility of effectively challenging entrenched gender roles and dynamics in the former case, and the unwitting reification of harmful gender ideologies – due to the external pressures of marriage migration, citizenship and immigration laws, and differing subject understandings of gender relations – in the latter case.

NOTES

1 It is noteworthy that the literature on the immigration patterns of Sikh women are separate and in a different field of study than the wider study of Sikh diaspora. Literature available on the general category of South Asian women in diaspora includes Balzani (2006); Charsley (2013); Gallo (2006); Gardner (2006); Gardner and Grillo (2002); Jain (2010); Qureshi (2014); Samuel (2010); Shaw and Charsley (2006); Werbner (2002; 2004; 2013).

2 Racial classifications were legislated to restrict immigration of non-preferred Asiatic races, such as the Chinese Immigration Act (1885), the Exclusion Act (1923), and the Continuous Passage Act (1909).

3 As a result of a changing international environment and Canada's high demand for labour during the 1970s and 80s, the Canadian Multiculturalism Act: An Act for the Preservation and Enhancement of Multiculturalism in Canada was instituted in 1988. Although this policy has characterized Canada as a country that accepts people of all nationalities, religions, and backgrounds, the social realities of non-white, non-European immigrants are replete with instances of ethnocentrism, racism, and/or sexism (Thobani 2007).

4 The consolidation of land holdings among agricultural tribes, such as the Jats, occurred in the colonial period with the passage of the Punjab Alienation of Land Act (1900) (Barrier 1965).

5 The development of the Sikh traditions (Sikhi) has, from the beginning, been intrinsically intertwined with the history and politics of Punjab and neighbouring regions. The choice to refer to the Sikh tradition as "Sikhi" as opposed to the more commonly used English term "Sikhism" is aimed at subverting this later construction imposed by colonialist and Orientalist observers (S.J. Singh 2016, 1).

REFERENCES

Legislation

CANADA
Chinese Immigration Act, 1885
Continuous Passage Act, 1909
Divorce Act, RS 1985, c.3 (2nd Supp.)
Exclusion Act, 1923
Immigration Act, 1953
Immigration Act, 1976–77
Points System, 1967

INDIA
Punjab Alienation of Land Act, 1900

Legal Cases

Burmi v. Dhiman [2001] OJ 2010
Kaur v. Brar [2005] OJ 475
Sidhu v. Chahal [2010] OJ 11

Books and Articles

Abu-Lughod, Lila. 1991. "Writing against culture." In *Recapturing Anthropology: Working in the Present*, edited by R.G. Fox, 137–54. Santa Fe, NM: School of American Research Press, distributed by the University of Washington Press.

Ames, Michael M., and Joy Inglis. 1973/74. "Conflict and Change in British Columbia Sikh Family Life." *BC Studies*, no. 20: 15–49.

Axel, Brian Keith. 2004. "The Context of Diaspora." *Cultural Anthropology* 19, no. 1: 26–60.

Ballantyne, Tony. 2006. *Between Colonialism and Diaspora: Sikh Cultural Formations in an Imperial World*. Durham, NC: Duke University Press.

Ballard, Roger. 1982. "South Asian Families: Structure and Process." In *Families in Britain*, edited by Rhona Rapoport, Michael Fogarty, and Robert Norman Rapoport, 179–204. London: Routledge.

– 1994. *Desh Pardesh: South Asian Experience in Britain*. London: Hurst.

– 2001. "The Impact of Kinship on the Economic Dynamics of Transnational Networks: Reflections on some South Asian Developments." Paper presented at the Workshop on Transnational Migration, Princeton University, 29 June–1 July. http://www.transcomm.ox.ac.uk/working%20papers/Ballard.pdf.

Bannerji, Himani. 2000. *Dark Side of the Nation: Essays on Multiculturalism, Nationalism, and Gender*. Toronto: Canadian Scholars Press.

Barrier, Norman G. 1965. "The Formulation and Enactment of the Punjab Alienation of Land Bill." *The Indian Economic and Social History Review* 2, no. 2: 145–65. https://doi.org/10.1177/001946466400200203.

Barrier, N. Gerald, and Verne A. Dusenbery. 1989. *The Sikh Diaspora: Migration and the Experience beyond Punjab*. Columbia, MO: South Asia Books.

Bhachu, Parminder. 1985. *Twice Migrants: East African Sikh Settlers in Britain*. London: Tavistock.

– 1991a. "Culture, Ethnicity and Class among Punjabi Sikh Women in 1990s Britain." *Journal of Ethnic and Migration Studies* 17, no. 3: 401–12.

– 1991b. "Ethnicity Constructed and Reconstructed: The Role of Sikh Women in Cultural Elaboration and Educational Decision-making in Britain." *Gender and Education* 3, no. 1: 45–56.

Bhatti, Rashmere, and Verne A. Dusenbery. 2001. *A Punjabi Sikh Community in Australia: From Indian Sojourners to Australian Citizens*. Woolgoola, Australia: Woolgoolga Neighbourhood Centre.

Brah, Avtar. 2005. "Locality, Globality and Gendered Refractions." *Journal of Punjab Studies* 12, no. 1: 153–65.

Brubaker, Rogers. 2006. *Nationalist Politics and Everyday Ethnicity in a Transylvanian Town*. Princeton, NJ: Princeton University Press.

Bryman, Alan, and Robert G. Burgess. 1994. "Reflections on Qualitative Data Analysis." In *Analyzing Qualitative Data*, edited by Alan Bryman and Robert G. Burgess, 216–26. London: Routledge.

Calavita, Kitty. 2006. "Gender, Migration, and Law: Crossing Borders and Bridging Disciplines." *International Migration Review* 40, no. 1: 104–32.

Chant, Sylvia, and Sarah A. Radcliffe. 1992. "Migration and Development: The Importance of Gender." In *Gender and Migration in Developing Countries*, edited by Sylvia Chant, 1–29. London: Belhaven Press.

Citizenship and Immigration Canada (CIC). 2012. Spouses and partners: Findings from the longitudinal immigration database (LMDB). Citizenship and Immigration Canada.

– 2016. "'Parallel Lives' or 'Super-Diversity'? An Exploration of Ethno-cultural Enclaves in Montreal, Toronto, and Vancouver, in 2011." Research Reports. Last modified 23 August 2016. https://www.canada.ca/en/immigration-refugees-citizenship/corporate/reports-statistics/research/parallel-lives-super-diversity-exploration-ethno-cultural-enclaves-montreal-toronto-vancouver-2011.html.

Charsley, Katharine, and Alison Shaw. 2006. "South Asian Transnational Marriages in Comparative Perspective." *Global Networks* 6, no. 4: 331–44.

Chilvers, Simon, and Margaret Walton-Roberts. 2014. "Introduction: Deconstructing the (Re)construction of South Asian Identities in Canada." *Diaspora: A Journal of Transnational Studies* 17, no. 2: 121–9.

Cho, Lily. 2007. "The Turn to Diaspora." *Topia: Canadian Journal of Cultural Studies* 17 (Spring): 11–30.

Dusenbery, Verne A. 1997. "The Poetics and Politics of Recognition: Diasporan Sikhs in Pluralist Polities." *American Ethnologist* 24, no. 4: 738–62.

Fairclough, Norman. 2005. "Critical Discourse Analysis in Transdisciplinary Research." In *A New Agenda in (Critical) Discourse Analysis: Theory, Methodology, and Interdisciplinarity*, edited by Ruth Wodak and Paul Chilton, 53–70. Philadelphia: J. Benjamins Publishing Company.

Ferguson, Robert. 1996. "*Untold Stories of the Law." In Law's Stories: Narrative and Rhetoric in the Law*, edited by Peter Brooks and Paul Gewirtz, 84–98. New Haven, CT: Yale University Press.

Fournier, Pascale. 2010. *Muslim Marriage in Western Courts: Lost in Transplantation*. Surrey, UK: Ashgate Publishing.

Gardner, Katy, and Ralph Grillo. 2002. "Transnational Households and Ritual: An Overview." *Global Networks* 2, no. 3: 179–90.

Goldring, Luin, and Sailaja Krishnamurti. 2007. "Introduction: Contextualizing Transnationalism in Canada." In *Organizing the Transnational: Labour, Politics, and Social Change*, edited by Luin Goldring and Sailaja Krishnamurti, 1–22. Vancouver: University of British Columbia Press.

Glick Schiller, Nina, Linda Basch, and Cristina Szanton Blanc. 1995. "From Immigrant to Transmigrant: Theorizing Transnational Migration." *Anthropological Quarterly* 68, no. 1: 48–63.

Guru, Surinder. 2009. "Obstacles and Oppourtunities – South Asian Women in Britain." *The Sociological Review* 57, no. 2: 285–305.

Hershman, Paul. 1981. *Punjabi Kinship and Marriage*. Delhi: Hindustan Publishing Corporation.

Herzig, Pascale. 2010. "Communal Networks and Gender: Placing Identities among South Asians in Kenya." *South Asian Diaspora* 2, no. 2: 165–84.

Ibbetson, Denzil. 1883. "The Races, Castes, and Tribes of the People." In *Report on the Census of the Panjáb Taken on the 17th of February 1881*, 172–90. Calcutta: Superintendent of Govt. Printing.

Jhutti, Jagbir. 1998. "A Study of Changes in Marriage Practices among the Sikhs of Britain." DPhil, Wolfson College, University of Oxford.

Jodhka, Surinder S. 2002. "Caste and Untouchability in Rural Punjab." *Economic and Political Weekly* 37, no. 19: 1813–23.

Judge, Paramjit S. 2003. "Social Construction of Identity in a Multicultural State: Sikhs in Canada." *Economic and Political Weekly* 38, no. 17: 1725–31.

Juergensmeyer, Mark. 2009. "Introduction: Religion and Social Rebellion." In *Religious Rebels in the Punjab: The Ad Dharm Challenge to Caste*, 1–7. New Delhi: Navayana.

Kofman, Eleonore. 2004. "Gendered Global Migrations." *International Feminist Journal of Politics* 6, no. 4: 643–65.

Kotiswaran, Prabha. 2008. "Born unto Brothels – Toward a Legal Ethnography of Sex Work in an Indian Red-Light Area," *Law and Social Inquiry* 33, no. 3: 579–629.

Lefebvre, Henri. 1991. *The Production of Space*. Oxford: Blackwell.

Leonard, Karen. 1996. "Nation and Migration: The Politics of Space in the South Asian Diaspora." *Journal of the Royal Anthropological Institute* 2, no. 3: 578–80.

Mahmood, Cynthia, and Stacy Brady. 2000. *The Guru's Gift: An Ethnography Exploring Gender Equality within North American Sikh Women*. Toronto: Mayfield Publishing Company.

Mand, Kanwal. 2008. "Marriage and Migration through the Life Course: Experiences of Widowhood, Separation and Divorce amongst Transnational Sikh Women." In *Marriage, Migration and Gender*, edited by Rajni Palriwala and Patricia Uberoi, 286–302. Vol. 5 of *Women and Migration in Asia*. New Delhi: Sage Publications.

Mason, Jennifer. 2002. "Qualitative Interviewing: Asking, Listening and Interpreting." In *Qualitative Research in Action*, edited by Tim May, 224–41. London: Sage Publications.

McLeod, W.H. 1986. *Punjabis in New Zealand: A History of Punjabi Migration, 1890–1940*. Amritsar, India: Guru Nanak Dev University.

– 2020. "Sikhism." *Encyclopedia Britannica*. https://www.britannica.com/topic/Sikhism.

Mendicino, M.E.L. 2020. *Annual Report to Parliament on Immigration. Citizenship and Immigration Canada*. Ottawa: Citzenship and Immigration Canada. https://www.canada.ca/en/immigration-refugees-citizenship/corporate/publications-manuals/annual-report-parliament-immigration-2020.html.

Menski, Werner. 1987. "Legal Pluralism in the Hindu Marriage." In *Hinduism in Great Britain: The Perpetuation of Religion in an Alien Cultural Milieu*, edited by Richard Burghart, 180–200. London: Tavistock.

– 1988. "English Family Law and Ethnic Law in Britain." *Kerala Law Times* 1, no. 1: 56–66.

Merali, Noorfarah. 2009. "Experiences of South Asian Brides Entering Canada after Recent Changes to Family Sponsorship Policies." *Violence against Women* 15, no. 3: 321–39.

Merry, Sally Engle. 1993. "Mending Walls and Building Fences: Constructing the Private Neighborhood." *The Journal of Legal Pluralism and Unofficial Law* 25, no. 33: 71–90.

Mongia, Radhika V. 2003. "Race, Nationality, Mobility: A History of the Passport." In *After the Imperial Turn: Thinking with and through the Nation*, edited by Antoinette Burton, 196–212. Durham, NC: Duke University Press.

Nayar, Kamala. 2004. *The Sikh Diaspora in Vancouver: Three Generations and Tradition, Modernity, and Multiculturalism*. Toronto: University of Toronto Press.

Palriwala, Rajni, and Patricia Uberoi, eds. 2008. *Marriage, Migration and Gender*. Vol. 5 of *Women and Migration in Asia*. New Delhi: Sage Publications.

Pew Research. 2012. *The Global Religious Landscape: A Report on the Size and Distribution of the World's Major Religious Groups as of 2010*. The Pew Forum on Religion and Public Life. Last modified 18 December 2012. https://assets.pewresearch.org/wp-content/uploads/sites/11/2014/01/global-religion-full.pdf.

Piper, Nicola. 2006. "Gendering the Politics of Migration." *International Migration Review* 40, no. 1: 133–64.

Purewal, Navtej K. 2010. *Son Preference: Sex Selection, Gender and Culture in South Asia*. Oxford: Berg.

Puri, Harish. 2003. "Scheduled Castes in Sikh Community: A Historical Perspective." *Economic and Political Weekly* 38, no. 26: 2693–701.

Ralston, Helen. 2000. "Redefinition of South Asian Women." In *Race and Racism: Canada's Challenge*, edited by Leo Driedger and Shiva S. Halli, 204–34. Montreal and Kingston: McGill-Queen's University Press.

Razack, Sherene. 1991. *Canadian Feminism and the Law: The Women's Legal Education and Action Fund and the Pursuit of Equality*. Toronto: Second Story Press.

– 1993. "Storytelling for Social Change." In *Returning the Gaze: Essays on Racism, Feminism and Politics*, edited by Himani Bannerji, 83–100. Toronto: Sister Vision Press.

Said, Edward. (1978) 1994. *Orientalism: Western Conceptions of the Orient*. New York: Vintage.

Sandhu, Kernial Singh. 1970. "Sikh Immigration into Malaya during the Period of British Rule." *Studies in the Social History of China and Southeast Asia: Essays in Memory of Victor Purcell*, edited by Jerome Chen and Nicholas Tan Ling, 335–54. Cambridge: Cambridge University Press.

Singh, Gurharpal, and Darshan Singh Tatla. 2006. *Sikhs in Britain: The Making of a Community*. London: Zed Books.

Singh, Nikky-Guninder Kaur. 2004. "Sacred Fabric and Sacred Stitches: The Underwear of the Khalsa." *History of Religions* 43, no. 4: 284–302.

Singh, Pashaura. 2004. "Sikh Identity in the Light of History: A Dynamic Perspective." In *Sikhism and History*, edited by Pashaura Singh and N. Gerald Barrier, 77–110. New Delhi: Oxford University Press.

Singh, Pritam. 2008. *Federalism, Nationalism and Development: India and the Punjab Economy*. London: Routledge.

Singh, Simran Jeet. 2016. "The Life of the *Puratan Janamsakhi*: Tracing the Earliest Memories of Guru Nanak." PhD dissertation, Columbia University.

Spivak, Gayatri C. 1988. "Can the Subaltern Speak?" In *Marxism and the Interpretation of Culture*, edited by Cary Nelson and Lawrence Grossberg, 271–313. London: Macmillan.

Statistics Canada. 2016. Canadian Demographics at a Glance: Second Edition. Statistics Canada Catalogue no. 91–003–X. ISSN 1916–1832. Ottawa: Minister of Industry. 19 February. https://www150.statcan.gc.ca/n1/pub/91-003-x/91-003-x2014001-eng.pdf.

– 2017a. Canada [Country] and Ontario [Province] (table). Census Profile. 2016 Census. Statistics Canada Catalogue no. 98-316-X2016001. Ottawa. 29 November. https://www12.statcan.gc.ca/census-recensement/2016/dp-pd/prof/index.cfm?Lang=E.

– 2017b. 2016 Census of Population, Statistics Canada Catalogue no. 98-400-X2016202. 25 October. https://www12.statcan.gc.ca/census-recensement/2016/dp-pd/dt-td/Rp-eng.cfm?TABID=1&LANG=E&A=R&APATH=3&DETAIL=0&DIM=0&FL=A&FREE=0&GC=01&GL=-1&GID=1341679&GK=1&GRP=1&O=D&PID=110558&PRID=10&PTYPE=109445&S=0&SHOWALL=0&SUB=0&Temporal=2017&THEME=120&VID=0&VNAMEE=&VNAMEF=&D1=233&D2=0&D3=0&D4=0&D5=0&D6=0.

Subramanian, Narendra. 2014. *Nation and Family: Personal Law, Cultural Pluralism, and Gendered Citizenship in India*. Stanford, CA: Stanford University Press.

Tatla, Darshan Singh. 2005. *The Sikh Diaspora: The Search for Statehood*. London: Routledge.

Taylor, Steve, Manjit Singh, and Deborah Booth. 2007. "Migration, Development and Inequality: Eastern Punjabi Transnationalism." *Global Networks* 7, no. 3: 328–47.

Thandi, Shinder S. 2013. "'Shady Character, Hidden Designs, and Masked Faces': Reflections on '*Vilayti*' Sikh Marriages and Discourses of Abuse." In *Sikh Diaspora: Theory, Agency, and Experience*, edited by Michael Hawley, 233–59. Leiden: Brill.

Thobani, Sunera. 2000. "Nationalizing Canadians: Bordering Immigrant Women in the Late Twentieth Century." *Canadian Journal of Women and the Law* 12, no. 2: 279–312.

– 2007. *Exalted Subjects: Studies in the Making of Race and Nation in Canada*. Toronto: University of Toronto Press.

Uberoi, Patricia. (1998) "The Diaspora Comes Home: Disciplining Desire in DDLJ." *Contributions to Indian Sociology* 32, no. 2: 305–36.

Umphrey, Martha Merrill. 1999. "The Dialogics of Legal Meaning: Spectacular Trials, the Unwritten Law, and Narratives of Criminal Responsibility." *Law and Society Review* 33, no. 2: 393–423. https://doi.org/10.2307/3115169.

Verma, A.B. 2002. *The Making of Little Punjab in Canada: Patterns of Immigration*. New Delhi: Sage Publications.

Virdi, M.K. 2016. *Marriage/Breakdown amongst Punjabi-Sikhs in Canada: A Legal Ethnography of Disputants, (Un)official Forums, and Access to Family Justice in Ontario, Canada*. PhD dissertation, SOAS University of London.

Walton-Roberts, Margaret. 2003. "Transnational Geographies: Indian Immigration to Canada." *Canadian Geographer* 47, no. 3: 235–50.

Werbner, Pnina. 1993. Review of *The Sikh Diaspora: Migration and the Experience beyond Punjab*, by N. Gerald Barrier and Verne A. Dusenbery. *American Ethnologist* 20, no. 2: 417–18.

Williams, Lucy. 2010. "Transnational Marriage within South Asian Communities." In *Global Marriage: Cross Border Marriage in Global Context*, 99–119. London: Palgrave MacMillan.

7

Chinese Buddhist Nuns in Canada

From Subservience to Spiritual Leadership

Henry Shiu

The forces of modernization in Chinese Buddhism, which can be seen in mainland China, Hong Kong, and Taiwan, have indirectly improved the traditionally subservient position of Chinese Buddhist nuns in Canada, with the nuns becoming a presence in the larger Chinese diaspora community. Rima Berns-McGown writes that in diaspora, "one doesn't lose one's old culture or have it replaced by a new one; one combines cultures and worldviews in ways that are, unsurprisingly, complex and constantly shifting" (2008, 15). The new face of Chinese Buddhist nuns in Canada therefore began with changes in Asia, were catalyzed by the challenges that migration poses to gender relations, and were further shaped by multiculturalism in Canada. This understanding can be read alongside the observation of Professor Victor Sōgen Hori, in his introduction to the volume *Wild Geese: Buddhism in Canada*, that "the development of Buddhism in Canada can only be properly understood against development of changes to Buddhism globally" (Harding, Hori, and Soucy 2010, 37). The modernized forms of Chinese Buddhism practised in Canada today had already been developed in Asia before they were introduced to Canada. The role of Chinese Buddhist nuns in Canada thus reflects both modernizing attitudes about gender in Buddhist communities in mainland China, Hong Kong, and Taiwan, and progressive attitudes about gender and multiculturalism in Canada.

As Jennifer Eichman has pointed out, cultural attitudes towards Taiwanese nuns have changed over the last fifty years: "From the

1960s onward, the Taiwanese nuns community slowly shed its image as a vocation of the undereducated, disaffected, and lovelorn. In the last thirty years, college-educated women have swelled the ranks of well-established Buddhist monasteries and also instituted their own female enclaves. These nuns have garnered the respect of the larger society and made numerous contributions to Taiwanese social welfare, environmental protection, Buddhist education, and many other areas of social and spiritual life" (2011, 345). In recent years, Chinese Buddhist nuns in Canada have been engaging with mainstream Canada in ways that are highly beneficial not only to the larger non-Buddhist community, but also to the establishment of the new role of Buddhist nuns as spiritual leaders. Through the influence of their more powerful Dharma sisters in China and Taiwan, they have rejected traditional expectations that trapped them in a subordinate position to male monastics. Leading masters of the major Buddhist temples have also encouraged Buddhist nuns to receive better education and take up more prominent roles in leadership and teaching.

I begin this chapter by looking at the gender roles and expectations for Chinese Buddhist nuns in China and in diasporic Chinese communities in Asia, briefly discussing gender attitudes in Buddhist teachings and practices, the traditionally subservient position of Buddhist nuns to Buddhist monks, and some recent developments. I then move the discussion to Canada, where I consider the demographics of Chinese Buddhists in Canada, taking into account the population of Chinese Buddhists from Southeast Asia. Finally, I talk about the remarkable change in social attitudes towards nuns, and the nuns' impressive accomplishments as a result of being empowered. I show how Chinese Buddhist nuns in Canada are taking on greater social engagement and responsibility, and are receiving greater respect from their communities in return. I consider the somewhat competitive relationships between various Buddhist groups in Canada and the important role of nuns in addressing this situation. I conclude by looking at the way Chinese Buddhist nuns in Canada have overcome linguistic and cultural barriers to engage with the Canadian community at large.

TRADITIONAL ROLES FOR NUNS IN CHINESE BUDDHISM

The traditional gender-hierarchical social structure in China is reflected in the gender inequality between monks and nuns. Chinese Buddhist monasteries have long adopted a paternalist structure reminiscent of family ancestry, naming the founding figure of the lineage as the "First Patriarch" and the subsequent patriarchs as his "Dharma-heirs." As each patriarch will have various Dharma-heirs, a family tree with relations identified through kinship titles like "uncle" and "nephew" are established. Within this Chinese Buddhist framework, the head monk is referred to as *shifu*, literally "teacher-father," and his disciples are like sons to the father. It is this fatherly figure who assumes absolute power and receives utmost respect from every monastic and lay practitioner inside the temple. The nuns, however, are only referred to as *shi*, or "teacher," and they are expected to provide domestic support to the monks. There is a monastic rule specifying that no matter how senior and respected a nun is, she must always consider all monks her seniors, regardless of how junior the monks might be. This aligns with the Chinese traditional norm according to which it is the Confucian ideal of "gentlemen" (*junzi*) who must bear the burden of the family, carry on the family lineage, receive proper education in order to serve as advisors to the ruler, and carry out the rituals of the state. Women, on the other hand, were believed best suited to domestic service, and were sometimes perceived as having a potentially negative influence on the "gentleman." Traditionally, women were often blamed for causing political problems. The transmission of the Dharma lineage, therefore, was entrusted only to the monks.

This patriarchal structure in Chinese Buddhism suggests a sense of carrying on a family lineage, and teacher-father monks are treated with respect and love, much like the Confucian virtue of "filial piety" in which gentlemen were expected to pay respect and service to fathers and grandfathers (Rainey 2010). In this way, the practitioners are socialized into a lineage that is said to reflect a patriarchal "family spirit" (*jiafeng*). Within such a structure, patriarchal succession is maintained, and the worthy heirs of each generation are considered as the "lineage holders." The nuns have no part to play in the transmission of lineages.

In Confucianism, the teachings were addressed almost entirely to men; women were not expected to receive educations. As a result, most women were uneducated. This traditional role of Chinese women was extended to the Buddhist order, and throughout the centuries of Chinese Buddhism, the nuns never received extensive training like the monks did. Male monastics were only interested in teaching male students and would refrain from teaching individual female students (Aronson 2004).

Some Buddhist canons suggest that a female rebirth is the result of weak, unwholesome karma. The texts also indicate that the Buddha initially hesitated to ordain females into his Sangha. He stated that the ordination of women would cause the Buddha Dharma to decline after 500 years and disappear entirely after 1,000. Culturally speaking, women were often perceived as sexual ensnarers who would be a distraction to the monks' practice. Monks were therefore advised to maintain ascetic wariness with respect to nuns. While the Buddha did not say women were spiritually inferior to monks, the Buddha made additional rules for nuns in the Vinaya. Among them was the rule that no matter how senior a nun was, she always had to defer to a monk even if he had been ordained for just one day. This created a sense of gender hierarchy within the monastic order. Even in terms of ordination, monks could be fully ordained by other monks, while nuns who have been ordained by a group of nuns must still have their ordination confirmed by monks (Harvey 2000). Although the Buddha acknowledged the potential for women to attain perfect enlightenment, he maintained the gender hierarchy of his day and entrusted monks with the authority to lead nuns in the monastic community.

It was not until the last century that efforts began to rectify the gender biases of Chinese Buddhism. Reforms at the beginning of the republican period in China gave girls access to formal education (Cong 2017). The Venerable Taixu, an early-twentieth-century reformer of Chinese Buddhism, also emphasized the importance of Buddhist training for women. The Wuchang Academy for Female Buddhists, established in 1924, was the first educational institute for female Buddhists in the history of Chinese Buddhism (Yuan 2009). But even Ven. Taixu concluded that "China's illness is caused by the fact that the nuns do not uphold the *vinaya*, and thus corrupted the *sangha*" (DeVido 2015), in a tone that aptly expresses the sexist view found in Confucianism.

The traditional Confucian preference for sons, when combined with the one-child-to-a-family policy in effect since 1979, made male progeny even more highly valued in the past several decades. The "only child syndrome" – selfishness and an inability to share – has created social problems. Chinese youth have been criticized for being materialistic, greedy and self-centred. The media have branded them the "me generation."[1] Counteracting perceptions of materialism, greed, and egoism, however, is the recent resurgence of Buddhism, which encourages non-materialistic and ego-less attitudes. Since the introduction of the one-child policy, it has become rare for a precious only son to renounce secular life for a monastic one, especially as the PRC limited the number of ordinations each year. That a young man would turn his back on the pursuit of fame and fortune for a life of religious devotion was perceived as wholly admirable. In the heavily gender-biased society of China, daughters who decided to be ordained were not admired to the same degree, because they did not have as much to lose. Chinese diasporic communities in Hong Kong, Taiwan, and Southeast Asia shared this cultural perception.

Although there have been important achievements accomplished by female monastic movements in China, such as the Three-Plus-One Project of the Pushou Temple at Mount Wutai (Mao 2015), Buddhist monks still occupy the highest positions in the traditional Buddhist religious hierarchy. The same can be observed in Fo Guang Shan and Dharma Drum Mountain, two of the four major Buddhist organizations in Taiwan. Both of these monasteries still operate on the basis of monks' superiority, though they rely heavily on large numbers of nuns who serve in teaching and functional roles. Fo Guang Shan, for example, has 1,000 nuns, in various positions of responsibility, and only 300 monks. Laliberté describes how "female members of Foguangshan are not only caretakers of the monastery, but also involved in public relations with outsiders, and act as scholars. The cliché that women who join the monastic life either have a shadowy past or are uneducated does not fit any of the individuals I met in Foguangshan and in the Taipei Temple" (2004, 84). The supreme head of Fo Guang Shan is the celebrated monk Master Hsing Yun, and his chosen successor, Venerable Hsin Bao, is also a monk. Nevertheless, the nuns' voices can no longer be silenced. The new cultural identity of the Buddhist nuns, as envisioned by Ven. Taixu, contributed to the revival of Buddhism in China. Nuns are also seen as leaders among Chinese women who were marginalized in traditional Confucian culture. Chinese Buddhist nuns have played an important role in "educating and transforming female Buddhist practitioners, who are the majority in the Buddhist community, and even all the women in China" (Yuan 2009). Although women may be the majority among lay practitioners, they remain a minority in monastic life. A 2009 article in a journal published by the Buddhist Association of China (BAC) claimed that there were approximately 80,000 Buddhist monks and nuns in China (Chen 2009).[2] The BAC also provided the number of monks and nuns who have received full ordination. From 1993 to 2003, 19,000 monks received ordination, compared with 9,800 nuns. The monks to nuns ratio is approximately two to one.

In Taiwan, there are about two-thirds more Buddhist nuns than monks, with the number of Buddhist nuns being around 7,000. The Buddhist nuns in Taiwan are very much engaged with secular society and make vital contributions to the development and growth of Buddhism in Taiwan. The numerical dominance of Buddhist nuns there is perhaps one of the reasons that nuns are allowed to have equal power with the monks. It has been estimated that in Taiwan 70 to 75 per cent of the Buddhist monastics are nuns (Cheng 2007). Many of these nuns have received higher education in addition to their training in Buddhist teachings, practices, and precepts.

Even though the status of Chinese Buddhist nuns has greatly improved in recent decades, the improvement is neither a revaluing of the status of female monastics nor a correction to centuries-old oppression from monks. Very often, Buddhist nuns simply do not want to maintain the gender distinction between male and female. Buddhist nuns in Taiwan, for example, often do not see themselves as "feminists" who are struggling against gender inequality; in other words, these nuns are not adopting a stance of protest against the monks, and are not encouraging laywomen to fight for gender equality in such a spirit. Indeed, Buddhist wisdom holds that the categories of "male" and "female" are illusory. Crane suggests that "compartmentalising and contextualizing gender symbols allow the nuns to see themselves both as men and as women without contradiction" (2007, 117). The nuns are striving to remove the ignorance that underlies gender inequality and hierarchy. The alternative ideal is the androgynous role model of *da zhangfu*, which, despite its literal meaning of "great, heroic man" or "big husband," and its affiliation with the putatively masculine characteristics of fearlessness and decisiveness, is understood by Buddhist women to be beyond gender. The term was used by the nuns to refer "not only to spiritually advanced monks but also when they talk about themselves and about one another" (Crane 2007, 27), as a metaphorical reminder to not be limited by the cultural descriptions of feminine qualities in any negative way. This understanding lays the foundation for Buddhist nuns to see themselves playing a role in the community that is significantly different from the traditional role of nuns.

Perhaps the most impressive Buddhist nun from Taiwan is Master Cheng Yen, who has been called the Mother Theresa of the Chinese.

Born in 1937, Cheng Yen established the Tzu Chi Foundation in 1966 with a membership of less than forty people. The foundation grew steadily in size. In 1986 it had 100,000 members, in 1990 1 million, in 1992 2 million, and in 1994 4 million members. By 2000, membership had reached 5 million, making the foundation the largest religious organization in Taiwan. The growth of the foundation may be attributed to the charismatic leadership of Cheng Yen, who developed the foundation into an enormous international network of charitable, educational, and disaster relief works. Huang has argued that the reason why overseas Chinese are particularly drawn to Tzu Chi's Buddhist practice is largely due to "the power of Cheng Yen's world-affirming charisma" (2009, 246). Cheng Yen and her Tzu Chi Foundation attracted Buddhist women who joined the organization wanting to contribute to society without abandoning their traditional family roles. Tzu Chi, although founded by a nun, is not categorized as a monastic institute, but as a lay organization. It is indeed the non-monastic nature of the foundation that contributes to its success in overseas Chinese communities.

In recent decades, the Chinese Buddhist nuns in Taiwan have been provided better access to educational opportunities and monastic training programs. Many of them have MBA degrees to help them with leadership and temple management; others have doctoral degrees in Buddhist studies. The nuns of the Luminary Buddhist Institute in Taiwan are a shining example. The Luminary nuns enjoy the reputation of being highly educated and well disciplined (Cheng 2007). The Taiwanese respect the institute as a place that provides Buddhist nuns with high-quality Buddhist education and which enhances their welfare. As a result of their improved educational background and leadership training, the nuns have also enjoyed improved social and spiritual status, and many are taking up leadership roles in a variety of Buddhist activities, such as offering Dharma teachings, leading meditative workshops, running hospitals, mobile clinics, and orphanages, providing disaster relief work, championing education, and delivering temple management. All these have contributed to the re-evaluation of nuns in the Buddhist tradition over the last few decades.

The three major Buddhist institutions in Taiwan all share the mandate of promoting Humanistic Buddhism. Under this vision, they are inspired to advocate gender equality within their own organizations, even though Buddhist women in the monastic community and the laity might still be under pressure to behave according to the traditional roles prescribed for them (Schak 2008). Nevertheless, the progressive nature of these major Taiwanese organizations has helped transform the images and expectations of lay and monastic Buddhist women in a patriarchal society.

Today, Buddhist nuns are gaining more respect as spiritual leaders in the Chinese community. Cass observes that "in considering gender in Chinese religions the lines of two competing narratives can be clearly traced: the hierarchical, masculine, institutionalized, often state-sponsored paradigm and, in contrast, the regional paradigm that is, in varying degrees, charismatic, vernacular, and often feminine" (2005, 3334). This aptly describes the reform of the role of Chinese Buddhist women set into motion by Ven. Taixu a century ago. In the course of the modernization of Chinese Buddhism, the successful reinvention of the gender identification of Taiwanese Buddhist nuns has played a very prominent role in moving toward contemporary Western perspectives on gender equality.

CHINESE BUDDHISM IN CANADA

Chinese Buddhist nuns are part of the modern Chinese diaspora in North America, which began with labour migration to the US and the Caribbean in the nineteenth century, and grew after China's defeat in the Opium War in the mid-1800s (Chaliand and Rageau 1995). In 1858 Chinese labourers working in the gold mines of California migrated to British Columbia to work in the gold mines there. They were eventually joined by more Chinese migrants, who worked in fish canneries and on grand infrastructure projects such as national railways (Scott and Shiu 2012). Most of these Chinese migrants hoped to return to China at the end of their working lives and retire on their savings. Indeed, the Canadian government hoped they would do just that, and to discourage migration from China in 1885 a head tax was imposed on almost every new Chinese immigrant. The heavy head tax led to disproportionately few women amongst the Chinese immigrants, as it became financially impossible for the Chinese workers to bring families along to Canada. Up until 1902, the population of Chinese wives was merely 0.7 per cent of the total Chinese immigrants, representing the highest gender imbalance among the ethnic groups in Canada. Many of these women were secondary wives (concubines) whose expected role was to meet the sexual needs of their husbands, while the first wives stayed behind to fulfill the traditional women's role as dutiful family caregiver.[3] However, the head tax proved ineffective in curtailing immigration. Thus in 1923 the Canadian government took more draconian measures and passed the Chinese Exclusion Act. This act was repealed in 1947, and Chinese residents of Canada were finally permitted to claim Canadian citizenship, though they still faced discrimination with respect to immigration policies. In 1967 the Canadian government abandoned race-based immigration policies and introduced a points system for evaluating applicants. The number of Chinese immigrants swelled a decade later in 1978, when the Chinese government lifted its own restrictions on emigration, creating an upsurge in family migration and an increase of Chinese women in the population. In 1997, when Hong Kong was handed back to China, many Hong Kong Chinese immigrated to Canada. In 2001, 45 per cent of immigrants came from the People's Republic of China, 30 per cent from Hong Kong, and close to 10 per cent from Taiwan. In 2011, it was estimated that 1,324,700 individuals of Chinese origin resided in Canada, making up to 4 per cent of the total population, or 21.1 per cent of the visible minority population (Statistics Canada 2003). The majority of people of Chinese origin reside in Ontario and British Columbia.

Between 1991 and 2011, Chinese Buddhism had a 124 per cent growth. In the Canadian 2011 National Household Survey, the Buddhist population is recorded as 366,830, or 1.1 per cent of the Canadian population. A survey of Canadian Buddhist Organizations (Negru 2013) shows that of the 558 organizations reporting, 150 of them are identified as Chinese Buddhist communities, representing the single largest ethnic Buddhist group in Canada. In addition, it has been reported that a very high percentage of the Chinese diaspora is unaffiliated with any religion: a survey of census data from several countries found that the largest numbers of religiously unaffiliated diasporic Chinese people are found in Canada (70.1 per cent) and Vietnam (74.7 per cent) (Skirbekk, Malenfant, Basten, and Stonawski 2012). Although they do not identify as Buddhists, many of these religiously unaffiliated Chinese diaspora groups take a syncretic approach to religion and "meld aspects of Chinese traditional religions with Christianity and Buddhism" (174). Such a syncretic approach allows religiously unaffiliated diasporic Chinese people to participate in the activities held at the Chinese Buddhist temples, which then serve as community centres for Chinese people in Canada beyond the merely 14 per cent of the Chinese Canadian population officially identified as Buddhists.

A survey of religious affiliations in the People's Republic of China shows that 18 per cent of the adult population declare themselves as Buddhists (Palmer 2011), compared to 24 per cent from Taiwan (Cheng 2007), and 10.6 per cent of Buddhists from Hong Kong (Yeung and Chow 2010). In the diaspora, Chinese people from different places of origin display different inclinations to religiosity. Chinese people from China, Taiwan, and Hong Kong together comprise 42 per cent of the Chinese Buddhist population in Canada, while Southeast Asians of Chinese origin comprise another 34 per cent (Boisvert 2005). It should also be noted that this group of Chinese from Southeast Asia actually represents the single largest Chinese Buddhist group in Canada, although only 8 per cent of these Southeast Asian Chinese speak a Chinese dialect (Beyer 2010).

Buddhist practice has allowed closer connection between Southeast Asian and Chinese Buddhists in Canada. A number of Buddhist temples in Canada were built by Vietnamese of Chinese origin, including the Fu Sien Tong Buddhist Temple (originally named the Buddhist Senior Society), founded by Venerable Po-Yu in 1982, and the Ching Kwok Buddhist Temple (originally named the Tai Bay Buddhist Temple), founded by Venerable Wu-De in 1984. These two Toronto temples provide services to the Chinese communities from Southeast Asia, as well as Hong Kong and southern China, with the primary language being Cantonese.

THE TRADITIONAL POSITION OF BUDDHIST NUNS IN CANADA

The traditional, hierarchical form of a Chinese Buddhist monastery can be observed in older temples, such as the Cham Shan Temple in Toronto. For decades, the Cham Shan Temple was led by two monks, Master Sing Hung and Master Shing Cheung. Within three decades, they developed Cham Shan extensively in the Greater Toronto Area, with branches established in Toronto, Whitby, Niagara Falls, and Hamilton; two of these were reserved as nunneries. The nuns, however, were subordinate to the two elder monks, who conducted the major ceremonies and teachings at the temple. With the passing of Shing Cheung in 2006, Cham Shan got a new, younger abbot, Ven. Da Yi, but the male-centred, hierarchical paradigm of the temple did not change.[4]

The paternal hierarchy is also found among Southeast Asian Chinese Buddhists in Canada. Soucy studied the Vietnamese Tam Bào Temple in Montreal and commented that the structure of the board of directors reflects the "'normative' dichotomy of women being part of the domestic sphere of activity (internal affairs) and men being part of the public sphere (external affairs)" (Soucy 1994, 153). Chinese Buddhists coming from Southeast Asia held the traditional view that women's place was in the home. This was extended to Buddhist monasteries, with nuns assuming the roles of housekeeping and providing domestic services. As Janet McLellan argues, "in most Asian traditions, Buddhism has long been the preserve of monks and male elders who provided representatives decision-making from positions of secular and sacred authority, while women participated as devoted worshippers, providing caretaking and domestic service for religious celebrations and creating merit by feeding monks" (1998, 231). Although a Vietnamese Buddhist institution, Tam Bào Temple caters to a large Chinese Buddhist community in Montreal. It has been suggested that the Sino-Vietnamese practitioners share "a linguistic and religious culture close to that of migrants from the People's Republic of China, Taiwan and Hong Kong" (Matthews 2006, 144).

Soucy presents a case study of the Venerable Thầy Phổ Tĩnh, a Vietnamese nun at the Tam Bào Temple who received a Master's degree in religious studies and refused to accept the subservient position of nuns vis-à-vis monks. The perception of Buddhist women at Tam Bào Temple reflects in many ways the older cultural identity of Buddhist nuns within a conservative and patriarchal culture. Thầy Phổ Tĩnh's education became a threat to the monks in the same way that a highly educated woman might be seen as a threat by husband; as Soucy points out, Vietnamese men "often feel uncomfortable in relationships where women have more social capital" (2014, 347). Many immigrant monks in this community were unprepared to fall under the leadership of a nun, and unfortunately Thầy Phổ Tĩnh was forced to leave the temple. It is important to note that second-generation Chinese and Southeast Asian Buddhist women are achieving higher levels of post-secondary education than men; Beyer notes that "first generation women … have less post-secondary exposure than their male counterparts, whereas the women of the second generation are reversing the trend" (2010, 123). However, these second-generation immigrants may not have a large impact on the Southeast Asian Buddhist communities because only a small number of them participate in temple activities, with many of them expressing frustrations towards parents and monks for their authoritarian stance.

As McLellan and White remark, "presently, monks and temples serve the community in traditional ways that are meaningful to the first generation." Many first generation women not only express utmost respect towards monks, but also find it uncomfortable to "accept any kind of role that could cause them to stand out" (2015, 427).

In Canada, due to the influence of the Taiwanese Humanistic Buddhist groups and the significant number of Chinese nuns, the role of nuns has been slowly becoming less subservient and more authoritative. Nuns are now expected to perform ceremonies and engage in administrative duties. This unfortunately consumes the time that might otherwise be spent furthering their Buddhist education, though the same challenges can be found among their male counterparts. As Boisvert concludes, "monks and nuns trained in Canada are generally less educated than their counterparts overseas" (2005, 78).

A transnational organization that appears to address this traditional attitude is Tung Lin Kok Yuen (TLKY), founded in 1935; it is the only seminary for Buddhist nuns in Hong Kong with an eight-year curriculum program. Its Canadian branch, the TLKY Canada Society, was established in Vancouver in 1994 as a Buddhist institute to meet the spiritual needs of Chinese Canadians, not limited to nuns or Buddhist females. The society was led by abbess Ven. Sik Yin-Tak until her passing in 2015. Crowe remarked that Ven. Yin Tak earned her doctoral degree in Buddhist studies in Japan in the 1960s (2010, 261). In 2004, the TLKY Foundation was established to promote Buddhist studies at major universities around the world, including the creation of the University of British Columbia's chair and program in Buddhism and Contemporary Society and the University of Toronto's Centre for Buddhist Studies. The TLKY Foundation has not, however, made any attempt to provide for Buddhist nuns in Canada.

The elevation of Buddhist nuns' social status in Taiwan coincides with the rise of Humanistic Buddhism, developed under Master Hsing Yun of Fo Guang Shan, Ven. Sheng Yen of Dharma Drum Mountain, and Ven. Cheng Yen of the Tzu Chi Foundation. All three institutions owe their success to the dedicated works of nuns, and all emphasize equality between monks and nuns in their community. Fo Guang Shan, in particular, is known for its participation in an ongoing discussion about reviving the Theravada nun order. Beginning in 1988, Master Hsing Yun included Theravada nuns in the ordination ceremonies, and accommodated the ordination of Tibetan nuns as well. Fo Guang Shan branches in Canada are exclusively led by nuns, most of whom are in their thirties and forties, and all of whom have received full training in Taiwan. They give regular Dharma discourses and other spiritual services to the laity. Fo Guang Shan's Toronto temple is currently run by six nuns on rotation from Taiwan.

It remains difficult to get an accurate picture of the total number of Buddhist monks and nuns in Canada, especially as many of the monastics, such as the nuns of Fo Guang Shan, are itinerant and in Canada only as visitors. These visiting nuns not only help to connect Buddhists in Canada with their home base in Taiwan, but also serve to "balance a community connection with a connection to the wider society" (Berns-McGown 2008). While 54.5 per cent of Chinese Buddhists in Canada are female (Beyer 2006), there are no statistics that indicate how many of them are nuns. As Heidi MacDonald notes in her study of Roman Catholic nuns in Canada, "although women religious (commonly called nuns) have historically been a large group of mostly professional women, they were regularly excluded from what the Census of Canada defined as the work force" (2010, 369). Unlike Taiwan, where the Buddhist Association of the Republic of China (BAROC) provides accurate figures of monastic ordination, no such figures are provided by Statistics Canada.

Very few Chinese Canadians have been ordained as monks or nuns in Canada. Most of the Chinese Buddhist monastics now in Canada were ordained elsewhere and came to Canada to fulfill their religious vocation. My interviews with the nuns at Fo Guang Shan and Dharma Drum Mountain confirmed that neither institution has ever held a full ordination ceremony for Buddhist nuns in Canada, although occasional ordination ceremonies for nuns took place at Cham Shan Temple. This suggests that the changing dynamic between Buddhist monks and nuns, the new role of nuns in Buddhist communities, and the level of appreciation of the nuns' role as spiritual leaders did not originate in the Canadian Chinese Buddhist community, but developed in overseas Chinese communities and then spread to Canada.

RELATIONS BETWEEN CHINESE BUDDHIST COMMUNITIES AND OTHER COMMUNITIES IN CANADA

Ethnic Buddhist groups in Canada are known for their exclusivity and their unwillingness to engage in activities with other Buddhist organizations or with mainstream secular society (Matthews 2006, xix). As a result, the conservative observance of traditional norms is often preserved and reified within Chinese Buddhist communities. Many Canada-based Buddhist groups acknowledge that they are divided from each other. Within ethnic communities like the Vietnamese, Taiwanese, mainland Chinese, and Burmese, the competition between temples can be fierce. The nuns at Fo Guang Shan and Tzu Chi in Canada are indeed "polite rivals."[5]

Another reason for the lack of communication between these Buddhist communities is that some of the communities and their leaders lack the English proficiency for such a purpose. To help overcome the language obstacles, an attempt was made in Vancouver to form a "United Sangha,"[6] with a coalition of thirty-eight Buddhist monks and nuns representing various eclectic Buddhist traditions. The initiative was organized by Ven. Zhihan to celebrate Vesak in 2015. It was the first attempt on the West Coast to bring together Buddhists of different ethnicities. As Ven. Zhihan remarked, the Buddhist monastics wanted to work towards the common vision to unite the Sangha, but they lacked the English facility to do so (Todd 2015).

Zhihan has certainly highlighted the difficulties that some Chinese Buddhist temples in Canada are facing. For now, the lack of English proficiency may only be an obstacle to communicate with other Buddhist groups, but what lies ahead is even more challenging. As second and subsequent generations in the Chinese diaspora community become less fluent in Chinese[7] there is a growing gap between the laity and the monastics, making the transmission of Buddhist practice to the second and third generations of Chinese immigrants increasingly difficult. Educated young women of the second and third generations are also unreceptive to the authoritative and patriarchal voice of the male monastics, and therefore seldom participate in Buddhist practices or activities. In addition, the monastics' lack of understanding of Canadian workplace culture, economics, the main policy differences between political parties, elections, etc., makes any meaningful conversation or spiritual exchange with young Chinese Canadians almost impossible. This could eventually threaten the very survival of these Buddhist groups, as there will come a time when they can no longer rely on the first generation of Chinese immigrants as followers.

The leading Chinese Buddhist organizations from Taiwan, however, have adopted a different strategy and have been bringing to Canada Chinese Buddhist nuns who are better educated and more fluent in English to help reach out to the larger non-Buddhist community. Described as the "new-age Buddhists" on BBC News,[8] these groups advocating Humanistic Buddhism have taken a neo-traditional approach to revitalize the religion in the modern world. They play down the traditional focus on devotional and ritual practice, and pay more attention to social service as a means of cultivating wisdom and compassion. In order to carry out the mission successfully, they need to have a good understanding of and relationship with the local communities, wherever in the world they build their chapters or branches. In Canada, for example, an interfaith panel on "Woman's Role in Public Life" was organized for International Women's Day (2015) by Fo Guang Shan Temple and the Intercultural Dialogue Institute, fostering a dialogue between four women representatives of Buddhism, Christianity, Judaism, and Islam, and moderated by a female interfaith and human rights activist. In addition, both Fo Guang Shan and Tzu Chi have established student clubs at the University of Toronto and University of Waterloo, thus ensuring they have close contacts with the younger generation of Chinese in Canada, as well as educated volunteers who are integrated into mainstream Canadian culture. This is a smart move to smooth the transmission of Chinese Buddhism to the second and third generations of Chinese immigrants.

Another good example that illustrates the trust in Buddhist nuns' ability and vision to lead the Sangha is the Great Wisdom Buddhist Institute (GWBI), a Taiwan-based Chinese Buddhist nunnery with a branch in Vernon Bridge, Prince Edward Island. The GWBI is currently constructing a multi-million-dollar temple complex on a 250-acre lot at Brudenell, PEI. The monastery is large enough to have dormitories that house up to 200 people. It is a sister organization to the Great Enlightenment Buddhist Institute Society (GEBIS), which runs a monks-only Buddhist monastery about 30 kilometres away. The two monastic communities function in tandem, rather than assuming a hierarchical relationship. According to the National Household Survey, in 2001 there were only 140 Buddhists in Prince Edward Island; the remainder of the population was mainly Roman Catholic. In 2011 there were 560 Buddhists, with 330 being immigrants. The founding of GEBIS in 2008 is largely responsible for this change in the religious landscape in PEI. The establishment of the GWBI will surely bring about further changes and introduce more Buddhists in the region.

With so few ethnic Buddhists in PEI, the nuns of the GWBI have been especially careful in reaching out to the local community, doing their best to blend in and minimize any possible hard feelings residents might have about the construction of a huge Asian temple in their community. For example, the nuns have preserved the historical barns on the land, made financial donations to community initiatives, participated in the clean up of roadside and pool facilities, met with the Women's Institute, and even celebrated Christmas with a big, decorated Christmas tree erected outside the temple. They gave out treats to the neighbours, fully affirming the importance of Jesus to the world. They do not want to be strangers to the local communities. Even their names are friendly to the PEI residents whose ancestry is overwhelmingly white, English-speaking, and Christian: instead of using Chinese Dharma names, these nuns have adopted names such as "Venerable Janet" or "Venerable Yvonne." This makes it easier for them to be accepted as counterparts of Catholic nuns. It is important to consider this practice in relation to the importance of Dharma names in Chinese Buddhism. Dharma names are not only expressions of Buddhist teachings, but they also reflect the transmitted lineage; occasionally, the names are given according to the generation poem used for generational naming.[9] That the Chinese Buddhist nuns at the GEBIS are willing to give up their Dharma names is both a capitulation to Christian norms, and a gesture that they are prepared to modify Buddhist teachings and practices to suit the spiritual needs of PEI's residents. The GWBI and the GEBIS together represent the new face of Chinese Buddhism on Prince Edward Island. Indeed, GWBI is particularly unique for being the nunnery that houses the greatest number of Buddhist nuns in Canada. Its existence in an area where there are not many Chinese residents, let alone Chinese Buddhists, has meant grappling with challenges that other Buddhist organizations in Ontario and British Columbia have not had to face. Instead of catering to a local Chinese immigrant community, the GWBI has adapted to mainstream PEI culture.

Although most Chinese Buddhist nuns seldom affiliate with other Buddhist groups, the creation of Sakyadhita Canada, a branch of the International Organization of Buddhist Women, has proven to be important for many Buddhist nuns in Canada. Fenn describes how the Canadian branch of Sakyadhita was established "to connect Buddhist women, especially nuns, across Canada providing both emotional and financial support to women who are often isolated by geography," the goal being "to establish an alliance of ordained and lay Buddhist women in Canada" (2013, 132). The establishment of Sakyadhita Canada is especially meaningful to the non-community-based Buddhist nuns, who lack financial security and the resources for training. It has supported, for example, the nuns at Po Lam Nunnery in British

Columbia for overseas training and attendance at the Sakyadhita conferences. Perhaps the nuns from the "United Sangha" in Vancouver can benefit from the Sakyadhita in developing its vision for the future.

It has been observed that "a strong feminist movement with regard to religious participation has not been as necessary among Chinese women as it has been among their Christian and Jewish counterparts" (Lai, Paper, and Paper 2005). Although the observation may be too generalized and context-dependent, it remains true that these Buddhist nuns do not actively seek converts among non-Buddhist Canadians, and neither have they called for religious gender equality. Writing about Taiwanese nuns, Eichman has observed that "very few nuns attribute their success to a women's rights movement or to Western-style feminism. Rather, many powerful nuns claim that such feminine and motherly virtues as compassion, nurturance, empathy, selflessness, patience, and warmth make it easier for them to administer to others while adjusting to communal monastic life" (2011, 349). These nuns are subtly making converts by being role models to inspire others to learn about Buddhism and live a life of caring and compassion according to its precepts. The androgynous egalitarian ideal is usually not emphasized, and the nuns display their qualities of perseverance, hard work, selfless devotion, and service to the public without reference to gender issues.

CONCLUSION

Traditionally, Chinese Buddhist nuns were treated as inferior to monks and were usually supposed to fulfill domestic roles that had little to do with a spiritual quest. The social and cultural transformations that began in Taiwan allowed Buddhist nuns to receive better education, earn higher respect, and take up leadership roles, although forms of traditional male chauvinism may still be detected in the Chinese Buddhist diaspora. Chinese Buddhist nuns in Canada could have clung to the traditions of the past, as many immigrant groups do. However, thanks to the influence of progressive Taiwanese Buddhist nuns, the traditional hierarchical relationship between monks and nuns is becoming less entrenched, allowing a spirit of gender equality to be embraced in Canada, where the empowerment of women as well as the promotion of their human rights are key values.

We are therefore seeing two very different attitudes towards Chinese Buddhist nuns in Canada, a traditional one that positions them as subordinate to monks, and a reformed one that places them on equal footing, enabling the nuns to determine the dissemination and development of their own Buddhist tradition in Canada. The latter model, inspired by some of the Taiwanese groups discussed here, allows nuns to receive a fuller education in Buddha Dharma and other leadership and management training. Not only that, but they are usually more fluent in English, which allows them to establish communications with other Buddhist communities and present Buddhism in a way that is more relevant to mainstream Canadian society. Having said that, the former patriarchal model retains a stronghold among some Chinese immigrants in Canada, who are more comfortable holding on to the older tradition as a means of staying connected to the "roots" of Chinese culture. Even after years of settlement in Canada, the dynamics of connections with the Chinese diaspora and progressive communities of nuns in mainland China, Hong Kong, and Taiwan are still paving the way for changes in attitudes towards Buddhist women.

The positive role of these transnational Chinese Buddhist nuns in Canada has implications for the spread of a more gender-equitable Buddhism world-wide. Not only are many of the nuns able to tap the rich resources of their host organizations in Taiwan for healthcare, education, and other services, but more importantly, their high social status, strong educational background, and willingness to communicate with other religions allow them to serve as role models with respect to the treatment of female religious professionals and the promotion of gender equality. Just as Chinese Buddhist temples are important statements of Chinese religious belief in Canada, so are Chinese Buddhist nuns making a visible statement about their new identity. Participation in the religious and social events organized by these groups has given Canadian Chinese Buddhists a sense of unity and a source of pride. Chinese Buddhist nuns in Canada can contribute to Canadian society at large by working with other religious communities in addressing issues of inequality in religious practices, education, charity works, and social services.

NOTES

1 One can see, for example, *Time Magazine*'s coverage of "China's Me Generation," 5 November 2007, http://content.time.com/time/magazine/article/0,9171,1675626,00.html.

2 The percentage of Buddhist lay practitioners in the overall population of China is said to be around 18 per cent (Wang 2011; Palmer 2011). This is a very loose estimate since religious practitioners do not have to register with the government, and many practitioners do not confine themselves to the practice of only one religion. A significant percentage of China's population practise Chinese folk religions, which blend aspects of Buddhism, Confucianism, Daoism, and ancestral worship. In addition, it is generally recognized that Chinese population statistics are often unreliable, and religious statistics are often compromised for political purposes. Lambert (2013) refers to a survey conducted by East China Normal University in 2006, which found that about 30 per cent of the adult population, or 300 million people, have maintained some forms of religious practice, with the majority of these being followers of Buddhism. This is significantly more than official estimates.

3 There were also other Chinese women who came as domestic slaves, serving girls, and prostitutes (Woon 2008). The stories and experiences of some of the earliest Chinese women who emigrated to Canada were captured in the documentary *Under the Willow Tree: Pioneer Chinese Women in Canada*, directed by Dora Nipp (1997).

4 Da Yi has taken on a highly ambitious multi-million-dollar project to replicate in the scenic countryside outside Peterborough, Ontario the Four Great Sacred Buddhist Mountains of China.

5 These rival groups' lack of willingness to communicate with one another led to the cancellation of an earlier enthusiastic effort to try to bring together the various Buddhist communities through the Buddhist Council of Canada (BCC) in 1985. As the Buddhist communities became stronger, they segregated into their own ethnic communities, and the BCC faded away within a decade. The BCC was revived in 2010, with its objectives redirected towards the promotion of social harmony and cultural vibrancy of Canada, by way of the application of Buddhist principles. It no longer maintains its original objective to promote greater communication and harmony among the Canadian Buddhist communities.

6 http://www.unitedsangha.org/vesak2015/

7 While the most recent Statistics Canada evidence suggests that Chinese language speakers have a high level of language retention in the home, more households are becoming multilingual or primarily use English or French. See "Census in Brief: Linguistic diversity and multilingualism in Canadian homes," Statistics Canada 2017 (Catalogue no. 98-200-X2016010).

8 http://www.bbc.com/news/world-asia-25772194.

9 An example of the importance of Dharma-naming is found in the Avatamsaka Sagely Monastery in Calgary. Verchery describes how a "nun's seniority is made apparent by her name. In accordance with standard pan-Buddhist practice, each monastic is given a Dharma name upon ordination that reflects her tonsure generation. All those ordained directly under Master Hua, as first-generation disciples, have the Dharma name Heng. The generation ordained under the Hengs are named Jin" (2015).

REFERENCES

Aronson, Harvey B. 2004. *Buddhist Practice on Western Ground*. Boston: Shambhala Publications.

Berns-McGown, Rima. 2008. "Redefining 'Diaspora': The Challenge of Connection and Inclusion." *International Journal* 63, no. 1, 3–20.

Beyer, Peter. 2006. "Buddhism in Canada: A Statistical Overview from Canadian Censuses, 1981–2001." *Canadian Journal of Buddhist Studies*, no. 2: 83–102.

– 2010. "Buddhism in Canada: A Statistical Overview from Canadian Censuses, 1981–2001." In *Wild Geese: Buddhism in Canada*, edited by John S. Harding, Victor Sōgen Hori, and Alexander Soucy, 111–13. Montreal and Kingston: McGill-Queen's University Press.

Boisvert, Mathieu. 2005. "Buddhists in Canada: Impermanence in a Land of Change." In *Religion and Ethnicity in Canada*, edited by Paul Bramadat and David Seljak, 69–88. Toronto: University of Toronto Press.

Bramadat, Paul, and David Seljak, eds. 2005. *Religion and Ethnicity in Canada*. Toronto: University of Toronto Press.

Butler, K.D. 2001. "Defining Diaspora, Refining a Discourse." in *Diaspora* 10, no. 2: 189–219.

Cass, Victoria. 2005. "Gender and Religion: Gender and Chinese Religions." In *Encyclopedia of Religion*, edited by Lindsay Jones, 2nd edition, vol. 5: 3338–45. New York: Macmillan, Gale.

Chaliand, Gerard, and Jean-Pierre Rageau. 1995. *The Penguin Atlas of Diasporas*. New York: Viking.

Chen, Xingqiao. 2009. "Aiguo aijiao liushinnian, yushi jujin pu xinpian [Sixty Years' Loyalty to Country and Religion, Keeping Up with the Times for New Progress]." *Fayan* (The Voice of Dharma) 11: 6–7.

Cheng, Wei-Yi. 2007. *Buddhist Nuns in Taiwan and Sri Lanka: A Critique of the Feminist Perspective*. New York: Routledge.

Choquette, Robert. 2004. *Canada's Religions*. Ottawa: University of Ottawa Press.

Cohen, R. 1997. *Global Diasporas: An Introduction*. London: UCLP.

Cong, Xiaoping. 2011. *Teachers' Schools and the Making of the Modern Chinese Nation-State, 1897–1937*. Vancouver: University of British Columbia Press.

Crane, Hillary. 2007. "Becoming a Nun, Becoming a Man: Taiwanese Buddhist Nuns' Gender Transformation." *Religion* 37: 117–32.

Crowe, Paul. 2010. "Chinese Religions." In *Asian Religions in British Columbia*, edited by Larry DeVries, Don Baker, and Dan Overmyer, 249–75. Vancouver: University of British Columbia Press.

DeVido, Elise A. 2015. "Networks and Bridges: Nuns in the Making of Modern Chinese Buddhism." *The Chinese Historical Review* 22, no. 1: 72–93.

Ebaugh, H.R., and J.S. Chafetz. 1999. "Agents for Cultural Reproduction and Structural Change: The Ironic Role of Women in Immigrant Religious Institutions." *Social Forces* 78: 585–612.

Eichman, Jennifer. 2011. "Prominent Nuns: Influential Taiwanese Voices." *Cross Currents* 61: 345–73.

Fenn, Mavis. 2013. "Sakyadhita Canada: Branching Out." *Canadian Journal of Buddhist Studies* 9: 131–41.

Harding, John S., Victor Hori, and Alexander Soucy, eds. 2010. *Wild Geese: Buddhism in Canada*. Montreal and Kingston: McGill-Queen's University Press.

Harvey, Peter. 2000. *An Introduction to Buddhist Ethics*. Cambridge: Cambridge University Press.

Huang, C. Julia. 2009. *Charisa and Compassion: Cheng Yen and the Buddhist Tzu Chi Movement*. Cambridge: Harvard University Press.

Lai, David Chuenyuan, Jordan Paper, and Li Chuang Paper. 2005. "The Chinese in Canada: Their Unrecognized Religion." In *Religion and Ethnicity in Canada*, edited by Paul Bramadat and David Seljak, 89–110. Toronto: University of Toronto Press.

Laliberté, André. 2004. *The Politics of Buddhist Organizations in Taiwan: 1989–2003, Safeguarding the Faith, Building a Pure Land, Helping the Poor*. London and New York: RoutledgeCurzon.

Lambert, Tony. 2013. "Religious Statistics in China." *China Source*, 7 January.

Li, Yu-chen. 2000. "Chujia Rushi – zhanhou Taiwan Fojiao Nuxiang sengiu zhi bianqian." *Huigu Taiwan, zhanwang xin guxiang – Taiway shehui wenhua bianqian xueshe yantaohui lunwangji*: 433–5.

MacDonald, Heidi. 2010. "Who Counts? Nuns, Work, and the Census of Canada." *Historie Sociale/Social History* 43, no. 86: 369–91.

Mao, Rujing. 2015. "Chinese *Bhiksuni*s in Contemporary China: Beliefs and Practices on Three-Plus-One Project." *International Journal of Dharma Studies* 3: 1–13.

Matthews, Bruce, ed. 2006. *Buddhism in Canada*. Abingdon and New York: Routledge.

McLellan, Janet. 1999. *Many Petals of the Lotus: Five Asian Buddhist Communities in Toronto*. Toronto: University of Toronto Press.

McLellan, Janet, and Marybeth White. 2015. "Changing Perceptions of Monasticism within Ontario Khmer and Lao Buddhist Communities." In *Understanding the Consecrated Life in Canada: Critical Essays on Contemporary Trends*, edited by Jason Zuidema, 419–32. Waterloo, ON: Wilfrid Laurier University Press.

Negru, John. 2013. "Highlights from the Survey of Canadian Buddhist Organizations." *Journal of Global Buddhism* 14: 1–18.

Palmer, David A. 2011. "Religion in the People's Republic of China: An Overview." In *Handbook of Contemporary China*, edited by William Tay and Alvin So, 293–326. Singapore: World Scientific.

Palmo, Tsultrim. 1999. "Life in Gampo Abbey – Western style." In *Blossoms of the Dharma: Living as a Buddhist Nun*, edited by Thubten Chodron, 49–60. Berkeley: North Atlantic Books.

Safran, W. 1991. "Diaspora in Modern Society: Myths of Homeland and Return," *Diaspora* 1: 83–99.

Schak, David C. 2008. "Gender and Buddhism in Taiwan," *Hsuan Chuang Buddhist Studies* (《玄奘佛學研究》) 9, no. 3: 145–74.

Scott, Jamie S., and Henry Shiu. 2012. "Buddhists." In *The Religions of Canadians*, edited by Jamie S. Scott, 261–306. Toronto: University of Toronto Press.

Skirbekk, Vegard, Eric Caron Malenfant, Stuart Basten, and Marcin Stonawki. 2012. "The Religious Composition of the Chinese Diaspora, Focusing on Canada." *Journal for the Scientific Study of Religion* 51, no. 1: 173–83.

Soucy, Alexander. 1994. "Gender and Division of Labour in a Vietnamese Canadian Buddhist Pagoda." MA thesis, Montreal: Concordia University.

– 2014. "Thấy Phổ Tĩnh: A Vietnamese Nun's Struggles in Canada." In *Flowers on the Rock: Global and Local Buddhisms in Canada*, edited by John S. Harding, Victor Sōgen Hori, and Alexander Soucy, 333–54. Montreal and Kingston: McGill-Queen's University Press.

Statistics Canada. 2003. *1971, 1981, 1991 and 2001 Census Custom Tabulations. DO0324.* CD-ROM. Ottawa: Statistics Canada, Advisory Services Division.

Todd, Douglas. 2015. "Vancouver Buddhists Strive to Overcome Ethnic Silos." *Vancouver Sun*, 12 May.

Velayutham, Sivakumar. 2012. "Diaspora as a Comparative/Competitive Advantage in a Global Economy: A Comparison of the British and Chinese Diaspora." *The Business and Management Review* 2, no. 1: 23–34.

Verchery, Lina. 2015. "The Avatamsaka Sagely Monastery (華嚴聖寺) and New Perspectives on Globalized Buddhism in Canada." In *Understanding the Consecrated Life in Canada: Critical Essays on Contemporary Trends*, edited by Jason Zuidema, 361–76. Waterloo, ON: Wilfrid Laurier University Press.

Wang, Zhiyuan. 2011. "Jiji Wenjian he Erlingyiling Nian Zhongguo Fojiao [Active and Steady Chinese Buddhism in 2010]." In *Zongjiao Lanpishu: Zhongguo Zongjiao Baogao (2011)* [Blue Book of Religions: Annual Report on Religions in China 2011], edited by Jin Ze and Qiu Yonghui, 19–53. Beijing: Social Sciences Academic Press.

Woon, Yuen-Fong. 2008."Between South China and British Columbia: Life Trajectories of Chinese Women." *BC Studies* nos. 156–7: 83–108.

Yang, Fenggang. 2004. "Gender and Generation in a Chinese Christian Church." In *Asian American Religions: The Making and Remaking of Border And Boundaries*, edited by T. Carnes and F. Yang, 205–22. New York: New York University Press.

Yeung, Gustav K.K., and Wai-yin Chow. 2010. "'To Take Up Your Own Responsibility': The Religiosity of Buddhist Adolescents in Hong Kong." *International Journal of Children's Spirituality* 15, no. 1: 5–23.

Yuan, Yuan. 2009. "Chinese Buddhist Nuns in the Twentieth-Century: A Case Study in Wuhan." *Journal of Global Buddhism* 10: 375–412.

8

Syrian Malabar Christian Diaspora in Canada

Women and the Rebuilding of Faith

Lina Samuel

The Malayali diaspora emerged in Canada in the late postwar period, and women played an important role. In this chapter, I deconstruct the role of religion in Malayali migration and focus on the role of women in building immigrant churches within the diaspora. I begin with a brief history of the Syrian Malabar Christian[1] Church and the role of religion in migration, arguing that the migration of Malayali nurses set the stage for later movements of Keralites both globally and in particular to Canada. I then examine the role of the Syrian Christian Church in the lives of Malayali immigrants and the role of women in the reconstruction of faith in the diaspora. Finally, I examine the ways in which faith and devotion are maintained or challenged intergenerationally; each generation has approached the question of worship and faith differently.

Drawing on face-to-face interviews with sixty-four respondents who trace their identities to the Syrian Christian Church of Kerala, India, this chapter examines the importance of the church in the Canadian Malayali diaspora and women's roles in the community. In addition to the formal conversations, I also had informal conversations with two priests from the two largest churches in the Greater Toronto Area (GTA) and two leaders of community cultural organizations. Since the 1960s, the church has been a central marker of identity within the Malayali diaspora in Canada. First-generation immigrants who arrived between the mid-1960s and 1980s worked hard to establish churches and bring qualified priests to preside over services and guide the spiritual needs of the community. However, their children, the second generation, are for the most part only marginally active in the church or do not attend religious services at all. Their relationship to the church is in sharp contrast to that of a third group, the now young adults who started to arrive with their parents as part of a new immigrant cohort in the 1990s. This group is the most active in the church, and identify most strongly with it. This chapter thus examines the changing role of the Syrian Christian Church and the shifting loyalties among different immigrant cohorts, exploring the reasons for rising religiosity among recent Malayali immigrants.

SYRIAN MALABAR CHRISTIANS OF KERALA

The state of Kerala is home to India's largest Christian minority.[2] They trace their origins to the arrival of Saint Thomas, the apostle, in north Kerala in 52 AD, and his subsequent establishment of many churches in the region (Mar Thoma Metropolitan 1985). Because many early converts were from Brahmin and other high-caste Hindu families, the Syrian Christians of Kerala occupy an elevated status within the caste hierarchy, and during the early years of the Christian era, they increased in numbers and prosperity as they came to dominate foreign and local trade. By the eighth and ninth centuries, they had attained several high privileges and were referred to as the *Nazranis*, because their status was similar to that of the high-caste Nayars (Kurien 2002, 47; Bayly 1989, 252). Under British colonial rule from the early eighteenth century, Syrian Christians in India further established their elevated status as the British sought to establish alliances with Christian groups in order to solidify their political authority. Moreover, Syrian Christians were early beneficiaries of the hospitals, schools, and other social programs established by missionaries. Syrian Christians were soon the most fluent in English and became disproportionately concentrated in the teaching and health professions. English proficiency and the privilege derived from these political alliances also meant that Syrian Christians were favoured as administrators not only on plantations in India but throughout the British Empire (Kurien 2002, 52). It became common for Syrian Christians to become teachers and, most importantly, doctors and nurses – a trend that continues to this day.

CHRISTIAN COMMUNITY AND NURSING

The Christian community of Kerala provides the state with 90 per cent of its nurses, as well as the majority of working nurses in a number of other Indian states (cited in Percot 2006, 44). The concentration of Christians in nursing and medicine is in part related to Hindu notions of purity and pollution, two key elements of the caste system that deter Hindus from entering the nursing profession. The caste system distributes the whole of society into a large number of hierarchically organized hereditary groups marked by social separation and division of labour (Dumont 1970, 21). These divisions between groups are based on notions of purity and pollution, and nursing, because it involves contact with substances such as blood, faeces, and vomit, is considered an "impure" occupation. At the same time, according to Hindu orthodoxy an upper-caste Hindu must not be touched by an untouchable person, so nursing cannot be left to untouchables. Although nursing is not a prestigious job (as my respondents attest), it has provided Indian Christian women opportunities to both pursue their education and career and meet certain gendered expectations, such as working with other women and being of service to others. The first nurses in Kerala were, in fact, religious sisters (Percot 2006, 44). Because nursing schools were run by Christian denominations, they allowed women to pursue their education in an environment that met their parents' strict standards. The Christian community continues to educate women and send nurses to countries around the world that are actively recruiting nursing professionals. According to Percot, the number of nurses trained in India has increased, particularly in response to growing labour markets in the West and the Persian Gulf. Thus, religion and occupational opportunities are together propelling Indian Christians, first into a profession, and then abroad to seek economic and financial security.

RELIGIOUS INSTITUTIONS AND SOCIAL CAPITAL

In *The Elementary Forms of Religious Life*, Emile Durkheim writes, "religion is an eminently social thing. Religious representations are collective representations that express collective realities" ([1912] 1995, 2). For Durkheim, religious beliefs, customs, and values serve to "recreate certain mental states" of the larger group (9). For immigrant groups, religious expressions are collective or social representations that hold a group together in spite of the challenges of migration. Durkheim's discussion of the central role of the collective conscience provides a conceptual framework and methodological tool for understanding the role of institutions in the lives of immigrant groups. For immigrants, religious beliefs, values, and cultural practices establish a way in which individuals come together; there is a conscience at the centre of these groups that allows them to form new collective spaces far from their country of origin. Etienne Wenger's social learning theory concurs (1998, 5). Individual identity and collective conscience are dependent on participation and mutual engagement within communities of practice – in this case religious communities of practice within the Syrian Christian diaspora.

Fenggang Yang and Helen Rose Ebaugh write that "historically, religious institutions were among the most important resources that immigrant groups used to reproduce their ethno-religious identity in new surroundings and to help them adjust to the challenges of surviving in a demanding and often threatening environment" (2001, 269). In the traditional paradigm of the sociology of religion, there was the expectation of "religious secularization" associated with modernization, but this has been challenged: not only is religion thriving, but those who might not have been terribly religious in their home country find a greater affinity for their religious faith in the new host country (270). In fact, studies on American religiosity find that American pluralism helps "energize and revitalize" religions from back "home" (269). Research on immigrant religions points out that "neither the functions of religion nor the significance of religion is declining among immigrants" within the diaspora (271). As Prema Kurien notes, religion is "the most common and most acceptable basis for community formation and expression for immigrants" (2013, 149). Religious institutions come to be one of the central institutions by which immigrant groups define themselves and maintain their cultural and ethnic life in the diaspora (ibid.).

As Kurien warns in her writings on the rise of Hindu nationalism in the United States, the process of migration can give support to immigrant nationalism (2004, 366). The various levels of dislocation (personal, spiritual, cultural, and social) that result from the migration process can lead to immigrant nostalgia for "home." Thus, the process of migration can work to strengthen ties to religion and religious institutions in ways that can undermine the formation of coalitions between and across various minority groups (380). In this way, to use

Robert Putnam's terminology, *bonding* social capital, which is exclusive, can prevent *bridging* social capital, which encourages broader inclusive identities based on connections with larger outside groups (2000, 22–4).

Expanding on the role of immigration, religion, and gender relations, Seongeun Kim's (2010) examination of working-class Korean women in the United States points to the ways in which women use religion to deal with patriarchal marriage practices. In one respect, Kim's study provides a startling contrast to earlier research by Yen Le Espiritu (2003), who points to middle-class Asian American women who use their advantages in the workplace to challenge patriarchal expectations around domestic work. However, among working-class Korean women who have embraced evangelical Christianity, Kim finds that teachings in the church that emphasize harmony and gender hierarchy encourage women to avoid conflict, suppress anger, and accept wifely submission (2010, 739). Thus, wives "rarely asked their husbands to share more parenting responsibilities and further kept their current [patriarchal] gender relations" (741). In this study, the evangelical church, through its religious teachings and faith, has reaffirmed the traditional gender ideology within the working-class Korean American diaspora.

Religious institutions, as a form of immigrant social capital, are important facilitators of social mobility not only within a given community but also externally between communities, particularly among migrants. Understood as a resource that individuals possess (Bourdieu 1990), social capital in the form of social networks of cooperation and reciprocity are fundamental to the ability of migrants to become established outside of their home communities, integrate into host societies, and create their own symbolic communities and identities (Faist 2000). In his 2000 work *Bowling Alone: The Collapse and Revival of American Community*, Putnam writes of the importance of participation in community affairs as a key aspect of social capital and collective action. Community engagement, he argues, is central to the building of collective goods such as mutual support, cooperation, trust, and institutional effectiveness (2).

Immigrant churches are not just places for religious services; they provide important social services for families through group activities and meetings, and they serve civic citizenship functions. In the diaspora, the function of the church exceeds spiritual matters and expands to include more and varied types of community events (garage sales, charity events, celebration of traditional harvest festivals) that bring members together in social settings and allow for the sharing and distribution of resources in new ways. On church websites, for instance, it is common to find information on acquiring citizenship, visa forms, employment information, and so on. The functions of religious institutions have remained diversified, particularly in colonial settler societies where local customs and institutions can seem intimidating for new immigrants. For example, on the website for the Canadian Mar Thoma Church Toronto, the section on "information for newcomers" contains links for securing a Social Insurance Number, a driver's licence, an Ontario Health Insurance Plan card, and the Canada Child Tax Benefit, as well as information on housing, education, transportation, and various health services (http://www.canadianmarthomachurch.com). The church provides valuable information and support beyond religious worship.

However, such forms of bonding social capital, through religious participation, can also encourage inward-looking tendencies (by choice or necessity), and reinforce exclusive identities and homogenous group affiliation (Putnam 2000, 22–3). Indeed, as the life stories of some of my respondents show, social capital in this form also has potential negative implications, working to limit and confine life choices and strengthen patriarchal structures.

THE SYRIAN MALABAR CHRISTIAN CHURCH IN CANADA

The literature linking religiosity and social capital formation in colonial settler societies is relevant to understanding the Malayali community's reliance on the expansion of religious institutions in Canada. Canada is unique in that the multiculturalism project has been enshrined in its constitution through law, reflecting an important historical context in Canada (Mahtani 2006, 164). Since 1971, multiculturalism has defined and framed Canadian discussions about diversity. As policy, multiculturalism focuses on immigrant ethnicity (and in this specific case, religious affiliation) as a primary marker of identification (166), looking backward in time to an immigrant's "homeland" as a central marker. The original policy objective of multiculturalism was to promote, on the one hand, the survival of ethnic groups and their particular cultures, and, on the other, tolerance for cultural minorities within the larger Canadian society. Within the Syrian Christian community, the process of religious identification has allowed for an entry into the dominant European Christian community; at the same time, it has allowed for a glorification of the "homeland." The intensity of religious identification in the Malayali community, as this chapter illustrates, varies by generation or cohort.

For the first cohort of immigrant respondents in my study – first-generation immigrants who arrived in the 1960s and 1970s – the practice of praying and singing together in private homes, initially in small groups of twenty or thirty families, was an important "structured" means of recreating community. It provided a means of social support for a community that was fairly small, but cohesive. What is particularly notable and unique to the Malayali community in Canada is the link with nursing, as many of the respondents in this first cohort were nurses (Samuel 2010b). Thus, in addition to the spiritual and cultural connections to the Syrian Christian Church, members of this cohort were also bound by occupation.

What started out as groups of families meeting in the basements of homes grew, as the "congregations" rented church spaces in existing local community churches and sponsored achens/priests who would come on three-year visas to administer and guide the congregation. According to the Canadian Mar Thoma website, the Mar Thoma Church in Toronto was founded in 1973 when the Most Rev. Dr Alexander Mar Thoma Metropolitan came to Toronto and advised the group to have a community with the local Anglican Church. In 1975, Rev. Geevarghese Mar Athanasius arrived and took a greater leadership role in guiding this group of believers. By 1983, the congregation was registered under the Corporations Act (Ontario) as a charitable religious organization. The church now boasts 250 families (www.canadianmarthomachurch.com). The St Thomas Orthodox Syrian Church, Toronto, another local congregation of the Orthodox Syrian Church of India, grew from about a dozen families in 1975 to sixty-four families more recently (www.stthomasosc.org).

In addition to allowing for greater connectivity among its followers, the Syrian Christian Church also plays an important role in distinguishing its members from other Indians. Their Christian identity allows members of this community to distance themselves from Hindu and Muslim Indians and align themselves with the Eurocentric value system. The alliances that were forged with the British in colonial India gave the Syrian Christians in Kerala an advantage both within India and abroad in overseas colonial offices. Edward Said (1993) argues that the culture of imperialism has ideological implications as well as political consequences. I argue that Keralites, through their adoption of the English language and Western religious forms, not only sanctioned these imperialist systems but used them to distinguish themselves from other Indians who did not have the same fundamental belief system, based on Christian ideology. This mode of distinction plays a central role in immigrant loyalty to the Christian church.

RESEARCHING THE MALAYALI SYRIAN CHRISTIAN DIASPORA

This chapter draws on interviews that I conducted with sixty-four members of the Malayali diaspora in the GTA. Of the sixty-four respondents, fifty were women and fourteen were men. The respondent profile is divided into three cohorts: (1) the first wave of Malayali immigrants to Canada in the 1960s and 1970s; (2) the children of the first wave of immigrants, or second-generation Malayali Canadians; and (3) the second wave of Malayali immigrants to Canada, who started arriving in the 1990s. All respondents except one are university educated, and all respondents trace their roots to the state of Kerala in India.

The first cohort, representing the first wave of first-generation Malayali Canadians, consists of seventeen respondents who arrived between 1965 and 1977. The majority of respondents from this cohort were women (sixteen). The nurses in this cohort entered into Canada as independent, professional skilled workers to fill a labour need for nursing professionals. The fifteen nurses in the respondent group were all educated in nursing schools in India. Two women in this cohort entered into Canada with their husbands and dependent children through the family class. For the respondents in this group the average age is 65.9 years. While the nurses were successful in finding work immediately after arriving, this was not the case for their husbands. Often, the nurses' husbands had to take work below their educational qualifications or go back to school to update their skill set.

The second cohort, representing second-generation Malayali Canadians whose parents immigrated between 1965 and 1984, consists of twenty-six respondents. In this group, twenty-two women and four men were interviewed. The average age of this group of respondents is 29.6 years. Of this group, some came as young children and others were born in Canada. Except for one respondent, they completed their elementary, junior, high school, and university education in Canada. Whereas the first-generation respondents are overwhelmingly concentrated in the health professions, the members of this second generation occupy a broad spectrum of occupations, expanding from the health and education sectors into business, computer software and information technology, science and engineering, teaching, dentistry, and a host of other professional and nonprofessional jobs.

The third cohort, representing a more recent immigrant group who arrived in the GTA between 1993 and 2005, consists of twenty-one respondents. In this group, twelve women and nine men participated, with an average age of 34.2 years. While some arrived in Canada directly from India, many entered after spending a number of years in other nations: Malaysia, Singapore, the Persian Gulf, South Africa, and the United States. Thus, entering into Canada was part of a larger migration journey. Their migration narratives speak to different motivations for leaving their countries of origin. While all respondents trace their identities to the Syrian Christian Church of India, some respondents, most notably in this third cohort, have moved to newer church communities.

WOMEN IN THE HISTORY OF THE SYRIAN MALABAR CHRISTIAN CHURCH

The first generation of Malayali immigrants, who were predominantly female and predominantly nurses, played a key role in the construction of early church communities. All of the women in this study either had work upon arrival in Toronto or found work immediately after arriving. Because their nursing qualifications were recognized in Canada, these women were able not only to find work but also to advance in their profession, and on this basis, despite patriarchal family relationships, many of them were looked up to within the community. Once settled in their professions, all but one married within the Syrian Christian community. Secure in their work, they returned to Kerala to marry a "suitable man" from among the Christian community in accordance with traditional marriage rituals. Upon their return to Canada these women were faced with the challenges of constructing a Syrian Christian community in Canada. The increasing number of young families in the community meant that there was a need for both a Syrian church and language (Malayalam) education. These were the early communities that met in basements and the homes of fellow worshipers, where a male elder would lead the liturgy and prayers. Respondents reflected warmly on these early community worship services. One of the Orthodox churches, the Canadian Mar Thoma Church, began to worship at Trinity College of the University of Toronto in 1972. In 1975, newly arrived Rev. C.I. George took a leadership role in the worship rituals of the early Toronto community.[3] For first-generation immigrants and their families, the religious community was integral to shaping their early immigrant experiences. They valued the time spent at the church and they valued the church community as a source of support and friendship.

Kamala, among the oldest of first-cohort respondents, remembers her early community fondly.

> We were a small group, there were about ten to fifteen families at the time. I cannot remember the number. We would meet in family basements each month on Sunday. All the families had our own liturgy books that we brought from back home so we would gather around and do readings and sing songs. Those who had children would bring them and they would sit and listen. Usually it was one of the older men who would do a bit of an informal sermon. There would always be a big meal at the end. Usually it was the member whose house we were meeting in that would serve the meal. When there was a visiting priest, he would lead us in the liturgy. We eventually moved to a rented church and then when the congregation grew, we had our own church. Now there are so many families.

While an older man would often lead the sermon, a significant amount of the organizing of these initial sessions occurred among the women participants. Many of the latter were nurses, and they formed important social networks with each other through their occupational affiliation and training. Their husbands ended up in diverse occupations, with some finding it difficult to land high-status and well-paying jobs, but nursing jobs were plentiful and virtually guaranteed. And although they were not exceptionally lucrative, nursing jobs did provide a solid foundation for middle-class life in Canada. Moreover, a job in nursing afforded these women a certain measure of both financial independence and status within the household.

This independence and status, however, did not necessarily translate to the church. According to the tradition of the Mar Thoma Church, women cannot be ordained as achens/priests, and, as in other patriarchal religious institutions and communities, the history of the church usually highlights the roles played by high-ranking males. Thus, the important work conducted by women in helping to establish and nurture such budding religious institutions as the Mar Thoma Church in diasporic settings is often overlooked. Although Canada's Malayali community may be somewhat distinct in having such a strong professional concentration of women, this example highlights how important women can be, and often are, in the establishment of diasporic institutions.

As Mar Thoma churches expanded and became formalized in their own permanent structures, and as the first generation of immigrants from Kerala aged and had children, women's roles in the church evolved, as did expressions of faith. In interviews with the second cohort of respondents – children of first-wave immigrants from Kerala – they highlighted, regardless of the path they chose in life, the importance of the church in their upbringing and in forming their identities, and the church's ongoing (albeit diverse) role in their adulthoods. All of the second-cohort respondents report that they were very active in the church community during their childhood and teenage years. They also said that they felt the church was instrumental in defining their parents' identities and abilities to integrate into Canadian society. In their younger years, many women in this cohort actively helped their mothers prepare for church meetings by organizing or making food. And their stories make clear how they, as children, were instrumental in their parents' ability to both establish social networks with other members of the community – particularly as this pertains to child-rearing and child socialization – and organize church activities that served to assimilate children into the value of the church and provide important adult socialization opportunities.

At the same time, as many in this cohort aged, they became critical of some of the values taught in the church, and a number of respondents stopped being active in the church as adults. This is particularly notable among female respondents. Of the twenty-two women in this cohort, only five are still active in attending services. The main criticisms of those who no longer attend church services or only participate occasionally (for instance, Easter or Christmas) pertain to marriage and dating norms within the community, which they feel are overly restrictive of women's rights, status, and independence. Although many respondents placed their origins and religion at the centre of their identity, growing up in Canada they also identified with calls for women's equality and viewed the norms they saw being promoted by the church as dated and patriarchal in relation to both secular and Christian values promoted in Canada. Many women in this cohort aspired to independence and expressed a desire to date outside of the community, while hoping for the community's emotional and spiritual support for this choice. However, they felt that they were not sufficiently able to express their opinions within the church, partly due to its patriarchal structure, and in turn were often not supported by their families in doing so. Ironically, many of their mothers, who came to Canada as nurses and were strongly independent, did not challenge religious norms around dating and marriage and instead pressured their children to marry within the community, leading to intergenerational family conflicts. The more critical female members often chose to leave the church when it became clear to them that expressing their voice would not be tolerated.

There is a related set of issues among respondents who were divorced or separated from spouses, particularly those who yielded to family pressures and married within the community. Those respondents perceived the church as unsupportive of them in their situations. Sybil, a thirty-four-year-old business consultant who is currently dating outside of the community, discusses her diminished involvement in the church community in a way that is typical of many of the second-generation respondents: "When I was younger, I was active in the Mar Thomite community in late high school and early university. And when I first moved to Toronto, I used to go to the Mar Thoma Church … Now I don't go … I do think that the Indian church is too strict and that is why so many are leaving. Kids can't relate to the Mar Thoma church anymore. It is very hard to relate to the church. I think the church is more social than it is spiritual." Sybil's comments on the church and the community in general provide context for the declining attendance of second-generation Malayali Canadians who have grown up in the Syrian Orthodox Church. Many women in the community who have gone through a divorce or who have married out of the ethnic group feel alienated from the church community. Many no longer feel that they are welcome, despite often having spent their entire lives as part of the church. Women who have challenged deeply held traditions around marriage often report they found no support from within the larger (religious) community. For the most part, respondents who have divorced or married outside the community find themselves estranged and maintain, at most, marginal connections (see also Samuel 2010, 106; 2015, 202–4). Despite the dynamism of the diasporic community and the evolution of Syrian Orthodox traditions in Canada, deeply held patriarchal traditions and socially constructed roles around marriage and the family have been much slower to change.

One result of this has been an ambivalence among women in this second cohort. While some have continued to participate in the church, a greater proportion has either stopped participating or moved to other (mostly Christian) churches. One may think of such declining participation as a reduction in the role played by women in the church, but it has also been important in provoking a shift within the Syrian Christian community, as well as a broadening of support for different and innovative approaches to religion. To a large extent, it was the very ambivalence of second-generation women and their uncertain participation that set the stage for how the church has evolved and the way that members of the third cohort have approached religion in the contemporary period.

CO-EVOLUTION: WOMEN AND FAITH IN CONTEMPORARY TIMES

As women who were the most critical of the church reduced their participation or stopped attending altogether, those who remained were relatively comfortable with the more traditional and conservative orientation of the church. While for some congregations this might present a problem of dwindling membership, in Canadian metropolitan areas, immigration rates remained strong and spurred the rapid growth of many congregations. Some of the third cohort – new immigrants to Canada after 1990 – came to Canada after living in South Africa or countries in the Middle East and Asia, and they reported that the Syrian Christian communities in those places were essential features of their lives there. They thus wanted to be part of the community in Canada as well. Many expressed their view that the church has been instrumental in smoothing their transition to Canada and affirming a sense of belonging in their new country. All of the twenty-one respondents in this third cohort report being active in the church and attending services on a regular basis. This contrasts strongly with the second cohort, the second-generation Malayali Canadians discussed above, who are similar in age to this third cohort.

As a result of this, the membership of the church has also changed, given the declining participation of the second cohort and the aging (and hence reduced participation) of the first cohort. The void left by the retreat of the first two cohorts has been filled by new immigrants who have a much greater diversity of occupational skills, experiences, and resources than the first wave. An important feature of the third cohort is that many hold on to more conservative values or espouse more fundamentalist Christian positions than do either of the first or second cohorts. These trends mirror those occurring across the Christian landscape, in which more traditional denominations (especially Protestant churches like the Anglican and United Church) have seen their memberships decline, while memberships in evangelical and fundamentalist churches rise (Ravelli and Webber 2016, 348). Indeed, a number of respondents in this third cohort are members of both the Syrian Orthodox Church and other (often charismatic) churches. Caroline, a respondent in this third cohort whose parents came to Canada from Malaysia in 1988, represents this pattern. She remains active in her local Mar Thoma church and identifies strongly with it, even to the point of taking on leadership roles and helping to organize national conferences. However, she also attends a Pentecostal church, and with her friends she sometimes attends two different churches on the same day. Unlike many members of the first cohort, who forged the first congregations and felt an intense loyalty to the community, many respondents in the third cohort did not feel any contradiction in belonging to two different congregations simultaneously. Another example of this is twenty-two-year-old university student Tessi. She is an active member of the Mar Thomas church, who, as secretary for the youth organization, feels that she can't "abandon ship" even though she admits that the Syrian Orthodox church does not fully represent her ideals of spirituality. "I do have more spiritual experiences at the Pentecostal Church, but I feel tied down to the Mar Thoma Church because of my position this year … [and] there is still the friendships and stuff I have there at the Mar Thoma Church, but in terms of the whole Sunday fulfillment experience I would get that from the Pentecostal Church … I feel that … church is important to me."

For members of the new immigrant cohort, the church (Orthodox or some newer charismatic variation) is very important to their identity and construction of self, more for spiritual reasons than out of the need to build a social community. They feel the "need to go to church," as respondent Agitha stated. Such a statement would be unlikely from respondents in the second cohort.

In the new immigrant cohort, both youths and parents were more likely to state that their close friends were from their church congregation, in contrast to the second cohort. Newer immigrants often said they chose their location of settlement based on proximity to the church and the community, and that this was an important decision in their immigration journey. Unlike the many critical voices among the second cohort, a number of young adults in the third cohort took a great deal of pride in belonging to the Syrian Orthodox community (whereas the majority of the second cohort are only marginally attached to the community). There appears to be an increase in the intensity of the bonds between new immigrant youth of the Syrian Christian community. The newer immigrant youth are more likely to be exclusive in their identification, when compared to earlier cohorts.

Perhaps most notably, once again, much of the organizing that is occurring within the contemporary church has been taken on by women. To take one example, all three of the daughters of Peter and Preeti, who immigrated from the Middle East to Toronto in 1994, are active in their local Mar Thoma church. Preeti was the secretary of the woman's group (Sevika Sanghom) and the daughters all held various administrative duties in the church. One of their adult daughters also spent time in the local evangelical church. When asked about her participation in the evangelical church, she too pointed to the higher levels of spirituality there as her motivation, but she continued to put in a lot of work with the Mar Thoma church. All three of the girls also still attend the annual North American Mar Thoma youth conferences. This level of active participation is reflective of this newer cohort.

Sherry, who immigrated with her parents from Singapore in 1990, is a twenty-four-year-old graduate of a local university and a self-defined "hard core Mar Thomite." She laments the decline of youth groups in Ontario: "I led the last regional local Mar Thoma youth conference. Montreal youth groups are all here now. The youth groups in Montreal, Ottawa, Kingston have all died out. The youth have gotten older and either they don't go or they move here. So the regional youth groups are all here in Toronto." Sherry also notes the draw of the Pentecostal churches: "Well, I was going to one [Pentecostal] as well when I was attending university. Because of the music and the sermon, you feel more uplifted with everything that is going on. They feel like they are getting more spiritual fulfillment in comparison with the Mar Thomite and Jacobite churches." She returned to the Syrian Mar Thomite services when she returned home, but she still feels the pull toward the evangelical churches despite her commitment to her Mar Thomite church community: "Last Sunday I went to a Pentecostal youth worship service and it was unbelievable. I have never felt so uplifted in my entire life. I came back and I was [wondering] why can't we do this in the Mar Thomite church. I don't know why everyone in the Mar Thoma church has such a problem with Pentecostal youth. The only thing you can do is try and change it otherwise you leave."

These conflicting sentiments resonated with many of the younger respondents in the third cohort. Their loyalty to their local community churches and the appeal of the newer evangelical churches force them to make compromises (such as attending multiple services on Sunday), including how much time and effort they can put into each commitment. Compared to the second cohort, who have largely chosen to leave the church, this newer younger cohort has opted to remain. Their criticisms are different, of course, but still relate to the conservative and less innovative nature of their home church – in this case based around spirituality rather than rights. Nonetheless, the challenge of the contemporary Syrian Orthodox Church is keeping the loyalty of youth members who are increasingly disengaging from the church of their parents. And once again, given the prominent role of women on the ground in key organizing positions (including the youth conferences), how women decide to address their needs will determine how the church evolves in the future.

FACING NEW REALITIES AND CHALLENGES

As the Malayali diaspora has aged, so have the institutions they created to build their communities. In addition to the changing foci of the church's new and youth members, the community has to face the challenge of how to deal with the needs of its aging members. One irony of this case study is that the establishment of Syrian Christian churches in the diaspora was disproportionately driven by the work and needs of nurses, but the church has not developed any way of addressing eldercare for its aging members – many of whom are nurses, and the vast majority of whom are female, since women tend to outlive men (Nelson 2010, 378).[4]

Respondents from the first cohort are increasingly concerned about their position as elderly women who cannot rely on care from their adult children (Samuel 2010b, 144–6). As members of this first generation retire, there is a growing need for eldercare. Within the traditional Indian family structure, elderly parents often live with their eldest male child. Research on aging immigrants has found that while many immigrant communities may continue to live in extended family settings, "the traditional reverence for parents has diminished" (Choudhry 2001, 377). There appear to be increasing intergenerational tensions as young adult children are unable to meet the needs of their aging parents. Ethel, a sixty-three-year-old retired nurse who immigrated in 1969, was very concerned about her retirement years. She told me, "I am not hoping a lot with regard to my children looking after me … My children so far tell me you are going to be in a retirement home or nursing home, we will come visit you."

Elderly respondents, such as Kamala, who is now widowed, do not attend church functions anymore. She finds that as her cohort ages, they do not feel the same sense of belonging they once did. Moreover, attending church is not always possible for elderly women (and men) whose driving skills are compromised. Adult children who have moved away or who do not attend Syrian Orthodox churches are usually unable to assist them. This presents significant challenges. Retired nurse Betty stated that when she does attend church, the more recent members often think she has just arrived from Kerala to babysit her grandchildren. "They don't know that I was one of the first members of the church. It makes me angry. There is no respect for us!"

The sentiments of the first cohort point to some of the current challenges of the Syrian Christian church. This early immigrant cohort of women, who paved the path for latter Keralite immigrants, are now finding that the church they helped build is neglecting to meet some of their basic needs. Not only is the church failing to retain the commitment of the second generation who grew up in it, but those young adults and the church community are neglecting the immediate concerns of their elderly founding members.

CONCLUSION

This chapter has pointed not only to the role of the Syrian Malabar Christian Church in the lives of immigrants from Kerala, but also to the specific role of women in the construction of immigrant churches in the diaspora. While first-generation women played a key role in the construction of the early church, as they age they feel their needs are not being met. The contemporary church faces challenges in addressing both the needs of their elderly patrons and the needs of young people.

For these migrants, faith institutions such as the Syrian Christian Church fulfilled a collective need for identification. Echoing Durkheim ([1912] 1995), their belief in the church feeds the collective conscience and allows for greater group cohesion, particularly for later immigrants who have lived in other countries prior to entering into Canada. The Syrian Orthodox Church works to reinforce group identification with Kerala and strengthen ties to the homeland. For the respondents in this study, belief in the church guides their actions and determines the extent to which certain cultural practices are retained. For many of the respondents, the church has played an important role in their lives. Even those who no longer attend as adults still speak fondly of the church. Much of their young lives was filled with attending and participating in church organization and cultural celebrations.

I have also argued that, for the respondents in this study, connections to the Syrian Malabar Christian Church are both empowering (as an important form of social capital) and debilitating (through cultural restrictions, particularly around marriage). Respondents who are perceived as bringing "shame" on the community, either through a divorce or by marrying out, are more critical of the institution because they feel they are not welcome in it. It is often women who are ostracized for their choices to divorce or marry out of the community. James Clifford correctly points out that "diasporic experiences are always gendered" (1994, 311); this is true for participants in this study, particularly those who have challenged traditions around marriage and mating (Samuel 2010a; 2010b; 2013; 2015). Women are often regarded as "keepers" of tradition and are thus subject to two sets of gender relations: those of the dominant host group and those that are internal to their own group, both of which are grounded in patriarchal traditions. Religious and cultural traditions work to renew and reaffirm patriarchal structures within the diaspora, which can limit the choices of individuals. The church needs to address these gendered challenges, both in terms of the younger adult cohort and the elderly cohort whose needs around eldercare are not being met.

NOTES

1 Syrian Christians of Kerala are also called Malabar Christians. Malabar refers to the South Western coastal region of India where the state of Kerala is located. I use both these key terms (Syrian and Malabar) so as to identify this unique group. For this paper, Syrian Christians refer to the Christian community from Kerala (cf. Lodrick 2021).

2 Only 2.4 per cent of India's total population identifies as Christian, compared to 20 per cent in Kerala (Percot 2006, 43).

3 See http://www.canadianmarthomachurch.com/pages.aspx?section=sub&ID=42.

4 Based on 2019 statistics, life expectancy at birth for males is 80 years, and for women it is 84.2 years (Statistics Canada 2019).

REFERENCES

Bayly, Susan. 1989. *Saints, Goddess and Kings*. Cambridge: Cambridge University Press.

The Canadian Mar Thoma Church. n.d. "Parish at a Glance." www.canadianmarthomachurch.com.

Choudhry, U.K. 2001. "Uprooting and Resettlement Experiences of South Asian Immigrant Women." *Western Journal of Nursing Research* 23, no. 4: 376–93.

Clifford, James. 1994. "Diasporas." *Cultural Anthropology* 9, no. 3: 302–38.

Durkheim, Emile. (1912) 1995. *The Elementary Forms of Religious Life*. Translated by K.E. Fields. New York: Free Press.

Espiritu, Yen Le. 2003. "Gender and Labour in Asian Immigrant Families." In *Gender and U.S. Immigration: Contemporary Trends*, edited by Pierrette Hondagneu-Sotelo, 81–100. Berkeley: University of California Press.

Faist, Thomas. 2000. *The Volume and Dynamics of International Migration and Transnational Social Spaces*. Oxford: Clarendon Press.

Kim, Seongeun. 2010. "Working-Class, Korean-American Women Navigating Marriage through Evangelical Christianity." *Journal of Contemporary Family Studies* 41, no. 5: 735–48.

Kurien, Prema A. 2002. *Kaleidoscopic Ethnicity: International Migration and the Reconstruction of Community Identities in India*. New Brunswick, NJ: Rutgers University Press.

– 2004. "Multiculturalism, Immigrant Religion, and Diasporic Nationalism: The Development of an American Hinduism." *Social Problems* 51, no. 3: 362–85.
– 2013. "Religious Life of Malayali Diaspora: Hindus and Christians in the United States. In *Malayali Diaspora: From Kerala to the Ends of the World*, edited by Sam George and T.V. Thomas, 149–60. New Delhi: Serials Publications.
Lodrick, D.O. "Syrian Christians in India." 2021. Encyclopedia.com. https://www.encyclopedia.com/humanities/encyclopedias-almanacs-transcripts-and-maps/syrian-christians-india.
Mahtani, Minelle. 2006. "Interrogating the Hypen-nation: Canadian Multicultural Policy and 'Mixed-Race' Identities." In *Identity and Belonging: Rethinking Race and Ethnicity in Canadian Society*, edited by Sean P. Hier and B. Singh Bolaria, 163–77. Toronto: Canadian Scholars Press International.
Mar Thoma Metropolitan, Alexander. 1985. *The Marthoma Church Heritage and Mission*. Houston: T&C Copy and Printing.
Nelson, Adie. 2010. *Gender in Canada*. 4th ed. Toronto: Pearson Canada.
Northeast American Diocese of the Malankara Orthodox Syrian Church. "About Northeast American Diocese." www.neamericandiocese.org/diocese/index.aspx (accessed 26 February 2017).
Percot, Marie. 2006. "Indian Nurses in the Gulf: Two Generations of Female Migration." *South Asia Research* 26, no. 1: 41–62.
Putnam, Robert D. 2000. *Bowling Alone: The Collapse and Revival of American Community*. New York: Simon and Schuster.
Ravelli, Bruce, and Michelle Webber. 2016. *Exploring Sociology: A Canadian Perspective*. 3rd edition. Toronto: Pearson Canada.
St Thomas Orthodox Church, Toronto. n.d. "About Us." https://www.stthomasosc.org/about-us.
Samuel, Lina. 2010a. "Mating, Dating and Marriage: Intergenerational Cultural Retention and the Construction of Diasporic Identities among South Asian Immigrants in Canada." *Journal of Intercultural Studies* 31, no. 1: 95–110.
– 2010b. "South Asian Transnationalism in Canada: Effects on Family Life." In *Family Geographies: The Spatiality of Families and Family Life*, edited by Bonnie C. Hallman, 131–50. Toronto: Oxford University Press.
– 2013. "South Asian Women in the Diaspora: Reflections on Arranged Marriage and Dowry among the Syrian Orthodox Community in Canada." *South Asian Diaspora* 5, no. 1: 91–105.

– 2015. "The Family, Religion, and the Re-Territorialization of Culture within the South Asian Diaspora." In *Engendering Transnational Voices*, edited by Guida Man and Rina Cohen, 193–212. Waterloo, ON: Wilfrid Laurier University Press.

Statistics Canada. 2019. "The Daily." https://www150.statcan.gc.ca/n1/daily-quotidien/201126/dq201126b-eng.htm.

Wenger, Etienne. 1998. *Communities of Practice: Learning, Meaning and Identity.* Cambridge: Cambridge University Press.

Yang, Fenggang, and Helen Rose Ebaugh, 2001. "Transformations in New Immigrant Religions and Their Global Implications." *American Sociological Review* 66, no. 2: 269–85.

9

Muslim Model Minorities and the Politics of Diasporic Piety

Nadia Z. Hasan

In the contemporary Islamophobic political climate in Canada, "Muslim model minority" seems like an oxymoron. Yet the Muslim community is not immune to the model minority discourse. Muslim mainstream media commentators on Islam, such as Tarek Fatah, Irshad Manji, and Salim Mansur, for instance, who relentlessly propagate Islamophobic understandings of Muslim practices in Canada,[1] gain favour and popularity in a white settler discursive terrain as Muslims who are willing and able to fortify structures of exclusion. Although fully attaining model minority status is an ontological impossibility in the context of a white settler colonial state such as Canada (Bannerji 2000; Haque 2010; Razack, Thobani, and Smith 2010; Thobani 2007), and although the category of model minority alludes to the limits of inclusion by maintaining a narrative of a racialized outsider being conditionally let in (Dhamoon 2013; Dua 2007), the trope of the model minority still sets in motion a powerful discourse that maps out the terms of inclusion and a seductive promise of belonging in the context of official multiculturalism.

To the extent that this discourse permeates minority communities in Canada, it influences diasporic formations by interjecting a compulsion to construct an identity that approximates the model minority in order to legitimize, or survive, its presence in Canada. For many this translates to having to cultivate a sense of belonging that is conditional on reproducing liberal multiculturalism's structures and codes of heteronormativity, neoliberalism, and secularism. However elusive the promise of the model minority may be, Muslims in Canada are implicated in these politics of aspiration in complex ways. While Fatah, Manji, and Mansur to some extent succeed in occupying the status of a model minority by publicly propagating a vulgar Islamophobia and a staunch secularism on mainstream media platforms, the everyday experiences of Muslims in Canada illustrate more nuanced engagements with the multicultural logics of the model minority.

In this chapter, I explore how these nuances emerge at the intersections of diaspora, religion, and gender. I ground my analysis in the stories of Pakistani Muslim women in Canada who are committed to developing their piety through participation in Al-Huda International,[2] a women's Islamic education organization that has gained notoriety within the Pakistani community and in the mainstream for practising a particularly conservative form of Islam. This notoriety would in some ways suggest that these women are precluded from the category of the model minority because of the practices that emerge out of their engagements with Al-Huda's teachings (such as defined domestic roles for women, patriarchal household structures, hijab and niqab). Drawing on interviews and participatory observations with a women's Quran class in Mississauga, Ontario, I trace how, despite this notoriety and related preclusion, these women engage, transform, and reproduce the trope of the model minority through the way they develop their piety in diaspora.

I argue that diasporic piety is articulated, practised, and developed in relation to heteropatriarchal[3] trajectories of migration and a diasporic sense of loss of nation, which is recuperated through multicultural categories of identity and enmeshed in the racialized politics of model minorities. Although diasporic engagements in processes of pious subject formation are responsive to hegemonic tropes of model minorities in a multicultural context, they also carry with them rearticulations of what it means to be a model minority. These rearticulations constitute a form of resistance to hegemonic Islamophobic ideas of model minorities, but, at the same time, they reinforce logics of liberal citizenship and multiculturalism.

AL-HUDA INTERNATIONAL

The women's piety group I conducted research with is an iteration of an increasingly popular Pakistani women's Islamic education organization called Al-Huda International, which considers itself a purveyor of a literalist form of Islam. Founded and led by Dr Farhat

Hashmi, an Islamic scholar who earned her PhD in Hadith Sciences from the University of Glasgow, Al-Huda began in Pakistan but has spread out to several locations around the world. Their campus in Mississauga was the first one outside of Pakistan. Al-Huda offers a diploma program at their campuses for women who are interested in developing skills and knowledge in *tajweed* (correct Arabic recitation), translation (from Arabic to Urdu), and *tafseer* (exegesis and implications for their everyday life).

As part of the ethic of *dawah* (inviting others to Islam) that is promoted through Al-Huda teachings, many women engage in proselytizing and charitable activities in their communities. One of the ways they do this is through forming home-based Quran classes in which an Al-Huda graduate teaches a group of women about the Quran and Hadith. While most of these Quran classes are not formally approved by the organization, they are the product of the emphasis on dawah in Al-Huda teachings, and they use Al-Huda teaching materials. These home-based Quran classes have become ubiquitous in major urban centres in Pakistan and in the Pakistani community in Mississauga. The Quran class I conducted research with was led by a graduate of Al-Huda. Meetings were held twice a week at one of the participant's homes, where women would gather to learn and practise tajweed, translation, and tafseer based on Al-Huda's teachings. For all of the women I met, the class was the first time they engaged with the Quran in this way.

Since its inception in 1994, Al-Huda has gained notoriety because the Islamic discourse they propagate is commonly characterized as being particularly inflexible, anti-women, and antithetical to modernity. Teachings that instruct women to veil, wear the niqab, adhere to men's *qawwam* (authority),[4] and confine themselves to gender roles that restrict their responsibilities to domestic duties are regularly held up as evidence of Al-Huda's anti-women impact on the Muslim community in Canada.

However, despite this reputation, there has been increasing participation in these groups by Pakistani women from the urban upper-middle classes in Pakistan and the diaspora – women who ostensibly belong to the demographic that would most vociferously reject these Islamic discourses as "backward" because they subscribe to ideals of liberal modernity. Not surprisingly, many of the women I conducted research with mentioned that their involvement with Al-Huda was often met with anxieties about the corrosion of a modern, liberal sensibility amongst their urban, educated, middle- and upper-class communities.

These anxieties are constitutive of and are constituted by prevailing Islamophobic ideas about the oppression of Muslim women. Gendered Islamophobic tropes,[5] such as the "imperilled" (Razack 2007, 3) or the extremist veiled woman, underpin the reactions received by the women I met because of their participation in Al-Huda. Such reactions took spectacular form in December 2015 after Tafsheen Malik was killed by police after she allegedly participated in an armed attack of an office gathering in San Bernardino, California. The Al-Huda campus in Mississauga was forced to shut its doors for several days because of the Islamophobic threats they received in light of the revelation that Tafsheen Malik had at one point attended classes at the Al-Huda campus in Multan, Pakistan. Malik's past and likely incidental affiliation with Al-Huda fuelled threats against the staff and students at the Al-Huda campus in Mississauga (note that little was made of her affiliations with any other institutions or experiences, giving way to popular understandings of her alleged actions as singularly caused by Islam in general and Al-Huda specifically). American and Canadian news media outlets churned out a flurry of headlines insinuating a direct link between Al-Huda's teachings and terrorism,[6] posing an existential threat to the organization's operations in Canada. This prompted the founder of Al-Huda, Farhat Hashmi, and the Al-Huda campus in Mississauga to release public statements that attempted to allay fears, distance themselves from Malik and her actions, and justify their presence in Canada by emphasizing their sense of civic duty and their interest in contributing to security measures.[7]

The media rhetoric and Al-Huda's response in the days following the San Bernardino shootings rehearse on a public stage the everyday struggles with Islamophobia that are navigated by the women I met in the Quran class. The moral panic over women's inscrutable involvement in Al-Huda echoes the logics mobilized by the families of the women I met who opposed their turn to piety. For the women I researched, engaging in processes of pious subject formation in a diasporic context through classes grounded in Al-Huda's teachings often butted up against suspicions held by their families, particularly spouses, about what Al-Huda represented and how it related to their aspirations to inhabit Canada as upwardly mobile model minorities. While this did not preclude these women from mobilizing model minority discourse themselves, as I show later in this chapter, it did create a number of challenges to the development of their piety in line with Al-Huda's teachings.

MUSLIM WOMEN RESISTING "GENDER EQUALITY"

The efforts of these women to develop their piety through Al-Huda were implicated in heteropatriarchal trajectories of migration. All of the women I interviewed migrated to Canada with their husbands – and their husbands' neoliberal trajectories and aspirations were central to their narrative of migration. Many women I met described how they immigrated to Canada because their husbands wanted to find better economic opportunities. What this also often meant is that their husbands imagined a place and role for their wives in Canada: this varied, from women functioning as the keepers of culture or authenticity, to women becoming the symbols and currency of modernity for their husbands.[8] The (perceived) control over the semiotics of women's bodies formed an essential part of model minority trajectories in the stories of the women I interviewed, with few exceptions. For most of the women, the central challenge they had to face in order to continue the development of their piety in line with Al-Huda's teachings was the instrumentalization of their bodies as symbols of their husbands' modernity.

In the context of Canadian multiculturalism, liberal conceptualizations of "gender equality" often come up as the prerequisite par excellence for the integration of Muslim immigrant communities. These Islamophobic logics of multiculturalism were perhaps best exemplified in the public debate and moral panic over Muslim religious arbitration in Ontario that erupted in 2004 (Bakht 2007; Bhandar 2010; Razack 2007). The proposed establishment of Muslim arbitration courts to settle civil disputes using sharia legal frameworks followed existing examples of Jewish and Christian courts, yet it yielded such an intense Islamophobic public backlash that the government of Ontario ended up enacting the Family Statute Law Amendment Act, which curbed religious arbitration across the board and ostensibly re-entrenched its commitments to secularism (Bakht 2007). Notably, as Bakht argues, this was less about separating religion and law and more of a capitulation to Orientalist discourses that render Islam a religion that is "less recognizable as being Canadian" (121). Central to the fear mongering that formed the opposition to sharia-based arbitration, and the concomitant "casting out" (Razack 2008, 19) of Muslims, was the figure of the "imperilled Muslim woman" (Razack 2007, 3). That is, the imagined possibility of Muslim women being subjected to "barbaric" Islamic laws became the cornerstone of the religious arbitration debate and the subsequent grounds for getting rid of religious arbitration altogether. "Gender equality," then, took on particularly patriotic meaning as a Canadian ethic in the face of a depiction of Islam as inherently and exceptionally patriarchal and barbaric.

In a Canadian context rife with such Islamophobic discourses, Muslim immigrant communities have been subjected to unrelenting scrutiny that erupts into a public spectacle every few years[9] but is felt profoundly in the everyday lives of Muslim communities. This scrutiny, together with the neoliberal imperatives of the Canadian immigration system, produce a tacit (and at times overt) understanding of what it means to be a model minority in Canada. The neoliberal desire for upward mobility must contend with racialized ideals of Canadian subjecthood. Thus, as a racialized prerequisite for belonging, notions of "gender equality" in the stories of the women I met were intertwined with heteropatriarchal trajectories of migration.

Several of the women pointed out that the roles they were cast in in their husbands' aspirations to integrate and belong within a neoliberal multicultural framework contradicted their own aspirations to develop their piety in significant ways. These semiotic tensions were made most visible in the way that women implemented and navigated their commitments to Al-Huda teachings about qawwam. As the women explained it, qawwam broadly refers to the authority of men over women with concomitant gender roles defined in terms of rights and responsibilities. The passages of the Quran that the women cited[10] in my interviews are perhaps some of the most contentious sections of the Quran as it relates to gender relations, and they have been the topic of much scholarly and public commentary on Islam and gender. The idea of qawwam and the gendered structures it perpetuates are often cited as the indisputable moment in Islamic scripture that authorizes a rigid patriarchy. These are the passages that led the prominent scholar of Islamic feminism Haideh Moghissi to proclaim that "no amount of twisting and bending can reconcile the Quranic injunctions and instructions about women's rights and obligations with the idea of gender equality" (1999, 140).

However, an inability to reconcile with universalized liberal notions of "gender equality" does not mean that women necessarily find qawwam to be against their interests. For many of the women

I interviewed, what their commitments to qawwam translated to in practice was that while they were working toward developing relationships with their husbands that ostensibly affirmed men's authority over women, the structure of this relationship was, paradoxically, not defined by their husbands. Committing to and inhabiting a spousal relationship defined by qawwam raised tensions between many women and their husbands. In particular, tensions arose in relationships where a woman's husband was aspiring to achieve liberal notions of model minority status, which often meant that their husbands wanted to structure their spousal relationship in line with concomitant notions of "gender equality." These paradoxical tensions between women's commitments to qawwam and men's commitments to "gender equality" reveal divergent trajectories of piety and model minorities in the diasporic context.

To elaborate on how the women I met understood qawwam, the qawwam of men over women did not refer to the authority of all men over all women. The qawwam of men was relevant to familial relationships, and only then in matters related to the domestic space and the functionality of the household. Having qawwam in the context of a spousal relationship meant that the husband would have the responsibility to ensure that the household was financially provided for and that there was harmony within the household, which also meant that men would ensure that their wives live up to their responsibility to provide reproductive labour in the household. These responsibilities could translate to the regulation of women's bodies and activities by the men in their family; however, it did not translate to absolute domination over women. So, for instance, in this interpretation men did not have direct qawwam over women's practices of piety, nor did husbands have qawwam over their wives' personal wealth and property (Hasan 2015).

Despite these common threads in the way the women I interviewed conceptualized qawwam, it was clear that qawwam is a shifting concept that acquired different dimensions of meaning and significance within particular contexts and circumstances (Hasan 2015). Qawwam operated through a conscientious, deliberate, and calculated arrangement in the lives of these women, and understandings of qawwam were constantly deepened and reformulated in consultation with study groups, teachers, and peers in the face of challenges to its implementation. Thus, it would be reductive to read it as women's submission to male domination, because more often than not, the women

I interviewed had a difficult time convincing the men in their lives to comply with their understanding of qawwam.

For many of the women who were engaged in developing their piety in line with Al-Huda's teachings about qawwam, this presented a dilemma. They maintained that women's "subordinate" position in a spousal relationship and taking care of domestic work were key sites in the development of piety, in accordance with their understanding of men's qawwam; however, many of their husbands felt that this was an antiquated and regressive division of labour. Essentially, the husbands were unwilling to lose their "modern" wives – who played an important role in their model migrant narratives – to religious conservatism. In this sense, the husbands occupied a paradoxical position, as both the key players in their wives' piety, and the primary obstacles to it.

These tensions were evident in many women's stories about how they managed the vociferous resistance they faced when they wanted to join Al-Huda or when they wanted to wear a hijab or niqab. One of my respondents, Sumaya, who was an avid participant in the Quran class, described an incident with her husband when she discussed wanting to join Al-Huda's more rigorous diploma program. Sumaya hoped to join the program to bring her passion for teaching to her religious praxis while still adhering to what she understood to be the ideal structure of Islamic domestic relationships. She asked her husband for permission, in line with her understanding of his qawwam over her activities. However, her husband would not permit her to do the program because of his concerns about the shape Sumaya's piety was taking. She explained:

> After taking many home-based Quran classes, I approached my husband, hopeful that the time was right to ask him for his permission to take the Al-Huda diploma course. He could see that this was something I really wanted to do but he was afraid he would lose his wife to what he was thinking was a religious cult or something. He hesitated but then said yes for the sake of freedom, equality, and all that – that I should be able to pursue whatever I like. I was so happy to have his permission because I would not want to disobey my husband's wishes. I was so happy because he even offered to drive me to the Al-Huda campus. I got all the registration forms together and got into the car with him and I was thanking him for his support the entire way. When we

> got there, I got out of the car and started running up the steps. I was so excited. But then I heard the car horn. My heart sank. I turned around and saw my husband gesturing for me to come back. I stood on the steps for a while and then walked back to the car hoping that he just wanted to give me something that I had left behind. He told me to get back in the car. I got in. We drove home in silence.

Sumaya's telling of her unfulfilled desire to join the Al-Huda diploma course reflects the tension that many of my interviewees faced in developing their piety through Al-Huda. As Sumaya mentions, Al-Huda reminded her husband of a cult, which speaks to suspicions of exclusively women's spaces outside the home that harboured the potential to alter women's practices of Islam without the participation of men. Frustrating the male gaze in this way, Al-Huda posed the risk of obfuscating Sumaya's husband's ability to observe, and perhaps control, his wife's practice of Islam.

Women's engagement in women-only spaces that redefined their Islamic practice and Muslim identity carries a particularly damaging potential for their husbands' notions of progress in the diasporic context. According to Sumaya, her husband wanted her to be a "moderate Muslim" – a charge that was meaningless to her. For example, she explained how one of the recurring points of contention in their relationship was his request for her to take off her hijab when attending his office parties. Already uncomfortable with attending "mixed-gender" social gatherings with people she did not know, Sumaya felt that taking off her hijab would be an even more egregious violation of her piety. She explained that for her husband, "just dressing moderately" was a sufficient practice of piety, and presumably one that would allow them to better fit in with his colleagues at the party. For her, the hijab was a vital practice of her piety that she wanted to further elevate by taking on the niqab. These divergent trajectories of subject formation form the context within which complex tensions over qawwam arise.

In her story about joining Al-Huda's diploma program, Sumaya expressed her commitment to obey her husband when she turned back from the steps and went home with him. As she explained, her desire to wait for his permission was driven by her devotion to developing a pious spousal relationship in which her husband would have authority over her activities. But, in some ways, this articulation of authority worked in contradictory ways as a barrier to the development of Sumaya's piety. When Sumaya described his momentary granting of permission as a matter of "freedom and equality and all that," she was referring to her perception of his commitments to a liberal rights-based discourse in which gender equality took a specific shape – a shape that she was not particularly interested in, as she made evident in her dismissive "all that." However, the withdrawal of his permission marks the limits of his liberal principles in the face of nonnormative practices of religion. In other words, Sumaya sought her husband's permission because his authority to give it was part of her conception of piety, but he invoked his authority to retract his permission in order to disrupt the development of this very conception of piety. Sumaya's description of her husband's fears and discomfort make it clear that only certain scripts of religiosity were intelligible within these ideas of "freedom" and "equality."

The tensions emerging at the interface of "gender equality" and qawwam reveal how trajectories of piety diverge from heteropatriarchal trajectories of migration. Note that Sumaya navigates this tension without completely capitulating to her husband's desire for her to behave like his gendered conceptualization of a moderate Muslim. Her act of obedience, and her husband's acceptance of this act, paints a contradictory picture in which his commitments to "gender equality" meet her commitment to qawwam. In this subtle act of refusal to perform "gender equality" the way her husband envisioned it, Sumaya continues to disrupt his heteropatriarchal trajectory of migration and aspirations to be a model minority.

AUTHENTICALLY MODERN

As mentioned in the introduction to this chapter, while women resisted elements of their husband's aspirations to become model minorities, they also cultivated a multicultural sense of belonging through the development of their piety. When contending with their husband's claims over their piety, the women I met mobilized model minority discourses to instantiate their practices of piety, differentiate themselves from other "bad" Muslims, and reproduce settler colonial logics of Canada and multiculturalism. Central to this mobilization was their understanding of their practice of Islam as rational and modern. To a large extent, for these women the appeal of the trajectory of piety that Al-Huda propagated was that it presented Islam as inherently and authentically modern. This representation of Islam was shaped by a disavowal of "inauthentic" practices of Islam that were, in turn, represented as backward and responsible for Islam's reputation for being anti-modern. The power of these disavowals was drawn from pedagogical practices that firmly established Al-Huda's version of piety as a rational and modern mode of subject formation for the women I interviewed.

Several women made it clear that they perceived themselves as engaging in a rational, methodical, and authentic form of Islamic learning that, for them, gained credibility because of its studied engagement with texts. This emphasis on text simultaneously facilitated their claims to authenticity and modernity. Several women identified Al-Huda's approach to scripture as taking the "literal" word of god and applying it to every aspect of everyday life. Al-Huda professes[11] a disavowal of interpretive traditions and histories of Islamic jurisprudence that generally mediate the practice of Islam. This disavowal was part of how they constructed their understanding of their approach as exceptionally authentic because they claimed that their approach facilitated women's "direct" access to scripture.

For nearly all the women I interviewed, their sense of modernity was grounded in the pedagogy of the Quran class. They variously described the classes as "logical," "accessible," "relatable," "rational," and/or "scientific."[12] The structured and methodical process of reading, translating, and relating the Quran to everyday life created a strong sense of credibility and marked a turn from how they had previously engaged with scripture. This pedagogy, for many of the students, was in contrast to the way in which they had learned about Islam and the Quran as children and adolescents in Pakistan, where they were taught how to read the Quran in Arabic without translation or exegesis.

The dual claim to authenticity and modernity put many women in a position where they could counter their husband's interventions in their piety. This authentically modern positionality, however, was based on the construction of a stark and exclusionary sense of others. For instance, using the example of the hijab, Kanwal, a student of the weekly home-based Quran class, made a distinction between women who were forced to wear it and those who chose to wear it through the development of their religious consciousness. She explained the difference as follows:

> There are definitely oppressed women like when you go to Saudi Arabia you can see that – the way some men treat their women … There are two kinds of people who wear the hijab. One, those who have chosen to wear the hijab – these are young girls who have chosen to wear hijab … and two, those who have been made to wear the hijab by their parents. The ones who have chosen to wear the hijab, they are the ones who, in my opinion, are really liberated women. Very self-confident, don't care what the world thinks, want to make a statement, and they are doing it only for one reason, to please Allah, and that's it. These women are really self-confident.

Kanwal mobilizes the stereotype of oppressed Saudi women in order to emphasize the agency of women who arrived at the practice of wearing the hijab through "choice." Kanwal's notion of "choice" is to some extent symptomatic of the ubiquity of liberal ideals of the autonomous individual who is free from coercion and/or the oppressive force of conformity.[13] The "liberated" status of Kanwal's ideal hijabi is thus dually linked to her condition of freedom and her ability to make a conscientious choice.[14]

DIASPORIC PIETY

The implications of women's identification with "rationality" for their diasporic positionality were exemplified in my respondents' understanding of Al-Huda's disavowal of "cultural accretions" to the practice of Islam – categorized as *biddat.* According to many of the women I interviewed, biddat refers to practices that are not required by Islam, as per the Quran and Hadith. This can include celebrating events such as birthdays, *basant* (spring festival in Pakistan), *milaad* (gathering to commemorate the Prophet Mohammed), or *mehndi* (a common ritual wedding event). These women's disavowal of biddat practices as un-Islamic emerges specifically through an association of biddat with practices common amongst Hindus and an understanding of the reproduction of these practices by Muslims in Pakistan as mindless and imitative. The ability to point out and refrain from practices considered to be biddat is key to how many of the women positioned themselves as rational diasporic Muslims who are conscientiously practising an "authentic" form of Islam.[15]

The reconciliation of authenticity and modernity produced through instantiations of "rationality" for these women is also intimately connected to the way they understood their piety as diasporic and how they perceived Canada and the West as a fresh start or a clean slate, harkening back to "new world" settler colonial logics (Upadhyay 2016, 235). Throughout my interviews, there was also a common thread lamenting a diasporic loss of nation, where the women described how the Pakistani religio-nationalist project failed to deliver on its promises. The formation of diasporic piety thus took place on the grounds of a lost religio-nationalist narrative, which was then (incompletely) recuperated through multicultural schematics of identity in Canada. Tracing how the concept of biddat travels through these narratives of loss and diasporic recuperation reveals how, despite their marginalization via Islamophobia, or perhaps because of it, the women I met used Islam to invest in the promise of the model minority. In other words, women use the Islamic concept of biddat to construct their Muslim identity in ways that allow them to inhabit and navigate Canadian subjecthood as (potential) model minorities.

Feelings of diasporic loss of nation were evident in several women's expressions of nostalgic longing for Pakistan. For example, Ayesha, a student of the Quran class, recalled the ease with which one can fulfill the Islamic duties of *namaaz* (prayer) and *roza* (fast) in Pakistan: "Every day you can hear the *azaan* [call for prayers] no matter where you are. In Ramzan, all the restaurants are closed during fasting hours, there are no ads for food, and people who are not fasting don't eat in public, so you see, it's so much easier to fast in a place like Pakistan because people have a lot of respect for these things." Others brought up examples of not having to worry about whether food was halal, not having the temptation of alcohol, and not having to feel awkward in their Islamically appropriate attire when in Pakistan. Dominant nationalist narratives of the creation of Pakistan as a safe place for Muslims reverberate throughout these expressions of nostalgia and memories of belonging.

However, as Fariha said, "Pakistan is not an Islamic state but it is an Islam-friendly state." Although many expressed a longing for this context, they simultaneously put those very feelings into question by drawing attention to the religious complacency produced through these amenities. Without undermining the importance of a "safe place" for Muslims, many suggested that being in this place can make one a "lazy Muslim." That is, many women in the diaspora worried that Islam is treated as a given in Pakistan because of hegemonic nationalist notions of being Muslim as synonymous with being Pakistani. The development of Islamic piety in Pakistan is at risk of stagnation, according to this assessment, because the nationalist project has failed to deliver an "Islamic state." So, even as the women I interviewed fondly remembered the sounds of the azaan in every corner of Pakistan, it still occupies a contradictory position as a place that both enables and obstructs the development of piety for them.

This contradictory position of Pakistan is in part developed through understandings of how biddat manifests in Pakistan. One of the women I met, Razia, put it this way: "If you want to know about Islam you should speak to women here [in Mississauga]." Her explanation for this was that "in Pakistan we are living in the past because we are too close to the past. It is right there next to us in India so it is not easy to let it go and move on to Islam." Razia went on to explain that the practice of Islam in Pakistan is so encumbered by the inadvertent accretions of Hindu rituals that what it means to be Muslim in Pakistan is "lost." Many other women described Pakistani Muslim identity as "confused" because they felt that people were in the habit of mindlessly engaging in practices that they (mistakenly) thought were part of Islam without knowing where the practice came from. The prospect of eternal geographic proximity to India, thought to be the main source of these accretions, produced for many of these women a dismal vision of the possibility of achieving an authentic form of Muslim piety in Pakistan.

In Razia's comment, a narrative of progress in which Islam is simultaneously the basis and the yet-to-be realized telos of the Pakistani nation is evident. She simultaneously locates India as a geographic neighbour and a spectre reflecting the past (and present) of Pakistan, which produces an anxiety of an ever-present, unrelenting threat to the nation's progress toward Islam. However, for Razia, through a migratory spatial displacement to Canada that mitigates this proximity (both in the sense of space and similarity), a different subjectivity is able to emerge. A booklet on biddat recommended to me by a teacher at Al-Huda suggests that Judeo-Christian contexts are considered relatively safe because "their falsehood is evident and less likely to cause us to stray," whereas, in cultures rife with biddat, "it is more difficult to shift the truth from falsehood," and they are "more prone to attract us to vanity and that which is pernicious"

(Ibn Mohar Ali 2006, 57). Thus, the diasporic context presented an opportunity for the practice and development of piety that many followers of Al-Huda's teachings in Mississauga felt was not possible in Pakistan because of its proximity to India/Hinduism and the related presence of biddat and the social compulsion, temptation, or desire to join in them.

This understanding of Canada, and the West more broadly, was reiterated in a few different ways. For instance, it is interesting to note how the women I interviewed mobilized the foreign influences of India and the West on Islam differently. Explaining the reasons for women's experiences of oppression in Pakistan, one of the women I met, Ghazala, explained:

> The reason being again, if you don't mind, is that we have lived with Hindus for nine hundred years. What they used to say about women is that they are just like dust on our shoes. They used to treat women as though she has no right to her life – she is only associated with a man. This is how Hindus think about women. The degree to which Islam protects women, the degree to which Islam has given women status by making her a mother, just look at all the conveniences Allah has provided for women through this. Woman herself doesn't know. Why? They of course weren't going to tell her, and woman herself didn't try to find out. The basic problem in Pakistan is that woman herself doesn't know her rights, what Islam gives. What she is running after is those rights that the West is talking about. See, the West, they never gave any rights to women. They always considered women as a body, as a commodity, as a thing that can be associated with selling. Like it's a creature that is sent to this earth to be humiliated always and is capable of nothing.

For Ghazala, the influence of Hindus is a historic circumstance that poses the threat of oppression to Pakistani women; she positions the West, however, as the means through which many women mistakenly think they will find refuge from these oppressive Hindu practices. Thus, she instead proposes an informed practice of Islam, in which women would know their Islamic rights, as a proven course for women to fight oppression as exemplified in Islamic history. In other words, Ghazala thinks of the West and Islam as competing solutions – although Islam wins out – to the problem of Hindu oppression.

The West figured prominently but contradictorily in my respondents' transnational discourse of piety, ranging from a knowable Judeo-Christian religious space to a depraved space of enlightenment-gone-awry, but always a less threatening space because it is relatively culture-free (where the culture in question is Hindu), and therefore biddat-free. In the first instance, the characterization of the West as Judeo-Christian situates it within familiar narratives of historic encounters between Islam, Christianity, and Judaism – encounters that are relayed in the Quran and *sunnah* and can thus be identified and dealt with in relatively straightforward ways by referring to scriptural examples.

The perceived depravity of the West poses a different set of issues in the diaspora, especially in relation to parenting; however, this depravity is seen as a degeneration of Christianity or Judaism, which, interestingly, is less threatening than degeneration caused by biddat (based in Hindu practices) that confuses Islamic identity in far more exhaustive ways. Thus, the West is represented as an easier and simpler route to piety by many of the women I interviewed.

The sense of expedited piety in the diaspora was key to the production of a rational student-subject of Islam, and the women I met felt that this was a form of engagement that ought to legitimize their practice of Islam in Canada. Indeed, it was this claim that facilitated a sense of ownership and power in their Islamic practice that was crucial to how they navigated heteropatriarchal diasporic contexts and how they inhabited the contentious notion of qawwam. However, what remains problematic about these understandings of the West is the forms of exclusion that they reify – so even though the women remain at the margins of an Islamophobic Canadian nationalist discourse, they also participate in the nationalist discourse of multiculturalism by creating a taxonomy of good and bad Muslims and by affirming Canada's contentious claims to being a Judeo-Christian space.

As mentioned earlier in this chapter, much Islamophobic vitriol has been directed at Al-Huda and women who participate in it. However, Islamophobic experiences are constitutive elements of many women's decision to join Al-Huda. Noreen, one of the founding members of the Quran class where I conducted research, described her reasons for starting the class in her home in Mississauga: "When I first came to Canada it was just before 9/11 and up until then I was not so interested in learning and practicing Islam in depth. After 9/11 so many people would ask me about Islam and why something like this is allowed in Islam and I didn't know how to answer this question. So I formed this group in order to answer other people's questions, but now I am here because I have my own questions." For Noreen, her need to learn about Islam emerges from an Islamophobic encounter in Canada. Taking place in the context of multicultural politics of representation, in which discrete and homogeneous categories are the lexicon of identity (Bannerji 2000), such encounters not only put her in the position of having to speak about and on behalf of all Muslims but they also implicated her own practice of Islam. As Noreen went on to explain, Al-Huda's teachings were particularly appealing to her because of their claim to follow a literal and, therefore, she thought, more authentic version of Islam. She felt empowered because Al-Huda facilitated her ability to go "directly to the source" (that is, the Quran), which also gave her a sense of clarity about Islam and her Muslim identity in Canada. Thus, through the Quran class, Noreen was able to define the contours of her diasporic Muslim identity, which, I suggest, was crucial to her feeling like she was intelligible within a multicultural framework.

However, the disavowal of other "bad" Muslims was foundational to the multicultural sense of belonging manufactured through participation in Al-Huda. For example, commenting on the merits of my project, Kanwal stated: "Canadians and everyone else needs to see what normal Muslims are like." Her statement implicitly constructs a sense of other Muslims who are abnormal, conjuring stereotypical images of those who engage in terrorist activities or partake in oppressive practices.

This sentiment was made more explicit in my interview with Fariha. When I visited Fariha at her home for the interview, I began with a short description of my project. I told her that I wanted to interview Muslim women who were engaged in activities to develop their piety to tell their stories about their relationship to Islam. Fariha responded with her thoughts on an "honour killing" that had recently made headlines in the local news. She showcased her knowledge of Islam by describing in detail the Quranic passages on murder and permissible violence and then concluded that "it is nowhere in Islam that you can just kill your daughter like that."

Fariha volunteered this analysis of "honour killings" as a response to my description of my topic of research. At first, this seemed to me like a disjointed conversation. However, on reflection, Fariha was probably performing the "good Muslim" for a researcher whom she believed would be taking her story to an audience outside of her community. The urgency with which she relayed her analysis of "honour killings" made it clear that she felt that this was a sticking point that needed to be cleared up immediately. At the same time, she also wanted to make it clear that a good Muslim is one who is knowledgeable of scripture. She distanced herself from "honour killings," and those she associated with it, by defensively asserting that real Muslims know what the scripture says, and insinuating that those Muslims who were involved in the so-called honour killing were ignorant and, by extension, "bad Muslims."

Fariha's rhetoric of distancing herself from and demonizing bad Muslims emerges in the context of an intensification of Islamophobia over "honour killings" when public outcries and moral panic reach a crescendo. This context compels a defensive posture that reproduces a version of a good Muslim-bad Muslim dichotomy in her denunciation of "honour killings." According to Fariha's logic, developing her piety and knowledge of the Quran through Al-Huda was the path to exonerating herself from such Islamophobic charges against her religion. In other words, she felt vindicated by the authentic, rational, and modern Muslim identity she was cultivating through Al-Huda's teachings.

CONCLUSION

While the idea of a Muslim model minority is typically equated with following a "moderate" form of Islam, the women I met were moving toward reconciling their "literalist" practice with Canadian ideals of multicultural belonging. While these reconciliatory efforts have, at best, mixed results in an Islamophobic context, they mobilize logics of rationality, authenticity, and modernity to construct a sense of ownership of a model minority trajectory. These efforts reveal the messiness of the intersections of Islam, diaspora, multiculturalism, and gender in Canada, and illustrate the multiple registers in which model minority discourses operate.

The ways in which my interviewees were implicated in their husbands' heteropatriarchal trajectories of migration, how they resisted it, and how they articulated their own sense of belonging through Islam, for example, demonstrates a set of competing notions of what it means to be a model minority in a multicultural context. As the women I met explained, while for their husbands the aspiration to become model minorities was articulated at the register of neoliberal progress, their own sense of being model minorities was tied to cultivating a "rational" form of diasporic piety and a sharpened Muslim identity. For them, their claims to engaging in a rational form of Islam through Al-Huda and their concomitant disavowals of biddat and "bad Muslims" wedged open a point of entry into the Canadian multicultural milieu and produced an expectation of recognition within a multicultural framework. However, the Islamophobia directed at these women and their Islamic praxis obscures how these women imagine themselves as part of a Canadian nationalist narrative through Islam. This obfuscation speaks to a larger problem of entrenched Islamophobia in Canada that renders it epistemologically impossible for Muslim women, like the ones I spoke with, to be intelligible.

NOTES

1 For instance, Fatah (2013) rejects the hijab and niqab as "symbols of servitude and misogyny imposed today by the worldwide anti-western Islamist movement." Manji, writing about the niqab, states that "to cover my face because 'that's what I'm supposed to do' is nothing short of brand victory for desert Arabs" (2004, 156). Mansur, who views Muslim immigration as a threat to Canada, describes the hijab as a "huge problem" in Quebec and Europe and generally for security in Canada (Canada 2012).

2 The interviews and participatory observations used in this chapter are part of a larger project examining Pakistani women's relationships with Islam in the diaspora in Canada. The larger project includes an analysis of women in other parts of Ontario, British Columbia, and Quebec.

3 Alexander defines heteropatriarchy as the "twin processes of heterosexualization and patriarchy" that structure the regulation of women's bodies and sexualities (1997, 65).

4 In this chapter, I transliterate based on how the Urdu-speaking women I interviewed pronounced Quranic concepts such as *qawwam* and *dawah,* instead of using Arabic pronunciations *qiwamah and da'wa.* I also use an explanation of qawwam and dawah that is based on how the women I interviewed understood it. For other academic analyses of qawwam/qiwamah, see Chaudhry (2013) and Mir-Hosseini, Al-Sharmani, and Rumminger (2015). For more on dawah/da'wa see Deeb (2006), Hafez (2011), and Mahmood (2005).

5 Zine suggests that there are specific attributes to "gendered Islamophobia" (2006, 240) that draw on histories of Orientalist representations of Muslim women as backward and oppressed.

6 Some examples of such headlines include: "Do Al-Huda Schools' Conservative Teachings Breed Extremism?" (CBC); "Founder of Pakistan Religious School Where San Bernardino Shooter Studied, Lives in Mississauga" (*Toronto Star*); "Tashfeen Malik, San Bernardino Suspect, Attended Conservative Religious School in Pakistan" (*New York Times*); "Canada's Growing Jihadi Cancery" (*Daily Beast*). "Understanding the Al-Huda Ideology," a 2015 report by the conservative think tank the Mackenzie Institute, in response to the association between Al-Huda and the San Bernardino shooting, concludes that "Al-Huda is on the path of bringing an Islamist revolution by indoctrinating women from influential families and future mothers of potential jihadis."

7 Imran Haq, the operations manager at the Al-Huda campus in Mississauga, gave a statement to the CBC: http://www.cbc.ca/news2/pdf/Statement-from-Al-Huda-Institute-to-CBC-News.pdf. Farhat Hashmi also posted a statement on the Al-Huda International website, http://www.alhudapk.com/officialstatement.

8 For an elaboration on the semiotics of women's bodies especially in relation to nationalist projects, see Abu-Lughod (1998), Chatterjee (1993), Kandiyoti (1991), and Yuval-Davis (1997).

9 See, for example, media coverage of so-called honour killings (Haque 2011); the 2011 high profile public debate and Zunera Ishaq's legal challenge against the Harper government's ban on wearing the niqab during the Canadian citizenship ceremony; and the Barbaric Cultural Practices Act (Carlaw 2015).

10 Surah al-nisa, 4:34.

11 While Al-Huda professes that they are independent of these traditions, whether or not they actually are remains unclear. The women I interviewed who mentioned this aspect of Al-Huda seemed convinced that Al-Huda was impartial in terms of conventional Islamic schools of thought (Hanafi, Hanbali, Maliki, Shafi'i).

12 In my doctoral dissertation (Hasan 2015), I examined how these characterizations of Al-Huda's approach also circulate amongst women participating in Al-Huda in Pakistan.

13 See Hasan (2015) for an elaboration on these ideals in Al-Huda's teachings. Also see Mehta (1999) for a salient analysis of how these liberal ideals are implicated in histories of colonialism.

14 It is important to note, as Mahmood (2005) cautions, that an ethic of individual choice does not necessarily reproduce the central assumptions of liberalism. For Mahmood, although the exercise of choice carries with it inflections of liberal individualism, it does not necessarily refer to the valorization of individual will that would be the basis of choice in liberalism. Instead, she argues, the notion of choice must be read within the field of possibilities laid out as part of a discourse of piety. That is to say, "choice is understood not to be an expression of one's will but something one exercises in following the prescribed path to becoming a better Muslim" (85). While Mahmood's point is salient in terms of teasing out the specificity of meaning accorded to concepts like "choice" that are often held hostage to liberalism's claims to universalism, I emphasize here the diasporic identity produced and affirmed through the deployment of such terms by the women I interviewed. The politics of representation underpinning Kanwal's portrayal of "liberated women," for example, operate through a process of othering that is constitutive of her piety as lived experience. In other words, the comfort drawn from the discursive othering of Saudi women (as well as Hindus and illiterate people) is integral to how many women I met submit to qawwam while maintaining their self-perception as rational, conscientious, educated, and modern women. So, while liberal ideas of "choice" may not be a comprehensive way of understanding how it is mobilized in the practices of piety of the women I interviewed, its significatory currency in the diaspora is drawn from its association with liberal modernity.

15 Biddat holds similar significance in Pakistan; however, it takes on different layers of meaning in the diaspora, especially through its intersections with discourses of Canadian multiculturalism, as I explain in this section.

REFERENCES

Abu-Lughod, Lila, ed. 1998. *Remaking Women: Feminism and Modernity in the Middle East*. Princeton, NJ: Princeton University Press.

Alexander, M. Jacqui. 1997. "Erotic Economy as a Politics of Decolonization." In *Feminist Genealogies, Colonial Legacies, Democratic Futures*, edited by M. Jacqui Alexander and Chandra Talpade Mohanty, 63–100. New York: Routledge.

Bakht, Natasha. 2007. "Religious Arbitration in Canada: Protecting Women by Protecting Them from Religion." *Canadian Journal of Women and the Law* 19, no. 1: 119–44.

Bannerji, Himani. 2000. *The Dark Side of the Nation: Essays on Multiculturalism, Nationalism, and Gender*. Toronto: Canadian Scholars Press.

Canada. 2012. Parliament. House of Commons. *Standing Committee on Citizenship and Immigration*. 41st Parliament, 1st Session, No. 051 (1 October). http://www.ourcommons.ca/DocumentViewer/en/41-1/CIMM/meeting-51/evidence.

Carlaw, John. 2015. "Coalition of the Winning: Neoconservative Multiculturalism in Canada." *The Ethnic Aisle*. http://www.theethnicaisle.com/new-blog/2015/9/24/moving-multiculturalism-to-the-right.

Chatterjee, Partha. 1993. *The Nation and Its Fragments: Colonial and Postcolonial Histories*. Princeton, NJ: Princeton University Press.

Chaudhry, Ayesha S. 2013. *Domestic Violence and the Islamic Tradition*. Oxford: Oxford University Press.

Cho, Lily. 2007. "The Turn to Diaspora." *Topia: Canadian Journal of Cultural Studies* 17 (Spring): 11–30.

Deeb, Lara. 2006. *An Enchanted Modern: Gender and Public Piety in Shi'i Lebanon*. Princeton, NJ: Princeton University Press.

Dhamoon, Rita. 2013. "Exclusion and Regulated Inclusion: The Case of the Sikh Kirpan in Canada." *Sikh Formations* 9, no. 1: 7–28.

Dua, Ena. 2007. "Exclusion through Inclusion: Female Asian Migration in the Making of Canada as a White Settler Nation." *Gender, Place and Culture* 14, no. 4: 445–66.

Fatah, Tarek. 2013. "Hijab Is Elephant in the Room." *Toronto Sun*, 27 August 27.

Hafez, Sherene. 2011. *An Islam of Her Own: Reconsidering Religion and Secularism in Women's Islamic Movements*. New York: New York University Press.

Haque, Eve. 2010. "Homegrown, Muslim and Other: Tolerance, Secularism and the Limits of Multiculturalism." *Social Identities* 16, no. 1: 79–101.

Hasan, Nadia Z. 2015. "Unscripting Piety: Muslim Women, Pakistani Nationalism, and Islamic Feminism." PhD dissertation, York University.

Ibn Mohar Ali, Abu Muntasir. 2006. *Understanding the Evil of Innovation: Bid'ah*. Riyadh: International Islamic Publishing House.

Kandiyoti, Deniz, ed. 1991. *Women, Islam and the State*. Philadelphia: Temple University Press.

Mahmood, Saba. 2005. *Politics of Piety: The Islamic Revival and the Feminist Subject*. Princeton, NJ: Princeton University Press.

Manji, Irshad. 2004. *The Trouble with Islam*. New York: St Martin's Press.

Mir-Hosseini, Ziba, Mulki Al-Sharmani, and Jana Rumminger, eds. 2015. *Men in Charge? Rethinking Authority in Muslim Legal Tradition*. London: Oneworld Publications.

Moghissi, Haideh. 1999. *Feminism and Islamic Fundamentalism: The Limits of Postmodern Analysis*. London: Zed Books.

Razack, Shrene. 2004. "Imperilled Muslim Women, Dangerous Muslim Men and Civilised Europeans: Legal and Social Responses to Forced Marriages." *Feminist Legal Studies* 12: 129–74.

– 2007. "The 'Sharia Law Debate' in Ontario: The Modernity/Premodernity Distinction in Legal Efforts to Protect Women from Culture." *Feminist Legal Studies* 15, no. 1: 3–32.

– 2008. *Casting Out: The Eviction of Muslims from Western Law and Politics*. Toronto: University of Toronto Press.

Razack, Sherene, Sunera Thobani, and Melinda Smith, eds. 2010. *States of Race: Critical Race Feminism for the 21st Century*. Toronto: Between the Lines.

Thobani, Sunera. 2007. *Exalted Subjects: Studies in the Making of Race and Nation in Canada*. Toronto: University of Toronto Press.

Upadhyay, Nishant. 2016. "'We'll Sail Like Columbus': Race, Indigeneity, Settler Colonialism, and the Making of South Asian Diasporas in Canada." PhD dissertation, York University.

Yuval-Davis, Nira. 1997. *Gender and Nation*. London: Sage.

Zine, Jasmine. 2006. "Unveiled Sentiments: Gendered Islamophobia and Experiences of Veiling among Muslim Girls in a Canadian Islamic School." *Equity and Excellence in Education* 39, no. 3: 239–52.

PART III

Building Relations, Imagining Futures

10

Brown Girl in the Ring

Caribbean Subversive Knowledges and the Discourse of Canadian Citizenship

Andrea A. Davis

This chapter intervenes into conversations about Caribbean women's immigrant location in Canada through the genre of speculative fiction and its portrayal of African-Caribbean spiritual practices and knowledges, reimagined as radical acts of recovery for Black people in the Americas. Through a close reading of Nalo Hopkinson's speculative novel *Brown Girl in the Ring* (1998), I consider how Caribbean women's presumed "transgressive" spiritualities might leak out, seep in, and settle into the in-between spaces of the nation in simultaneous processes of "contamination," healing, and transformation that complicate narratives of dis/location. By situating Toronto, Canada's most diverse multicultural city, as a "diaspora space" (Brah 1996, 178) within which a productive entanglement of women's histories, dreaming, and futures takes place, the chapter suggests that Black peoples' memories not only thwart Western neoliberal attempts at management and containment, but also exert a powerful diasporic influence on the nation itself, unsettling and transforming the white, British Canadian imaginary (Barrett 2015, 5). Hopkinson specifically suggests a critical relationship between social and spiritual ill-health through the African Caribbean trope of spirit thievery, which dramatizes the sociopolitical, cultural, and psychological losses experienced by Black people and the poor in Canada. In so doing, her novel reconsiders African spiritual practices and Caribbean women as important sources of retrieved African memory and as a potential source of Canada's healing.

LA CULTURA CURA / CULTURE HEALS

Margarite Fernández Olmos and Lizabeth Paravisini-Gebert (2001) argue that "Caribbean writers and intellectuals ... have turned to the discourse of healing – particularly that of healing through African-derived religious and cultural practices – to articulate a contestatory discourse of cultural and political liberation." They argue that this re/turn to Africa and its historically discredited spiritualities has been made necessary by the crisis of colonization and cultural imperialism. Within the post/colonial Caribbean, sickness cannot be understood solely in biomedical terms. It has to be understood, rather, as part of a continuing negotiation of discourses of race, power, and gender that construct Caribbean peoples as powerless and culturally disabled. If the post/colonial condition leads to expressions of dis/ease and ill-health, then one of the primary tasks of Caribbean writers and intellectuals, they argue, has been to offer an alternative "discourse of healing" nurtured within counter-discursive religious and cultural practices. In this sense, the healing metaphor symbolized in the Spanish Caribbean phrase, *la cultura cura* (culture heals), has become "perhaps the most frequent and most effectively deployed tool against colonial discourse" (xx).

In an essay in the same volume, Opal Palmer Adisa takes this argument further by situating Black women writers as the self-conscious media of their communities' healing (Davis 2013, 525). Black women writers in the Americas "have helped to move and heal many black people from the amnesia and brutal, historical pain in which so many of us were and are still drowning" (Adisa 2001, 181). Living in the afterlife of slavery and colonialism, Caribbean men and women continue to live threatened lives (Davis 2013, 525). Understanding the relationships between history, memory, and healing as inextricably linked, Black women writers help their readers confront histories of violence and powerlessness, and repair fragmented memories, by revalorizing African-derived cultural traditions (526).

M. NourbeSe Philip argues similarly that her writing, especially her poetry, is a self-conscious attempt to resist a certain kind of post/colonial management made possible through deeply entrenched social discourses of power located in the intersections of language, race, and gender:

> In working on the poems that comprise the manuscript *She Tries Her Tongue*, I came up hard – to use a Jamaican expression, I "buck up" against the weight of Eurocentric traditions and became aware that even poetry and the way it was brought to, and taught in, the Caribbean was a way of management. I was, in fact, working in a language that has at best omitted the reality and experience of the managed – the African in the New World – and at worst discoursed on her nonbeing. The challenge for me was to use that language, albeit the language of my oppression, but the only one I had, to subvert the inner and hidden discourse – the discourse of my non-being. (1990, 296)

For Philip, a Black Trinidadian woman living in Canada, the refusal to be managed demands a certain kind of transgressive behaviour, a deliberate unmanageability, necessary not just to subvert and challenge the overarching imperialist discourse, the colonial metanarratives, but necessary to recover Black women's beings, bodies, and voices from erasure, powerlessness, and the margins of the societies in which they live and work. In an act of linguistic transgression, Philip, therefore, rearticulates the margin as a new frontier – a site of power, imagination, and discovery: "When we think of ourselves as being on the frontier, our perspective immediately changes. Our position is no longer one in relation to the managers, but we now face outward, away from them, to the undiscovered space and place up ahead which we are about to discover" (300). While Philip's cultural geographic re/ordering draws on an uneasy metaphor of colonial re/conquest, what she seeks ultimately is to dream new locations for the region's managed peoples (Indigenous communities, non-white peoples, women, and the poor). Philip rewrites the marginalized, in this way, as constitutive of the region's history and imagined future.

Nalo Hopkinson is similarly involved in the mapping of a new kind of literary and social frontier. Through the use of speculative fiction, Hopkinson attempts a critical reassessment of African-derived spiritual practices that locates those traditions not on the *margin* of American societies but on the *frontier* of a new radicalized social order – as necessary entanglements within the diaspora space of the city. According to Brah, diaspora space is the site "where multiple subject positions are juxtaposed, contested, proclaimed or disavowed; where the permitted and the prohibited perpetually interrogate; and where the accepted and the transgressive imperceptibly mingle even while these syncretic forms may be disclaimed in the name of purity and tradition" (1996, 205). Diaspora space thus breaks down and obscures the neat boundaries of the nation. Rather than thinking of diasporas as located on the margins of the nation – which is itself imagined as a complete and finished product – diaspora space suggests a messy but productive entanglement. The diaspora space as a metaphor of the everyday living and dwelling of diaspora signifies the place where multiple diasporas meet to produce, reproduce, narrate, and reimagine the nation never as a finished product but as the site of creation, recreation, and transformation. In other words, the nation is not separated from its diasporas but becomes itself diasporic (Barrett 2015). Set in the inner core of a near-future Toronto, Hopkinson uses the genre of speculative fiction to graft African Caribbean belief systems onto the Canadian landscape, site of the deep colonial management of Indigenous and African peoples. By disrupting a centre-periphery (majority/minority) dichotomy, she succeeds in demarcating a diaspora space that dramatically alters the collective national consciousness.

REIMAGINING A SUBVERSIVE CITY

In *Brown Girl* (1998), Toronto's booming metropolitan and multicultural economy is reimagined as the Burn: a desolate, abandoned wasteland in need of political, spiritual, and economic recovery. The once-powerful metropolitan centre has been reduced to an inner-city garrison of rubble, poverty, and crime. Hopkinson explores this possibility of Toronto's demise precisely by insisting on a necessary relationship between physical dis/ease and social ill-health. If the source of the social dis/ease is not identified and cured, there is the strong suggestion that the disease will continue to spread beyond the borders of the abandoned city to infect an entire Canadian nation. The novel constructs this possibility, however, not as loss but as a moment of dramatic possibility. By challenging the construction of the hegemonic, neoliberal nation and settler colonial state as the only useful configurations of government and citizenship, the novel re-narrates the diaspora space of the multicultural city as a more productive site of shared belonging. Put another way, the novel imagines a Canadian society in which multiculturalism moves beyond empty political policy to radical interventionist practice. Indeed, as Paul Barrett argues in *Blackening Canada*, it is precisely the "simultaneously disabling and enabling quality of Canadian multiculturalism" that is "parodied, seized upon, challenged, and celebrated within black diasporic writing in Canada" (2015, 9). For Barrett, the diaspora space of day-to-day entanglement identified by Brah functions as a "space of diasporic articulation" for Black Canadian writers. This practice of narration importantly "stresses not merely the movement of diasporic people across nations, but the recasting of the nation itself as diasporic through the struggle to establish and uncover the links between the local, the national, and the diasporic" (13). By locating Canada as part of a wider Americas, entangled in the histories and memories of the Caribbean, Africa, and South and Central America, Hopkinson radically expands our understanding of a Canadian national identity. Instead of mourning the loss of "home" for Caribbean immigrants both in the Caribbean and its diaspora, Hopkinson's novel reclaims home. The diasporic home – as "the lived experience of a locality" (Brah 1996, 188) – is the site where multiple sources of memory converge and are recovered, shared, and transformed.

By positioning formerly discredited African knowledge systems at the heart of conversations about Canadian national identity, Hopkinson's fiction reimagines radical acts of recovery for people of African descent in the Americas, as well as the Canadian nation. These acts of recovery are themselves literary acts of transgression, of unmanageability, overturning hegemonic, imperialist narratives and challenging sociopolitical hierarchies. The novel thus thematizes the importance of developing anticolonial narratives that can help effectuate the recovery and social well-being of Caribbean and Canadian societies in which Black people, in both instances, are still at risk. If, as Olmos and Paravisini-Gebert argue, Caribbean societies, like others in the Americas, are afflicted by social dis/ease occasioned by brutal histories of fragmentation and loss and by cultural and spiritual alienation, then Hopkinson's *Brown Girl* reaches precisely into those brutalized histories to recover the language and medium of healing.

Ioan Davies's (2000) attempt to articulate a theory of Toronto centres the city's Scottish, English, Presbyterian, Catholic, and Anglican roots and reinforces a history of settler colonialism, but he also provides an unexpected opening through which to demarcate new city boundaries and histories. The boundaries of "the habitable city," Davies suggests, is constructed "both in the imagination and in the everyday" (15). The imagined city, in addition, is "equally significant to our understanding as the 'real' city," and the connection between the two must be explored (16). Hopkinson's novel goes further to suggest that Toronto is a city that "must be imagined, invented, before it can be inhabited" (Davis 2018, 76), and that Caribbean women writers are central to this project of reimagining new livable futures. The rewriting of the diasporic city and nation ultimately is a contest over multiple geographical, cultural, and social borders. Borders, Brah explains, constitute "forms of demarcation where the very act of prohibition inscribes transgression; zones where fear of the other is the fear of the self; places where claims to ownership – claims to 'mine', 'yours' and 'theirs' – are staked out, contested, defended, and fought over" (1996, 195). In *Brown Girl*, the "habitable city" is thus re/invented and re/bordered to create the kind of place in which Black people might be able to dwell. Hopkinson, thus, challenges questions of national origin, cultural authority, and class privilege by reimagining a subversive city saturated by the myths of Caribbean immigrants and shaped by their oral histories; a city that depends on the reinsertion of a previously absented Black humanity.

What the novel achieves, however, may not seem immediately hopeful, because the Toronto it reimagines relies on a complete dismantling of the consumerist impulses and capitalist economy that sustain Davies's "real" city. The city Hopkinson projects demonstrates the dystopian effects of national decay and global capitalism, and it is transformed beyond recognition. The city's abandonment has been precipitated by a mass out-migration of the upper and middle classes into the surrounding suburbs: "Those who stayed were the ones who couldn't or wouldn't leave. The street people. The poor people. The ones who didn't see the writing on the wall, or were too stubborn to give up their homes. Or who saw the decline of authority as an opportunity" (Hopkinson 1998, 4).[1] The novel imagines this abandonment as a postcolonial struggle over the ownership of the land. Temagami Indians[2] have filed a lawsuit against the Ontario government over land claims that are supported by Amnesty International and have resulted in a global trade embargo and reduced transfer payments. Reductions in government revenue have led, in turn, to an Ontario recession, increased crime, the relocation of big corporations, the mass walkout of the Toronto police, and the Riots that mark the city's final transition to the Burn. Left to its own devices and increasingly alienated, Hopkinson's reimagined Toronto is like Davies's "suburban garrison state," the ultimate nightmare of the "'old' bourgeoisie" (2000, 21).

This fictional movement of the middle classes away from Toronto – one of the most culturally and racially diverse cities in North America – may also be read as a movement away from multiculturalism, precisely the social condition that Canada is supposed to celebrate. Himani Bannerji (2000) argues that the problem with Canadian multiculturalism is its insistence on being read only in relation to an ideologically homogenous identity. "This core community," Bannerji writes, "is synthesized into a national we, and it decides on the terms of multiculturalism and the degree to which multicultural others should be tolerated or accommodated. This 'we' is an essentialized version of a colonial European turned into Canadian and the subject or the agent of Canadian nationalism" (42). Canadian nationalism, always under threat from diversity, paradoxically uses a discourse of multiculturalism to translate concerns of racism, legal discrimination, and family reunification into questions of culture and to reduce the framework within which structural inequalities can be addressed (44–5). Since immigrants are the only ones considered to be "really" diverse, they have to be ethnicized, culturalized, and then forced into "insulated communities" (48). For Bannerji, there are clear colonial tendencies in Canada's discourse of nationalism: "The genealogies of these reified cultural identities which are mobilized in Canada are entirely colonial though they are being constantly reworked in the modern context of state formation and capital's transformation" (49).

In "Racializing Culture/Culturalizing Race," Augie Fleras argues similarly that the privileging of a "monocultural" multiculturalism is a powerful tool of management and containment directed against othered cultures to force them to conform to the dominant cultural and political ideology of the Canadian nation, even as these cultures are fooled into thinking they can exercise agency (2004, 431). Diversity is tolerated only to the extent that differences do not get in the way of "normal" Canadian life and do not challenge taken-for-granted Canadian values and social institutions regardless of how oppressive these values may be when deployed against these very "minority" cultures. There is always, then, an invisible pressure on communities that stand outside the Canadian cultural "ideal" to prove they belong, not by celebrating difference but by managing difference. Since the Black Caribbean immigrants, the street children, and the bag ladies who overrun Hopkinson's reinvented Toronto are often literally diseased, they must be permanently isolated from the rest of Canada; they must be contained. This inner-city garrison, in fact, has only one unguarded exit from the city, over water and by plane: "from the Toronto Island mini-airport to the American side of Niagara Falls" (4). McKittrick identifies the crisis of cultural management as resulting in part from a public discourse of spillage that "repeats Canada's history of marking nonwhite communities through discourses of disease, vice, cleanliness, and health ... The geographic 'problem' of blackness, after its existence is surprisingly unearthed, is often recast as something/someone who threatens to launch a criminal, or a non-Canadian, or a diseased surprise attack on the nation" (2006, 102). But the real threat to the city-nation, Hopkinson's novel suggests, is not posed by these kinds of threat. The real damage portends from precisely the post/colonialist tendencies to reify some cultural identities at the expense of others. The possibilities for re/imagining a "habitable" Toronto are, indeed, possible only within a willing engagement with difference (Bannerji 2000). For Caribbean diasporic communities residing in Toronto, there is an imperative to construct, to invent, "alternate public spheres, forms of community consciousness and solidarity" that can "maintain identifications outside the national time/space in order to live inside, with a difference" (Clifford 1997, 251). This is precisely the radical subversion that *Brown Girl* imagines: a Toronto in which displaced Caribbean bodies no longer occupy the margins but are essential to the city's political and cultural health, a "habitable" city where Black bodies "live inside, with a difference" (ibid.).

Speculative fiction offers Hopkinson a genre through which she can explore this potential to reimagine a new political future by dislodging oppressive colonial ideologies: "something fundamental about the nature of humans or human understanding has to change. That's one of the places where science fiction and fantasy can really be exciting, where they can envision how that change might come about" (Glave 2003, 153). In another interview with Gregory Rutledge (1999), Hopkinson identifies a particularly creative and subversive potential in the speculative fiction she writes: "I think that a speculative literature from a culture that has been on the receiving end of the colonization glorified in some sf could be a compelling body of writing ... It's very important to me to be a voice coming from one flavor of black experience, and Caribbean, and Canadian, and female, and fat, and from feminist and sex-positive politics" (591). Hopkinson's embodiment of a wide range of political positions and her conflation of the body as writer and the body as text gives her a vantage point beyond that of Du Bois's double consciousness – the ability to articulate a radically transformed environment that can account for the presence of multiple national subjectivities. Her experiences of having lived in Jamaica, Trinidad, Guyana, and the United States before arriving in Canada shape this radical multicultural perspective, which has a concrete goal: "If black people can imagine our futures, imagine – among other things – cultures in which we aren't alienated, then we can begin to see our way clear to creating them" (593). This is the future she sets out to reimagine in *Brown Girl.*

The city in *Brown Girl* further allows for an exploration of the local in order to make comments about the limits and possibilities of the nation-state. By stripping the Toronto core of its technological advantages, reducing its imposing architecture, and isolating it from the rest of the country, Hopkinson creates a kind of "rural" city where people are forced to eke out their living in cooperation with nature and the land. Paula and Pavel, former lecturers at the University of Toronto before the Riots, for example, are now local farmers who use the Allan Gardens Park and its greenhouse to grow produce for the city core and to trap animals (13). The Burn is isolated, set apart from its suburbs and the rest of the nation. Not only is it a kind of "rural" city within a developed city (its suburbs) but it is also an impoverished nation within a developed nation (every exit into the rest of Canada is guarded).

SOCIAL AND SPIRITUAL ILL-HEALTH AND THE TROPE OF SPIRIT THIEVERY

Within the context of diversity that the novel establishes, Hopkinson specifically explores the co-relationship between social and spiritual ill-health through the use of the African Caribbean trope of spirit thievery. *Brown Girl* relies on the trope of spirit thievery to symbolically dramatize the sociopolitical, cultural, and psychological losses experienced by Caribbean and other Black people in Canada. In so doing, Hopkinson's novel not only portrays African spiritual practices as important sources of retrieved African memory, but also points to these understandings of spirituality and human relationships as a potential source of Canada's national healing. By locating the site of disease and ill-health not in the Caribbean but in Canada, not in the "underdeveloped" South but in the Global North, she inscribes that African memory as inseparable from the Canadian past and challenges dominant discourses of power, belonging, and ownership. In line with

Canada's and her own multiculturalism, Hopkinson uses a syncretized version of African-derived religious traditions – combining the practices and philosophical worldviews of Myal, Shango, Santería, and Vodou – as her entry point into an examination of the ill-health of Canadian society and the implications of a kind of cultural sorcery.

Brown Girl suggests that the belief systems of African-derived spiritual practices may contain the clues to help Canadians traverse the complex and dangerous boundaries of race, gender, and class. By locating her discussion within Toronto, Hopkinson is able to radically challenge and redefine understandings of Canadian multiculturalism and contest the specific expressions of racism experienced in "first-world" spaces like Canada. This chapter, then, reads Canada's practice of multiculturalism as one kind of spirit thievery. On the one hand, the practice of multiculturalism in Canada represents a kind of empty and easy appropriation of othered cultures through food, music, and dance, without any cultural knowledge or history. There is certainly a way in which Canadian multiculturalism legitimizes cultural appropriation, so it becomes taken for granted. But multiculturalism, in its demand for integration under the guise of celebrating diversity, also represents another kind of spirit thievery: it zombifies individuals and communities by forcing them to conform, to behave like willing, obedient machines within the carefully delineated boundaries of a Canadian "ideal." As Evelyn O'Callaghan explains, zombification "results from the trauma of being forcibly rewritten by imperial discourse, and then attempting the futile task of living as a subject in relation to one's scripted Otherness" (1993, 71). The "other" culture, the never-quite-equal cultural group, has to prove its loyalty by being rigidly obedient, never daring to challenge social codes of behaviour or challenge cultural hegemony.

In Hopkinson's novel the trope of spirit thievery is explored most clearly through the character development of the antagonist, Rudy. Trained in the art of Caribbean healing practices, Rudy uses his knowledge and memory of West Africa learned from his wife, Mami Gros-Jeanne, for selfish material gain at the expense of the wider community's well-being. According to Robert Stewart, during enslavement African Caribbean communities distinguished between the roles of two African spiritual practitioners: the Ashanti *okomfo*, a priest who through public ritual "influenced the spirits for the health and well-being of the community," and the *obayifo* or obeah man (1992, 136). African traditions of healing, Stewart argues, still function as an important "expression of black identity and resistance" in societies "in which the European presence continued to be the sign and source of political, economic, and cultural oppression" (144). In *Brown Girl*, while Mami Gros-Jeanne understands her role as mirroring that of the *okomfo* priest, the character of Rudy is deliberately aligned with that of the *obayifo*.

Exploiting the absence of the police in the abandoned and destitute city, Rudy combines Western capitalist values and the destructive and competitive forces of obeah to establish a powerful drug and sex work cartel, meting out brutal punishments to anyone who refuses to conform to his self-imposed rule of law. Using a form of paralysis derived from toad poison, Rudy transforms his victims into zombies, as he does with Melba, the sex worker who dares to assert signs of sexual agency by withholding part of her earnings. The novel thus extends Rudy's sphere of control by linking the widespread drug addiction that plagues large cities like Toronto to the early stages of national and cultural paralysis. As such, Sarah Wood understands Rudy's absorption of Western capitalist values as clearly antithetical to the social health of the local community: "It's interesting that the 'specific ends' that Rudy aspires to in his ritual practice of obeah are the Western elixir of youthful appearance, material wealth and gain and physical prowess and power at the expense of both community and family. The correlation of Western capitalist values and the form of obeah Rudy practices signifies a perversion of traditional Caribbean knowledge" (2005, 322). Rudy's obsession with Western capitalism and his abuse of Caribbean cultures and knowledges, in fact, have far-reaching ideological implications. As he explains to Ti-Jeanne, zombification is a powerful form of ideological control: "Combine the paralysis and the suggestibility with the right kind of um, *indoctrination*, and the zombie go do anything me tell it" (Hopkinson 1998, 212). Mindless slaves, however, can only follow simple instructions. Spirit thievery offers complete mastery of control: "A duppy from a dead somebody not too smart. Smarter than a zombie, but you still can't give it nothing too complicated to do, seen? But if you split off the duppy from the body while the body alive! Well then you have a servant for true. One that could teach you everything it did know in life" (213). By commanding the accumulated knowledge of his victims for his own ends, Rudy controls a wide sphere of political and ideological power and influence that is difficult and dangerous to dislodge. He replicates a colonial endeavour of appropriating Caribbean cultures and resources for the enrichment and empowerment of Western capitalist imperialism.

The political, socioeconomic, and cultural domination Rudy practises combines elements of both sexual and mental control. As he watches a partially paralyzed Tony and senses his own complete power, "Rudy felt the familiar tightening in his crotch that that sense of power always brought him" (134). The homoerotic desire expressed toward Tony is juxtaposed by his patriarchal tirade against Black women's power in the domestic sphere: "Poor all me born days. Come up to Canada, no work. Me wife and all kick me out of me own house. Blasted cow. If it wasn't for me, she woulda still be cleaning rich people toilets back home, and is so she treat me. Just because me give she little slap two-three time when she make she mouth run away 'pon me" (131). Rudy fails to recognize the ways in which the capitalist values he models reproduces Black men's socioeconomic disempowerment. By identifying his wife as the cause of his potential emasculation, he obscures the fact that in the Caribbean diaspora Black women suffer multiple forms of oppression: as Black people, immigrants, workers, and women. Black women are located at the bottom of the social hierarchy after Black men, and this is emphasized by Rudy's unchallenged violence against women. In this way, Hopkinson successfully links a discussion of "the racism and sexism of globalism's cultural reifications" to certain destructive practices of obeah (Rogan 2008, 88).

By aligning Rudy with a corrupted Ontario government that espouses empty political rhetoric but coldly disregards the needs of its citizens, Hopkinson also reveals a national willingness to consume and profit from othered cultures. But by representing the needs of the nation-state as antithetical to those of the abandoned city, she also reemphasizes Toronto's position as a "special kind" of city even within Ontario, whose encroaching diversity might be seen as a threat to Canadian nationalism: "The Premier's request for a heart procured from within the Ring concretizes both the heartlessness of capitalist political and economic interests *and* the sense in which the life of the inner city is constantly threatened by the invisible power structures that contain it" (Rogan 2008, 90). The government's complicity with colonial and imperial capitalist exploitation is also signalled by its refusal to recognize the land claims of the Temagami Indigenous communities. This represents a failure of multiculturalism at all levels of Canadian government that have refused to recognize the losses that Canada's Indigenous communities have suffered as a result of Canada's expansionist and imperialist goals: "Hopkinson extrapolates from existing tensions between different levels of Canadian government to show how the idealized structure of Canadian unity-through diversity was able to fragment" (Reid 2005, 301). The novel further suggests that while Rudy steals the spirits of those around him, he himself is also completely trapped, zombified, in the corruption of a neocolonial Canadian political system that recognizes him only as a Caribbean outcast who can be used to keep other designated non-Canadian citizens powerless, marginalized, and contained.

"SHOW ME YOUR MOTION": CARIBBEAN WOMEN'S HEALING PRACTICES

Still, in *Brown Girl* there is an insistence that "white Western philosophical and intellectual traditions" have to make a place for "the discourse of Afro-Caribbean culture's folkloric resistances to colonization" (Rogan 2008, 89). This is the dilemma at the centre of Derek Walcott's 1958 play *Ti-Jean and His Brothers* (1991), which Hopkinson references in her speculative fiction.[3] In Walcott's play, which is an allegory of the Caribbean colonial experience, Ti-Jean and his brothers engage in a war of wits with the Devil that he alone wins because of his ability to draw on a range of anticolonial strategies of resistance that honour folk knowledge and the traditions of family and community (Baugh 2006, 76–7). Hopkinson rewrites the earlier male-centred Caribbean discourse about nation-building from a woman-centred, diasporic perspective, charting the lives and struggles of three generations of Caribbean women in Toronto trying to overcome the shared difficulties of their lives. The novel suggests that the survival of Caribbean communities within the region or its diaspora will depend on the survival of African folk memories and the use of the power those memories offer in responsible, community-conscious ways (Davis 2013, 530). But, even more importantly, the novel insists that the project of Canadian nation-building must take into account the most marginalized of Canada's citizens: non-white, immigrant women. Hopkinson positions women, therefore, as critical to the recovery of the Canadian city-nation symbolized by the Burn.

Mami Gros-Jeanne, the head of the family and the community's healer, represents the critical curing function in Hopkinson's novel and calls for a revalorization of African-derived religious traditions:

"I don't work the dead, I serve the spirits and I heal the living" (Hopkinson 1998, 59). In *Brown Girl,* there is a critical difference between the *okomfo* she practises and the *obayifo* she defends her family against. Trained as a nurse and a midwife, Mami Gros-Jeanne is a herbalist who heals and gives life. In this way, Mami is contrasted not just with Rudy, whose evil she must help to exorcize, but also with Tony, himself a nurse, who abuses drugs and allows himself to be manipulated by Rudy.

The syncretic body of African Caribbean spiritual practices that Hopkinson calls on is reflective also of her characters' location in the Caribbean diaspora in Toronto. The diaspora that Hopkinson represents is one that is pan-Caribbean in scope; it is not boundaried by island affiliation. This is perhaps most evident in the characters' linguistic movements between different Caribbean creoles. Rudy's question, "Oonuh need a heart transplant for she, and she nah let you put no Trenton in she body?" (2), for example, demonstrates his ability to draw equally on the rhythm and vocabulary of Jamaican and Trinidadian linguistic registers.[4] Collier explains this linguistic intervention: "*Brown Girl* involves a linguistic blending of creoles, anglophone and francophone, as a medium to convey cultural practices that can no longer be identified solely with say, St. Lucia or Dominica or Haiti, Trinidad or Jamaica" (2003, 445).

This melding of languages is, indeed, critical to the Caribbean diasporic nature of Toronto. The fact that this syncretism might make the novel difficult to read only further demonstrates that a genuine multicultural practice is never easy and always demands a certain kind of difficult personal commitment.

This syncretism also occurs in Hopkinson's representation of the novel's healing traditions and her incorporation of African Caribbean religious rituals that combine diverse regional influences: Shango from Trinidad; Santería from Cuba; Vodou from Haiti; Condomblé from Brazil; Myalism from Jamaica, and all their diverse Christian influences. Mami introduces her granddaughter, Ti-Jeanne, to these African spiritual knowledge sources by teaching her to honour the spirits: "The African powers, child. The spirits. The loas. The Orishas. The oldest ancestors. You will hear people from Haiti and Cuba and Brazil and so call them different names. You will even hear some names I ain't tell you, but we all mean the same thing" (Hopkinson 1998, 126). But she also warns that the power these spirits encode is vast, and they open the door to both good and evil. Hopkinson also draws equally from the region's folklore, so that the novel is replete with appearances of La Diablesse, the Jab-Jab, the Soucouyant, the Duppy Conqueror, and Prince of Cemetery, all of which have a specific spiritual function.[5] Almost all of these Caribbean folk characters appear exclusively to Ti-Jeanne, who shares her grandmother's gifts. Ti-Jeanne is terrified by these appearances and by her dreams until she learns of their cultural significance and value in her own life – that they appear to warn her of danger and to protect her from evil. By using the genre of speculative fiction, Hopkinson is able to suspend her readers' disbelief in her revelation of these religious practices in the diaspora. Hopkinson thus normalizes Caribbean cultures within a Canadian landscape not only through her invocation of African Caribbean religious deities and folk characters but also through the stories, sayings, proverbs, and songs that she uses to frame each chapter and are embedded in various sections of the novel. The ring game from which the novel derives its title, for example, encourages improvisation by challenging each dancer in the centre of the ring to "show me your motion." Ti-Jeanne, the symbolic "brown girl in the ring," will have to rely on her inventiveness, her creative potential, if she is to save herself and this already endangered city.

The healing potential in Hopkinson's novel, importantly, extends equally to all members of the Burn regardless of race or colour. As Anatol insists, the "strict black versus white, Caribbean versus European struggle of earlier independence and black nationalist movements no longer apply to Hopkinson's futuristic Canadian landscape" (2004, 2). And Hopkinson agrees: "My experience of being 'raced' ... is a complex one that has to take into account the cultures and histories of many races, not to mention class and economics. It cannot be a simple binary" (Rutledge and Hopkinson 1999, 592). Understanding her role, Mami ministers to the entire Burn, even the street children who have nothing to barter. She is even patient with the children's expression of the dominant culture's fear of the alternative knowledge she shares. The healing Mami practises is also sensitive to her environment. She replaces the Caribbean healing herbs she can no longer find with new North American plants, and her Romany friend, who also attends the syncretized Caribbean rituals over which Mami presides, teaches her to read the tarot cards.

When Mami is killed by Ti-Jeanne's boyfriend, Tony, who has been instructed to deliver her heart to Rudy as an organ donation for the sick Ontario premier, her knowledge and healing function passes to her granddaughter, Ti-Jeanne, on whose shoulders the healing of the community finally rests. Ti-Jeanne will challenge her father's corrupted power and free the soul of her mother, Mi-Jeanne, which he has trapped in his dead bowl and uses to fulfill his evil desires. But the power of Rudy's ideological brainwashing is strong. The offer to live free of responsibility, with no need to mourn her grandmother or feel the guilt and pain of her mother's death, is seductive: "*Heart couldn't hurt she … she coulda go wherever she want, nobody to trap she*" (215). Hopkinson's use of italics helps readers register this as an attack not against Ti-Jeanne's body but against her mind. It is Ti-Jeanne's ambivalence about the gifts she possesses that makes her susceptible to her father's evil. As the Jab-Jab explains to her, "It have plenty names for what Gros-Jeanne was. Myalist, bush doctor, iyalorisha, curandera, four-eye, even obeah woman for them that don't understand" (218–9). But, he continues, "Gros-Jeanne woulda tell you that all she doing is serving the spirits. And that anybody who try to live good, who try to help people, who try to have respect for life, and age, and those who go before, them all doing the same thing: serving the spirits" (219). With this understanding, Ti-Jeanne uses the centre pole of the CN Tower as the bridge between the worlds and calls eight of the Oldest Ones into a spiritual warfare on behalf of the inhabitants of the Burn. These are joined by the children Rudy has killed and his victims of zombification. This gathering, importantly, is not about revenge; it is about balancing the power in the world. As Ti-Jeanne emerges from this ordeal, she must face her grandmother's death and the betrayal of Tony. The responsibility is hers not only to live but to live connected to a community that needs her to offer what Mami can no longer give.

At the end of the novel, Mami's heart is transplanted into the body of the white Ontario premier, Premier Uttley, and another kind of spirit possession takes place. The doctors have to fight hard to establish a symbiosis between body and heart. While Catherine Uttley is grateful for the organ, she resists the sharing of power involved in the exchange. This is typical of the dominant culture's refusal to yield its hold on the centre. Uttley's body will have to be paralyzed before she will acquiesce: "And then she was aware again. Her dream body and brain were hers once more, but with a difference. The heart – her heart – was dancing joyfully beneath her ribs … In every artery, every vein, every capillary: two distinct streams, intertwined. She had worried for nothing. She was healed, a new woman. 'Stupidness,' she said, chiding herself for her unnecessary fears" (237). It is only at the end of this interior sequence that we realize that we are hearing both women's thoughts. In this merging of the Caribbean and Canada, the Global South and the Global North, Africa and its diaspora, in the heart of multicultural Toronto, there is the beginning of a radical politics in which Ontario, at least, may offer a government with "a social conscience" (239). It is not accidental, however, that this transformation results from another kind of spirit possession. As Carolyn Cooper cautions, spirit possession is both a positive and negative metaphor: "As metaphor spirit possession doubly signifies both the dislocation and rearticulation of Afro-centric culture in the Americas; divine possession mirrors its subversive other – zombification – that diabolical ownership of the enslaved in the material world" (1992, 64). *Brown Girl* thus attempts multiple and layered acts of transgression in the persistent search for far-reaching social and national transformation.

CONCLUSION: REFUSING A POLITICS OF POLARIZATION

In Hopkinson's reimagined Toronto, Caribbean immigrant women in low-paying jobs and stereotyped as poor, illiterate, and unskilled save the city and offer its members an alternative value system (Davis 2013, 530). In this way, Hopkinson has radically reimagined a "habitable city" where her characters can "live inside, with a difference" (Clifford 1997, 251). By demarcating Caribbean cultural traditions' potential in the healing of the Canadian nation, Hopkinson offers a Canadian society in which multiculturalism moves beyond empty political policy to radical interventionist practice. Again, by writing Caribbean immigrants not simply as marginalized noncitizens but as productive, socially and politically responsible citizens, Hopkinson realigns the boundaries of Canadian society to find Philip's frontier. By locating Canada as part of a wider Americas, she radically expands our understanding of a Canadian national identity. Instead of mourning the loss of "home" for Caribbean immigrants both in the Caribbean and its diaspora, Hopkinson's novel reclaims home. Home is the site where memory is recovered and fragmented diasporic African identities are healed. Home is also, therefore, of necessity a *shared* space, where communities (both dominant and marginalized) recognize not only that each other exist, but also begin to take responsibility for each other. The assumption has always been that the taking on of responsibility is the function of the dominant culture. But if that assumption of responsibility is left only to the dominant culture (which continues to have a primarily colonizing function), then what may result is a deeply fragmented and segregated society in which diversity is a disease rather than a cure. It is only when historically marginalized communities begin to take ownership of their diasporic spaces that we can reach toward any meaningful understanding and practice of multiculturalism.

Brown Girl, thus, insists on a radical definition of community and nation that can take into account the complex historical and sociopolitical experiences of the African diaspora in the Americas. The novel is animated by particular and localized concerns, but the working through of these concerns has critical meaning for the larger societies and wider world its characters inhabit. By linking Toronto to the Caribbean, Hopkinson recognizes that the social and political well-being of societies in the Americas are deeply interwoven. By refusing to rely on a politics of polarization, the novel escapes the trap of an essentialist "us" versus "them" binary and offers instead more complex and sophisticated strategies of resistance and self-empowerment.

NOTES

1 All further page references for the novel are to Hopkinson 1998 unless otherwise specified.

2 The Teme-Augama Anishnabai (TAA) and/or the Temagami First Nation (TFN), together referred to as the Temagami Indians, have been involved in a long dispute with the Ontario government over land claims since the 1980s. In 1984, the Ontario Supreme Court denied the Temagami Indians approximately 9,000 square kilometers of land they claimed as their homeland around Lake Temagami, and the Ontario Court of Appeals upheld this judgement in 1989. The TAA accepted a preliminary agreement reached in 1993, but the TFN rejected it. Negotiations were ongoing until 2008 when they were suspended. For further discussion, see Bray and Thomson (1996).

3 Hopkinson's father, Slade Hopkinson, a Guyanese actor, poet, and playwright, participated in Derek Walcott's Trinidad Theatre Workshop. See Hopkinson's interview with Rutledge (1999, 589, 498).

4 While the sentence itself has a largely Trinidadian rhythm, the insertion of the word Trenton highlights its linguistic and cultural complexity. Trenton

is a specifically Jamaican word for pork, which many Jamaicans do not eat for religious, philosophical, or health reasons.

5 For a more detailed elaboration of folklore in the novel, see Giselle Liza Anatol (2004).

REFERENCES

Adisa, Opal Palmer. 2001. "A Writer/Healer: Literature, a Blueprint for Healing." In *Healing Cultures: Art and Religion as Curative Practices in the Caribbean and Its Diaspora*, edited by Margarite Fernández Olmos and Lizabeth Paravisini-Gebert, 179–93. New York: Palgrave.

Anatol, Giselle Liza. 2004. "A Feminist Reading of Soucouyants in Nalo Hopkinson's *Brown Girl in the Ring* and *Skin Folk*." *Mosaic* 37, no. 3: 33–50.

Bannerji, Himani. 2000. *The Dark Side of the Nation: Essays on Multiculturalism, Nationalism, and Gender*. Toronto: Canadian Scholars Press.

Barrett, Paul. 2015. *Blackening Canada: Diaspora, Race, Multiculturalism*. Toronto: University of Toronto Press.

Baugh, Edward. 2006. *Derek Walcott*. Cambridge: Cambridge University Press.

Brah, Avtar. 1996. *Cartographies of Diaspora*. New York: Routledge.

Bray, Robert Matthew, and Ashley Thomson, eds. 1996. *Temagami: A Debate on Wilderness*. Toronto: Dundurn Press.

Clifford, James. 1997. *Routes: Travel and Translation in the Late Twentieth Century*. Cambridge, MA: Harvard University Press.

Collier, Gordon. 2003. "Spaceship Creole: Nalo Hopkinson, Canadian-Caribbean Fabulist Fiction, and Linguistic/Cultural Syncretism." *Matatu* 27–28: 443–6.

Cooper, Carolyn. 1992. "'Something Ancestral Recaptured': Spirit Possession as Trope in Selected Feminist Fictions of the African Diaspora." In *Motherlands: Black Women's Writing from African, the Caribbean and South Asia*, edited by Susheila Nasta, 64–87. New Brunswick, NJ: Rutgers University Press.

Davies, Ioan. 2000. "Theorizing Toronto." *Topia* 3 (Spring): 14–36.

Davis, Andrea. 2013. "Women and Healing in Anglophone Caribbean Literature." In *Encyclopedia of Caribbean Religions*, vol. 1, edited by Patrick Taylor and Frederick I. Case, 525–34. Champaign: University of Illinois Press.

– 2018. "The Black Woman Native Speaking Subject: Reflections of a Black Female Professor in Canada." *Atlantis: Critical Studies in Gender, Culture, and Social Justice* 39, no. 1: 70–8.

Fleras, Augie. 2004. "Racializing Culture/Culturalizing Race: Multicultural Racism in a Multicultural Canada." In *Racism, Eh? A Critical Inter-Disciplinary Anthology of Race and Racism in Canada*, edited by Camille A. Nelson and Charmaine A. Nelson, 429–43. Concord, ON: Captus Press.

Glave, Dianne D. 2003. "An Interview with Nalo Hopkinson." *Callaloo* 26, no. 1: 146–59.

Hopkinson, Nalo. 1998. *Brown Girl in the Ring*. New York: Warner Books.

McKittrick, Katherine. 2006. *Demonic Grounds: Black Women and the Cartographies of Struggle*. Minneapolis: University of Minnesota Press.

O'Callaghan, Evelyn. 1993. *Woman Version: Theoretical Approaches to West Indian Fiction by Women*. New York: St Martin's Press.

Olmos, Margarite Fernández, and Lizabeth Paravisini-Gebert, eds. 2001. *Healing Cultures: Art and Religion as Curative Practices in the Caribbean and Its Diaspora*. New York: Palgrave.

Philip, Marlene NourbeSe. 1990. "Managing the Unmanageable." In *Caribbean Women Writers: Essays from the First International Conference*, edited by Selwyn Cudjoe, 295–300. Wellesley, MA: Calaloux Publications.

Reid, Michelle. 2005. "Crossing the Boundaries of the 'Burn': Canadian Multiculturalism and Caribbean Hybridity in Nalo Hopkinson's *Brown Girl in the Ring*." *Extrapolation: A Journal of Science Fiction and Fantasy* 46, no. 3: 297–314.

Rogan, Alcena Madeline Davis. 2008. "Tananarive Due and Nalo Hopkinson Revisit the Reproduction of Mothering: Legacies of the Past and Strategies for the Future." In *Afro-Future Females: Black Writers Chart Science Fiction's Newest New-Wave Trajectory*, edited by Marleen S. Barr, 75–99. Columbus: Ohio State University.

Rutledge, Gregory E., and Nalo Hopkinson. 1999. "Speaking in Tongues: An Interview with Science Fiction Writer Nalo Hopkinson." *African American Review* 33, no. 4: 589–601.

Stewart, Robert, J. 1992. *Religion and Society in Post-Emancipation Jamaica*. Knoxville: University of Tennessee Press.

Walcott, Derek. 1991. *Dream on Monkey Mountain and Other Plays*. New York: Noonday Press.

Wood, Sarah. 2005 "'Serving the Spirits': Emergent Identities in Nalo Hopkinson's *Brown Girl in the Ring*." *Extrapolation* 46, no. 3: 315–26.

11

Towards a Canadian Islam

The Change-Making Power of Young Muslim Women

Rima Berns-McGown

Public narratives about Muslim women often portray them as submissive, trod-upon creatures who are to be pitied for their unfulfilled subservience and who need to be saved from narrow lives in which they are forced to wear headscarves and hide their light. These narratives, held by many mainstream politicians, policy-makers, and media alike, inform Quebec's Bill 21, which makes it illegal to perform a government job or receive government services while wearing the hijab. These same narratives permeate the "West," and Canada is no exception. In the name of "saving" women, they are profoundly Islamophobic and are used to justify legislation that itself serves to solidify Islamophobic public narratives, in an apparently endless vicious circle that deems Muslims and Islam as incompatible with Western ideas of feminism and equity.

But the lived experience of Canadian Muslim women is a far cry from that infantilizing portrayal. Operating at the intersections between diasporic and public spaces and institutions, many young Muslim women in Canada work to define and redefine their practice and embodiment of Islam as both feminist and socially just, in a variety of ways that are respectful of and demonstrate difference, from each other and from the practice of many of their elders. This chapter argues that young Muslim women from a wide variety of geographic and ethnic backgrounds – including but not limited to Somali,

Sudanese, Eritrean, Malaysian, Guyanese, Panamanian, Indian, Pakistani, South African, and Arab – are at the forefront of social change in Canada, in multiple ways that employ an anti-oppression, antiracism framework and which combat patriarchy, anti-Black racism, anti-Indigenous racism, homophobia, transphobia, and anti-Semitism. This action occurs within their communities and in the wider society, in addition to the growing and ever-present fight against Islamophobia that operates at both incidental and systemic, institutional levels. Their collective work and learning from each other and from racialized non-Muslim Canadians and Indigenous people is creating a practice of Islam that grounds it firmly in the Canadian context, and fuses together Canadian and Muslim notions of social justice.

The chapter is based on interviews and conversations with hundreds of Muslim women across Canada, as well as examples of public initiatives launched by Muslim women in the Toronto-Hamilton corridor. The excerpts quoted here have been drawn from interviews for two studies (Berns-McGown 2013; Monahan, Berns-McGown, and Morden 2014) that explored identity, belonging, and the enduring nature of trauma.[1] I work with a theoretical framework that holds that "diaspora" is a vibrant and ever-evolving space of connection between community and the wider society, as well as between "back home" and the adoptive home (Berns-McGown 2008, 8). I argue that within a global climate obsessed with identity politics, diasporic communities – and perhaps none more than Muslim women – play an enormous role in (re)creating the idea of what it means to be Canadian and what, indeed, the idea of "Canada" represents.

Diaspora is "best defined as a space of connections," and specifically two sets of tensions: that between the imagined homeland and the adoptive country, on the one hand; and between the "community" and the wider "mainstream" society on the other. To be "in the diaspora," then, "is to perceive oneself as linked to multiple places and to hold a complex identity that balances one's understanding of those places and the way one fits into each of them." It is not, by any means, necessarily nostalgic. It forces one to think deeply about "home" and "belonging" (Berns-McGown 2008, 8).

The young Canadian Muslim women I spoke to, most of whom were born in Canada to parents who were not, and whose knowledge of "back home" exists primarily through diasporic spaces and sometimes occasional visits, inhabit these tensions in ways that are fundamentally different from the ways that their parents do. Home is indisputably Canada, yet ever since 9/11 they have been faced with a climate of rising racism and Islamophobia and a public discourse that not only "others" Muslims but which regards Muslims, of all immigrant groups and communities, as perhaps uniquely un-Canadian, with values that are somehow incompatible with Canadian values.

I once, quite some time before I had embraced Islam myself, wrote a book review for a Canadian literary journal. In it, I argued that the authors' perspective on Islam and Muslims was, effectively, racist and Orientalist. The authors took issue with the review and complained to the editor of the magazine, which the editor took great pains to tell me. She challenged me to find some examples of Muslims with an understanding of what she took to be Canadian values of equity and inclusion. I told her about a young jilbab-wearing Muslim woman who insisted that queer Canadians have as much right to be accepted as she does, and I said that she is emblematic of her generation. The editor snorted, "good luck finding others who agree with her."

In fact, I knew a great many, and now I know a great many more. The editor was wrong, but in the years since, racism and Islamophobia have only increased, and many people in positions of power and influence continue to hold opinions like those of the former editor of the magazine.[2]

One of the tasks of combatting racism, in whatever form it occurs, is the need to make its sufferers fully human in the eyes of its perpetrators. This is what Desmond Cole writes about in his Twitter feed, his book, *The Skin We're In* (2020), and the 2017 documentary of the same name that he made with director Charles Officer about anti-Black racism in Canada. This is the essence of the Black Lives Matter movement. Black lives have to be declared to matter because the perpetrators of systemic racism do not hold that fact to be self-evident.

The Truth and Reconciliation Commission (2015) seeks in its Calls to Action to establish precisely the same understanding with regard to Indigenous people in Canada: horrors were perpetrated upon them because they were not seen as fully human. Horrors and indignities continue to be perpetrated upon them because they still are not seen as fully human. To see someone as fully human is to make inexcusable acts of racism or racist perceptions that, even unconsciously, lead to acts and systems that perpetrate racism.

Since 9/11, the "Islamophobia industry" in one way or another feeds and embellishes a narrative that diminishes the humanity of Muslims and demonizes Islam as a faith (Lean and Esposito 2012). Decades of federal legislation have, in the name of improving security, sharpened and reinforced the narrative that the Muslim community is problematic and uniquely troubled in its struggles to adapt or "integrate" into Canada. This is so despite mountains of evidence showing that violent extremism is an individual, not a community, trajectory.[3] Security experts repeatedly argued that Bill C-51, the Harper government's anti-terrorism act, does not make Canada safer (Forcese and Roach 2015). The Zero Tolerance for Barbaric Cultural Practices Act does not necessarily make women safer and may in fact make them less safe, but, despite the prevalence of domestic violence in all cultures, it does succeed in perpetuating the narrative of Muslims as uniquely given to violence against women (Sheikh 2015; SALCO 2018).

The media continue to describe murderous acts as "terrorism" only if they involve a Muslim perpetrator. After the 29 January 2017 massacre of six worshippers at a Quebec City mosque, for instance, the media tended to shy away from the term "terrorism" to describe the mass murder once it was determined that the perpetrator was a white Christian Québécois (Lum 2017). Quebec politicians were among those who agreed that their political rhetoric may indeed have emboldened the murderer and other perpetrators of hate crimes (Perreaux 2017).

Federal politicians, including recent Conservative Party of Canada leadership hopefuls such as Kellie Leitch and Chris Alexander, both former ministers in the Harper government, openly enable and encourage the Islamophobic narrative. These candidates have participated in such events as the 15 February 2017 Rebel Media forum at which at least one participant appeared to have given a Nazi salute (Kandaker 2017). The Conservative Party has not officially denounced these tactics and voted almost en masse (with two exceptions) against MP Iqra Khalid's post-massacre Motion 103 asking the House to condemn and study Islamophobia in Canada (Canadian Press 2017). Some mainstream commentators and organizations also objected to M-103 on the grounds that Islamophobia is a confusing concept that, they argued, precludes the right to critique Islam (Coren 2017). It is this environment of societal racism, in addition to the conservatism of many of their elders, that young Muslim women must navigate to create space for themselves.

"GOD AND I HAVE BEEN THROUGH A LOT"

The following excerpts of conversations are emblematic of strains of thought among young Canadian Muslim women. None of them are anachronistic or unusual. In this first excerpt, we see both analysis of the place of faith in a diasporic life and a regendering of the idea of "God," in addition to the speaker's clear understanding that there is no contradiction between being queer and being Muslim – regardless of the perceptions of others inside or outside the community. This speaker, twenty-four years old at the time of the interview, also discusses her connection to Canada and some of the complex ways in which she understands the Canadian diasporic space:

> God and I have been through a lot. I have come to know Her. It is not a ritualistic understanding. What God wants you to be is what you need to be for your own sake.
>
> I'm queer and have been in love with people who identify in different ways. It's been a struggle for others and for me and God. I have struggled to be in the affirming relationship with God that I grew up with. And then realizing that what God wants me to do is what I want to do.
>
> People's relationship with God evolves when they come here. In a conflict zone you have a bargaining relationship with God: help me through this and I will fast or pray or whatever it is. And there is also anger with God if you want someone to come back and they don't, or when you believe that bad things won't happen to good people and they do. You see people lose so much, it's easy to be angry.
>
> When you come here, God sits on the back burner for while, or God becomes a cultural, not a spiritual thing. Things I used to pray for were trivial compared with ten years ago when I was praying to Allah for an uncle to come back or my father to come and live with us. Now I was praying for the streetcar to come on time.
>
> I have a personal relationship with God, not structured by ritual. It is informed by my politics. God is in everything, not an omniscient being in the sky hanging on to the True Islam. I see God in people. That is political.
>
> The political me is the reason I have that understanding of God. Culturally I consider myself Muslim. I love the ritual. It is who I am. I love the community.
>
> The political me is a feminist. I understand my struggle in relation to everyone else's story. My struggle and lack of privilege and privilege are constructed in terms of others' privilege and lack of privilege and struggle.

> The way I see the world is coloured by my body and my being an African queer Muslim Black woman. Loss, war, community, healing, all inform the way I see politics. I know that I don't know.
>
> A lot of my perspective is due to being Canadian. Living in the space that is Canada has given me the ability to meet people who are extremely different from who I am.
>
> I do what I do because the reflections of me and people who look like me are rarely generated by people who look like me. I thought a counter-narrative was necessary. I felt a need to connect with my people in a positive way.
>
> I want to give people emotional uptake. I want to believe people. I know what it is to be told your experiences are not real. I want to give you a platform without telling you what to write or not to write. (S., North Sudanese woman, age twenty-four, born in Cairo; moved to Canada at thirteen.)

The following excerpt speaks to a point that a number of women have made: ironically, it is sometimes easier to embrace life as a Muslim in Canada than it was in the Muslim-majority countries where she grew up, not because of Canadian secularism but because of her freedom to reimagine and redefine Islam and her practice of it. This speaker is also clear that queer positivity and feminism are an important part of her Islam.

> I am very much Muslim now. This city has allowed me the freedom to see different ways of practicing Islam. There are so many rich practices, many of which embody resistance to mainstream Islam. I can embrace social justice, queer-positive, leftist, feminist Islam. I can have a Muslim identity and still express all those other parts of myself.
>
> It is inspiring to be in Toronto and see all those communities merge. It's a journey and I am still in the early stages of it.
>
> It is my own personal jihad.
>
> This city showed me you can leave all that baggage behind and can live with people as neighbours even if you don't agree. (M., Kenyan/Arab woman, age twenty-nine, moved to Canada at eighteen after many years of living in Saudi Arabia.)

People often turn to their faith as a way of dealing with the aftereffects of trauma, regardless of which spiritual tradition they belong to (Monahan, Berns-McGown, and Morden 2014). In the following excerpt, Islam offers refuge from trauma and a comforting constant in a world of flux, uncertainty, and alienation, both in the war "back home" and during a period of sometimes painful adjustment in Canada. In addition, this young woman describes how *not* wearing the hijab had "hidden" an important part of her identity, and how donning the hijab allowed her to become visible in a way that felt important to her:

> Once you go through those experiences, you want something to give you hope. We all suffered from severe depression ... Over the course of this everyone in the family became more religious. We did it individually, not as a group ...
>
> My perspective on all of this is definitely a result of my Canadianness. When I put the hijab on, I became more confident. I had always felt like I was hiding a part of me. I always had the desire and then afterwards I felt like I had nothing to hide. I can voice my opinions without being scared of how people will judge me ... I always am keen to tell stories about Afghanistan and about my religion. You can ask me anything. (N., Afghan Pashtun woman, age twenty-three, born in Kabul; moved to Canada at ten.)

The following excerpt illustrates the box in which many women find themselves diasporically: a Black Muslimah, born in Saudi Arabia and exposed to terrible racism both in the country of her birth and also in Canada, searches for ways to square the circles of her multiple identities and finds it through both intellectual and spiritual pursuits.

> Islam had always been part of my life: I respected and admired it and I was well-versed in the Qur'an. And Arab racism made me ask why being dark can possibly be a bad thing? I had been sheltered by money in Egypt but was very exposed to it in Canada.
>
> I am repelled by Arab racism, but I love and practice Arab culture. I began to feel a need for a connection to God. Deep down I had always had an interest and I had curbed it for many years.
>
> In university I took on a more proactive approach. I took courses in Near and Middle Eastern Civilization, I joined the Muslim Students Association, I had Muslim friends. It was nice to connect.

> There was pressure to wear the hijab that I resisted, but I began to pray. It was my way to unload. I was doing it because I wanted to.
>
> My own respect, appreciation, love for Islam grew. It has definitely affected me deeply. (A., Eritrean woman, born in Saudia Arabia; in her late twenties; moved to Canada at nine.)

Respondents sometimes spoke expressly of the importance of creating a "Canadian Islam," which reflects Canadian cultural norms and values:

> We need to create a Canadian Islam. It is very necessary … Saudi Islam can't be the measure.
>
> And we need a Muslim leader who understands Canadian society, politics, the fabric of society – as well as Islam – and who is respectable. Not to import someone from Egypt who can't speak English. (S., Somali woman, twenty-two, born in Toronto.)

Many women – and not only those who are young – spoke about the concurrence between what they see as Canadian and Muslim values:

> The values my parents instilled in us are good civic values – that there should be no borders, that you should treat people with compassion, kindness, caring. These are Muslim values and Canadian values; the only difference is the *shahada* [the Muslim declaration of faith]. (F., Pakistani woman, fifty-two, born in Pakistan; moved to Canada at thirty-nine.)

Many thought carefully about what it means to be in a diasporic space in Canada:

> Somali girls are doing amazing things. I have friends who are in medical school, law school, doing their MA – and we grew up in underprivileged neighbourhoods and didn't have all the advantages of kids who grew up knowing they were going to succeed.
>
> Being Canadian allows me to compare and contrast, to employ critical thinking, to see things from different sides and different perspectives. (L., Somali woman, twenty-six, born in Hargeisa; raised in Ottawa)

Several women spoke specifically of the suffocation and pain of Islamophobia and why, in an Islamophobic environment, they make the clothing choices they do:

> Ever since I put on the hijab and embraced Islam people have been more open and interested in learning and engaging. I work in the bank and one-on-one people always ask me questions.
>
> I don't feel it personally, but you can smell the Islamophobia in the ways that Islam is portrayed subliminally and otherwise in the media.
>
> It makes me want to speak out. I have freedom of expression. At the same time, always having to explain makes me suffocate: having to explain things that should be understood. (T., Afghan woman, born in Afghanistan, 1987; moved to Canada at eight.)

> There is domestic violence in every country, and I want to be the voice for Muslim women. I do sympathize with women who wear the hijab. Just because I don't wear it doesn't mean I don't support it, or women who do.
>
> My older sister has decided to wear it. I want to change the way women who wear it are viewed.
>
> People here choose to wear it – it takes a lot of strength and power. I have considered it but won't do it until I have gained the strength to do it.
>
> Women are objectified and subjectified in so many ways in the west. I know the showing off of bodies is seen by some people to be liberating but it is also objectifying women, which is its own form of oppression. The hijab is the respect of the body and the protection of it. But people who wear it do get glances, looks, call attention to themselves – it takes strength. (S., Afghan woman, born in Nova Scotia, 1989.)

> Two years ago I put on the hijab: I decided I believed it and had wanted to do it for a long time. I examined the things that were stopping me and decided they were not as important as God.
>
> One day my neighbour said to me, "I miss your beautiful hair." Which was her way of saying she didn't like the hijab. I said that I had cut it and there wasn't so much of it now. But also, I said she could come to my house and I would show it to her because I don't wear it everywhere.

> But I would never comment on her personal choices. It is because of a lack of equality, I think – people from the dominant society believe they have a right to comment on my choices. (B., Turkish woman, forty-four, born in Turkey; has lived in St John's for ten years.)

Sometimes the racism and Islamophobia that Muslimahs feel becomes their bridge to understanding the racism that Indigenous peoples experience. This woman's experience of Islamophobia also became the bridge to her rejection of homophobia and transphobia and to her open support for queer rights.

> I was the only Muslim girl in my high school and the only girl who wore the hijab. There were some younger girls in middle school who started wearing it because I did, so I was happy about that. I really loved the idea. I was tired of people judging me. I didn't know why they did. The staff were really judgemental. There was one teacher I was close to who said they were always talking about me in the staff room.
>
> There is a great deal of racism, much of it directed against Aboriginal people, and I have learned a lot about their culture. I can relate to a lot of it. I understand them. A lot of people are racist toward them. It's about ignorance.
>
> I think Aboriginal studies should be a requirement in university. I went to my first pow-wow this year. It was cool!
>
> People who grew up outside of Canada are more judgemental. I am different from my parents. I support queer rights and queer people. I have loved learning about different genders and helped out at Pride. I had an awesome time. (O., Libyan woman, twenty-two, born in Libya; moved to Saskatoon, Canada as a child.)

They learn different strategies for dealing with racism and Islamophobia:

> My mother wears it [hijab], and when we moved to Woodbridge and she was in the backyard starting a garden the Italian lady next door came out and said, we're nice people. As if to say, don't hurt us. And my mother said, "We're nice people too." And six years later when my parents left all the neighbours came out

> to see them and this lady cried and cried. I was angry but my mother's reaction got a better outcome. They are still friends. (T., Palestinian woman, thirty, born and raised in Jordan; moved to Canada at sixteen.)

Living in Canada and meeting Jews with different perspectives on Zionism and Palestine means that many Muslims, including those from Arab countries, separate their understanding of Jews from Zionism and do not make assumptions about what Jews believe about Israel/Palestine.

> My mom did not used to wear the hijab but when I was growing up, we were taught to pray and to fast – it was as much tradition as religion. My dad fasts and prays, although not always five times per day. My mom became devout about ten years ago and I was encouraged by that. I had wanted to put on the hijab before that.
>
> I got very involved with the MSA [Muslim Student Association] but became devout on my own. My sister made a promise to God that if she survived the war she would put on the hijab, but I was already wearing it. I began to wear it in high school.
>
> I went to a Catholic high school and there were a lot of Lebanese Catholics but also some Muslims and we all did it together. My mother had begun to listen to an Egyptian imam, Amer Khaled, and she really got into it. Then she took religion classes.
>
> My parents were generally against my wearing it. It was not about 9/11 and I never felt an Islamophobic backlash. I don't feel like I experienced anything bad afterwards.
>
> During the war I do remember thinking that I was not acting like a person who was about to die. Aside from saying the *shahada* in the taxi – because I thought I might die then and if I did I wanted those to be the last words on my lips – I didn't read the Qur'an more than usual. It was odd.
>
> My own understanding is that different people have different ways of being devout. God instils different passions in different people: some pray, some do community work, some show leadership. For me it is my academic work. I feel blessed to do it and it seems to be what I am supposed to be doing.

> I do identify as Arab Canadian most of the time. I do wear my Islam on my sleeve, so I don't declare it. Partly that's because I think I don't need to – it's obvious – but also, it's personal, it's about my relationship with God. I don't want to make it a political act. That's dangerous territory to get into, when people equate religion with politics.
>
> As a person who has suffered a cultural stigma, I am very aware of the problems of labelling people and refuse to do it. It's not about being Jewish. It has nothing to do with that. When I meet Jews here, I make no assumptions about what they think or their knowledge.
>
> I don't want people to make assumptions about me, so I don't make them about other people. (A., Palestinian woman, twenty-six, born in Abu Dhabi; moved to Montreal as an infant.)

The following excerpt illustrates the perception, held by many young Muslimahs, that wearing the hijab is both a performative and political act. For these women, wearing the hijab is a demand to be treated with respect.

> My decision to wear the hijab was about changing the perception of Muslims and being Canadian. I want to let people know that I am a Muslim person who cares about Canadian issues, Canadian politics, Canadian environmental issues …
>
> I wanted to change the perception of Muslims in Canada. I am Muslim and covered and Canadian. It was my way of asking people to accept me as I am. I want it to be a norm that one can be covered. It helps me too. This is why I decided to wear hijab. It wasn't really about my spirituality. I can be spiritual without wearing hijab. It was political – a political expression of identity. (Y., Sudanese woman, twenty-four, born in Sudan; moved to Canada at eight.)

CREATING SPACES FOR SOCIAL JUSTICE

There are numerous examples of public initiatives that young Muslim women have organized or undertaken recently that exemplify these various social justice concerns. The examples cited here are primarily focused on the Toronto-Hamilton-London region, but one can find initiatives like them across the country. Young Muslimahs have been at the centre of organizing initiatives with Muslim youth and Indigenous elders intended to work toward meaningful solidarity-based relationships with Indigenous people. They aim to broaden ties, increase understanding, and build activist solidarity between the two communities. Young Black Muslim women have been at the forefront of forums and discussions aimed at identifying and dismantling anti-Black racism and homophobia in Muslim spaces, including mosques and Muslim Student Associations on various campuses. These are difficult, tense, and pain-filled conversations, but that has not prevented them from being well attended, solutions-driven, and ongoing.

Young women are pushing for changes to the way mosques are run and to mosque boards – even at some of the largest and most well established in the country – in order advocate for changes in policies that will benefit them and to ensure their voices and perspectives are heard. Women have been active participants in the El-Tawhid Juma Circle, which has grown by leaps and bounds since it was created by El-Farouk Khaki, his husband, Troy Jackson, and University of Toronto lecturer Laurie Silvers in 2009. Its weekly *jummah* prayers once consisted of half a dozen people in El-Farouk and Troy's living room.[4] Now, Friday prayers invariably include between forty and sixty people. El-Tawhid is an LGBTQ-affirming, gender-equal space. Women give khutbahs, lead prayer, and give the call to prayer. People of all genders pray side by side and the mosque has no dress code. Its participants are enjoined to remember that Islam is not a monolith and to speak in terms of "my understanding," and "I believe ..." in the weekly discussion period so as not to shame others with different understandings of the faith. Participants are invited to introduce themselves at the end of prayers and to indicate their preferred pronouns. Young women are key to the mosque's administration.

Young Muslim women co-created Outburst! for the Barbra Schlifer Clinic in Toronto in 2013. Outburst! was a program aimed at giving space to young Muslim women and girls to define and achieve safety from violence on their own terms, in contrast to those who would define safety for them and dictate how it ought to be achieved. Above all, the program sought to create space for Muslim women and girls' agency, empowerment, and voice, within their communities and within the wider society.

Muslim women have also played a critical role in the Canadian media. Shireen Ahmed, for example, advocates powerfully for the right of girls to play sports in hijab. Ahmed uses the voice and platform she has earned, in traditional and social media, to denounce all forms of oppression, not only those aimed at Muslims (www.shireenahmed.com). Azeezah Kanji is a young Muslim columnist at the *Toronto Star* and program director at the Noor Cultural Centre. Kanji writes fearlessly and provocatively about official and systemic racism, including specifically anti-Black and anti-Indigenous racism; Islamophobia; the need for governments to address the Truth and Reconciliation Commission's Calls to Action; and equity throughout society.[5]

Young Muslim women are an integral part of social media campaigns that push back against Islamophobia – including Facebook groups such as the Coalition against White Supremacy and Islamophobia – and which also explicitly condemn anti-Semitism. Young Muslim women are pushing back against institutional racism and Islamophobia, and are being heard. Young Somali Muslimahs were key to the formation of the Justice for Abdirahman Abdi campaign after the thirty-seven-year-old Somali-Canadian with mental health issues was beaten to death by Ottawa police in July 2016. The group advocated for police accountability and has continued to make public presentations that push for the end to systemic racism. In late April 2017, taxi driver Vijay Bhatia was murdered by a fare. A couple of days later, the *London Free Press* included a profile of the accused, without any attempt to determine his motive, and no profile of the victim. Selma Tobah and Leila Almawy, two young Muslim Londoners, took issue with the newspaper. Why was the white murderer worthy of a profile when his brown, Muslim victim was not? In addition, without an attempt on the part of the reporter to understand the killer's motive, there was no lesson to draw on concerning how to keep other taxi drivers safe. The two women took to social media to shame the *London Free Press*'s approach to the story. By the end of the day, the paper had revisited the story and written a tribute to Bhatia, a community member beloved by many (De Bono 2017).

Some Muslim women are purposefully vocal on social media about their histories of sexual abuse and their insistence that rape culture change. They write about misogyny within their communities at the same time that they navigate and write about the violence of the wider community's anti-Black racism, Islamophobia, and misogyny. Although they deal with intense backlash, denial, and online attack, they stand strong, often with support of key family members, including parents. Riya Jama's social media presence provides an example of this form of activism (https://twitter.com/hausofriya).

The National Council of Canadian Muslims (NCCM) is staffed by young Muslim women, some of whom expressly support the rights of queer Muslims to be respected for who they are, as well as the necessity of the Canadian government addressing the Truth and Reconciliation Commission's Calls to Action. Amira Elghawaby, NCCM's former communications director, campaigns against anti-Semitism as assiduously as she does against Islamophobia (see Elghawaby and Farber 2016). She, and other activists within the community, act from the perspective that these two "isms" are intimately linked: to promote one is to make way for the other, and to eliminate one requires the elimination of the other.

Muslim women have been integral to recent campaigns to combat racism in Toronto and throughout Canada. Muslim women are central to Black Lives Matter Toronto (BLMTO) and to York Region District School Board (YRDSB) Kids Need Help, the lobby group that worked for the resignation of the YRDSB trustee who called a parent a particularly horrific racial slur, as well as working to have the board investigated by the Ministry of Education for its inequitable practices (Shum 2017). Muslim women are members of Salaam-Shalom, a group that reaches across the Muslim-Jewish divide to create bonds of understanding and meaningful discourse.

Yusra Khogali is a young Sudanese Muslim woman who is one of the founders of BLMTO and who works tirelessly to assert an anti-oppression, anti-racist, queer-positive, intersectional framework for social change, with the unwavering support of her family. In a striking illustration of the nexus of anti-Black racism and Islamophobia, Yusra, an actual Muslim woman pushing back at Islamophobic and racist narratives, has been attacked by columnists in mainstream media outlets for being an angry Black Muslim woman on more than one occasion when her comments at a rally and on Twitter were taken out of context.[6] She has continued to be a vocal and visible activist despite these attacks.

Young Muslimah lawyers such as Naseem Mithoowani and Zoya Alam have been working on civil rights cases, fighting for the rights of women to wear the niqab while taking the oath of citizenship (the Zunera Ishaq case) and the right of Muslim students to write their own khutbahs at jummah prayer when it was contested within the Peel District School Board (*CBC News* 2015; Alphonso 2017).[7] Both lawyers have had to contend with public, Islamophobic attacks for their work.

With regard to participation in mainstream politics, it is notable that young Muslim women signed up in droves to work on Jagmeet Singh's campaign to lead the federal NDP party, drawn to his social justice perspectives, his insistence that Canada fix its broken relationships with Indigenous peoples, and his framework that equity entails belonging for all Canadians, regardless of their race, skin tone, ethnicity, faith, sexual or gender identities, or background.

INTERSECTIONALITY AND DIVERSE VIEWS ON CANADA AND ISLAM

Some of the Muslim women discussed and quoted in this article are hijabis, a very few are niqabis, and some wear no identifying garments. They attend different mosques, are members of different communities, and have families and traditions rooted in different parts of the world. A great many were born in Canada; some came as young children (generation 1.5); and some as older children. Some are mothers themselves; some are married (at least one to another woman); some are single; some are divorced; and some are in relationships. They have in common a political awareness but no singularity of approach or way of expressing their Islam or their politics.

What they do share is an understanding that their interests – a Canada free of Islamophobia, where they are treated equitably and without harassment at school, at work, when accessing services, and when living their lives – are the same interests as those of non-Muslims who are also marginalized and the victims of intolerance, inequity, abuse, or stigma. That understanding also prompts them to examine Muslim institutions and to work toward ridding the latter of the same stigmas that are problematic in the wider society. In discussion groups and activist circles, and as they continue to tackle one specific issue after another, they find themselves in conversations with each other and with others who may point out perceptions that they may not have considered; viewpoints they had not taken into consideration but that are logically consistent with their own politics. They learn, unlearn, and adjust their positions.

Young Muslim women think increasingly from an intersectional perspective – understanding different intersections of oppression – but also an anti-oppression, antiracist framework, which necessitates working toward the elimination of all forms of oppression. In fact, it necessitates the understanding that those who are not affected by any specific form of oppression have privilege in that area and therefore a greater moral obligation to work for its elimination. This is not to say that each and every one of these women becomes an advocate for LGBTQ rights, but it does mean that they increasingly support those who are comfortable taking such public stances. It does mean that they increasingly push back at anti-Black racism or anti-Indigenous racism or anti-Semitism in Muslim spaces.

In June 2016, during Ramadan, after a gunman killed forty-nine people and wounded another fifty-three in an Orlando nightclub, a number of non-queer-identifying Muslims came together with Muslim and non-Muslim members of the queer-identifying community in Toronto to hold an *iftar*.[8] It was held at the 519 Community Centre in Toronto and was well attended. Non-queer-identifying Muslim women were among the organizers. The organizers experienced pushback from some members of their communities, but that pushback did not prevent joint statements of support from being written and signed by prominent imams and community members (Zhou 2016).

At a May 2017 fundraiser for NCCM, the keynote speaker was a young physician who was born and raised in Saskatoon, Alaa Murabit. Murabit finished high school at the age of fifteen and completed medical school in her parents' native Libya. She is also a UN High Level Commissioner on Health, Employment, and Economic Growth and a MIT Media Lab Director's Fellow. Murabit, who wears the hijab, spent her talk taking aim at mosque spaces and how narrow and unsupportive they can be for women. She made it clear that she has no time for racism or intolerance for queer people – Muslim or not. While she may have ruffled feathers, Murabit received a standing ovation from the packed hall.

The vast majority of adult Muslim women in Canada make their own decisions, for their own reasons, over whether or not to wear the hijab or other clothing that identifies them as Muslim. To be a visible Muslim can expose a woman to danger and harassment, especially in a time when open Islamophobia is on the rise. Visibly Muslim women face everything from rudeness on the street to verbal harassment and even physical abuse. Some women who choose to wear the hijab do so in spite of their families' concerns for their safety. Those who choose to wear the hijab do so for a variety of reasons, ranging from believing that the Qur'an's enjoinder to be "modest" encompasses covering their hair to a political desire to perform an important aspect of their identity.

Muslim women who are social justice advocates, whether or not they wear clothing that identifies them as Muslim, are united in their quest to create a country in which they are treated equitably *as Muslims*. Sometimes this means building up community institutions, networks, and forums. Sometimes it means engaging with Canadian institutions, systems, and frameworks of belief so as to make space for themselves and their communities. Sometimes it means doing both.

Regardless of how observant they are or how they observe their faith, their ability to be accepted unapologetically and to belong as Muslims in Canadian society is paramount. Among other things, this means advocating for changes in laws and public procedures that target Muslim Canadians; changes in political rhetoric that treats Muslims as uniquely incapable of being fully Canadian; and changes in the way Muslims and Islam are treated by media. It means combatting Islamophobia in the institutions that Muslims navigate on a daily basis, from school to universities to workplaces to healthcare and other services.

For many Muslims, civic engagement begins with understanding that Canada is a settler nation whose original sin – its genocide of Indigenous peoples – has yet to be rectified. Therefore, for many, being an ethical Muslim in Canada requires solidarity with Indigenous peoples in Canada. Indeed, for some Muslim women, identifying as proudly *Canadian* is dependent upon Canada's rectification of that original sin.

IMAGINING HOME

To be in the diaspora is not to constantly attempt to recreate "back home" in the adoptive home, but rather to navigate between the present and the past, between community (or communities) and society. It is to navigate between and among identities. It is to carve out belonging in a space that is not always immediately welcoming, in a way that feels true to oneself. In precisely this manner, the young Muslim women social activists profiled here are reshaping their practice of Islam in Canada, just as Islam has always been shaped by local conditions in every country around the world in which it is practised.

Obviously, not all Canadian Muslim social justice activists are either young or women, but young Muslimahs are the focus of this article precisely because the prevailing narrative that Muslim women need to be saved has had such mainstream salience. They share the belief, however they practise it and whether or not they perform it publicly or on their person, that Islam is a key part of their identity, and they are unapologetic about their adherence to it. They insist upon being treated with respect. They value the Canadian space to express themselves and their beliefs freely and they value the ideas that inform inclusivity and diversity. At the same time, they are horrified at the hypocrisy of white normativity: they are horrified that whiteness continues to be understood as the default institutional norm and that those who hold unconsciously to this norm uphold the image of diversity as honourable but do not see the disconnect between that image and ongoing racist and Islamophobic laws, practices, histories, and institutions.

For these young women, the practice and ethos of Islam is integrally tied to social justice, and not just social justice for Muslims, but for the entire society in which they find themselves living. It is global – reaching back to their homelands but not stopping there – and it is local, encompassing the lived reality of Muslim and non-Muslim individuals and communities across the country.

Young Muslimahs illustrate the tensions of living at the intersections of the wider society and their various diasporic communities – and insist upon reshaping those intersections to reflect their perspectives of what a good, Muslim life entails. There is nothing in that tired Islamophobic stereotype of the trod-upon Muslim woman that resembles the lives of these vibrant, engaged, and change-making Muslimahs, who are demanding that they be recognized and respected for who they are, and who insist upon observing Islam as a code for daily living whose emphasis is on social justice for everyone: a consciousness that is very much a product of the very particular Canadian diasporic spaces that they inhabit.

NOTES

1 The interviews for *"I Am Canadian"* (Berns-McGown 2013) were conducted between 2007 and 2011 and the interviews for *Perception and Reality* (Monahan, Berns-McGown, and Morden 2014) were conducted between June 2012 and July 2013.

2 The May 2017 public fracas over cultural appropriation and the resulting resignations of three editors from high-profile media positions (as of this

writing) indicate that attitudes like these continue to be prevalent in Canadian publications and media.

3 See, for example, the writing and commentary of Dr Stephanie Carvin, former security analyst for the government of Canada and assistant professor of International Relations at the NPSIA School, Carleton University, as well as the security analysis of Michelle Shepherd (2017), a *Toronto Star* security reporter whose Atkinson Fellowship gave her a year to research and write about these issues full-time.

4 *Jummah* prayers are communal prayers, held Friday around midday.

5 See, for instance, Kanji (2017).

6 For a sense of the controversy, see Baglow (2017).

7 *Khutbahs* are sermons delivered at *Jummah*.

8 An *iftar* is the meal that breaks the fast at sundown each day during Ramadan.

REFERENCES

Alphonso, Caroline. 2017. "Peel School Board Changes Controversial Decision on Muslim Prayers." *Globe and Mail*, 6 January.

Baglow, J. 2017. "White People Have No Right to Criticize Yusra Khogali's Anger." *rabble blogs*, 20 February 20. http://rabble.ca/blogs/bloggers/j-baglow/2017/02/white-people-have-no-right-to-criticize-yusra-khogalis-anger.

Berns-McGown, Rima. 2008. "Redefining 'Diaspora': The Challenge of Connection and Inclusion." *International Journal* 63, no. 1: 3–20.

– 2013. *"I Am Canadian": Challenging Stereotypes about Young Somali Canadians*. IRPP Study no. 38. Montreal: Institute for Research on Public Policy. http://irpp.org/wp-content/uploads/assets/research/diversity-immigration-and-integration/i-am-canadian/IRPP-Study-no38.pdf.

Canadian Press. 2017. "House Passes Anti-Islamophobia Motion M-103." *Global News*, 23 March. https://globalnews.ca/news/3330776/anti-islamophobia-motion-m-103-approved/.

CBC News. 2015. "Zunera Ishaq, Who Challenged Ban on Niqab, Takes Citizenship Oath Wearing It." 5 October. https://www.cbc.ca/news/politics/zunera-ishaq-niqab-ban-citizenship-oath-1.3257762.

Cole, Desmond. 2015. "The Skin I'm In." *Maclean's*, 21 April.

Coren, Michael. 2017. "The Rebel Hits a New Low." *The Walrus*, 14 March. https://thewalrus.ca/the-rebel-hits-a-new-low/.

De Bono, Norman. 2017. "Slain Cab Driver Remembered as Hard-Working, Funny Man Who 'Always Had Time for Family.'" *London Free Press*, 3 May.

Elghawaby, Amira, and Bernie Farber. 2016. "It Takes a Village to Combat Hatred." *Ottawa Citizen*, 23 November.

Forcese, Craig, and Kent Roach. 2015. "Bill C-51: The Good, the Bad … and the Truly Ugly." *The Walrus*, 13 February. https://thewalrus.ca/bill-c-51-the-good-the-bad-and-the-truly-ugly/.

Kandaker, Tamara. 2017. "Anti Anti-Islamophobia." *Vice News*, 16 February. https://news.vice.com/en_ca/article/wjzmj4/hundreds-rally-against-motion-calling-on-canadian-government-to-condemn-islamophobia.

Kanji, Azeezah. 2017. "Quietism Is Activism for the Status Quo." *Toronto Star*, 11 May.

Lean, Nathan, and John Esposito. 2012. *The Islamophobia Industry: How the Right Manufactures Fear of Muslims*. London: Pluto Press.

Lum, Fred. "The Quebec City Mosque Attack: What We Know So Far." *Globe and Mail*, 10 February. https://www.theglobeandmail.com/news/national/quebec-city-mosque-shooting-what-we-know-so-far/article33826078/.

McGillivray, Kate. 2019. "York Region Parent Files Human Rights Complaint against School Board over Trustee Byelection." *CBC News*, 22 March. https://www.cbc.ca/news/canada/toronto/charline-grant-human-rights-complaint-yrdsb-byelection-1.5066815.

Monahan, John, Rima Berns-McGown, and Michael Morden. 2014. *The Perception and Reality of "Imported Conflict" in Canada*. Toronto: The Mosaic Institute. http://mosaicinstitute.ca/wp-content/uploads/2016/05/15.pdf.

Officer, Charles, director. 2017. *The Skin We're In*. Toronto: 90th Parallel Film and Television Productions.

Perreaux, Les. "Quebec Media, Politicians Express Regret in Wake of Mosque Attack." *Globe and Mail*, 31 January.

Sheikh, Nabeelah. 2015. "Farrah Khan Speaks about Gender Violence." *The Medium*, 26 October 26. https://themedium.ca/features/farrah-khan-speaks-about-gender-violence/.

Shepherd, Michelle. n.d. "Five CSIS Employees Are Accusing the Spy Agency of Islamophobia, Racism and Homophobia in a $35-Million Lawsuit." *The Star* (accessed 31 July 2019). https://www.thestar.com/news/canada/2017/07/13/five-employees-accuse-canadas-spy-agency-of-islamophobia-racism-and-homophobia-in-35-million-lawsuit.html.

Shum, David. 2017. "Ontario Government Launches 'Urgent Review' of York School Board amid Racism Allegations." *Global News*, 26 January. https://globalnews.ca/news/3207433/ontario-government-launches-urgent-review-of-york-school-board/.

South Asian Legal Clinic of Ontario, 2018. "Perpetuating Myths, Denying Justice: 'Zero Tolerance for Barbaric Cultural Practices Act.'" https://www.salc.on.ca/FINALBILLS7STATEMENT%20updated%20nov%2018.pdf.

Truth and Reconciliation Commission of Canada. 2015. *Truth and Reconciliation Commission of Canada: Calls to Action*. Winnipeg: Truth and Reconciliation Commission.

Zhou, Steven. 2016. "Muslim Leaders Break Bread with Toronto Queers." *Now Magazine*, 29 June. https://nowtoronto.com/news/muslim-leaders-break-bread-with-toronto-queers/.

12

Diaspora, Spirituality, Kinship, and Nationhood

A Métis Woman's Perspective

Chantal Fiola

This collection foregrounds experiences of women and religion in diaspora; I was invited to provide an Indigenous perspective. As a Métis woman who is first-degree Midewiwin[1] and participates regularly in ceremonies, I was excited to focus on, for example, Métis women returning to the Midewiwin lodge. Elsewhere, I examine Red River Métis spirituality (Fiola, forthcoming); now, I had an opportunity to focus squarely on Métis women. However, I quickly realized that degree of specificity may be premature. Except my books, *Rekindling the Sacred Fire: Métis Ancestry and Anishinaabe Spirituality* (2015) and *Returning to Ceremony: Spirituality in Manitoba Métis Communities* (forthcoming), almost nothing has been published regarding Métis people going to ceremony, never mind a women-centred analysis that considers diasporic discourse. Discussing Indigenous women and spirituality in diaspora cannot be disconnected from the larger history of colonization. Considering Métis women returning to the Midewiwin lodge only makes sense when we understand Métis dispossession from our home territories, forced separation from our First Nations relatives, systematic devaluation of Indigenous women, forced Christianization, and internalization of colonial hierarchies of indigeneity. Therefore, this chapter examines such contexts and lays some of the necessary groundwork in the hopes of inspiring future dialogue on Métis women, spirituality, and diaspora.

Since the 1960s, the discourse on diaspora has grown from a historical focus on a few classic examples (Jewish, Greek Armenian) to include scholarship in the fields of anthropology, sociology, cultural studies, and political studies, and on the experiences of diverse peoples including African, Chinese, Filipino, and Iranian (Butler 2001; Clifford 2007; Pulitano 2007; Tölölyan 1996; Tölölyan 2012; Vertovec 2000). Indigenous experiences of dispossession, forced migration, and dispersal complicate this discussion; some scholars wonder if diasporas reach their limits with claims to indigeneity (Brydon 2000), while others contemplate Indigenous-specific diasporas (Clifford 1994; Haig-Brown 2009; Lilley 2006; McCall 2012; Rolls 2001). I aim to contribute to the discussion by exploring Métis and Anishinaabe kinship, spirituality, and nationhood, and how these can inform the discourse on diaspora and improve relationships between Indigenous peoples, settlers, and newcomers (diasporan and non-diasporan) living on Indigenous lands on Turtle Island (North America).

The Métis, a seminomadic, post-contact Indigenous people whose territory was disrupted by the international border between Canada and the United States (Hogue 2015), were forced from our birthplace after the Red River Resistance (1869–70) and the Manitoba Act (1870). The Métis attempted to establish new communities in places like St Laurent and Batoche, Saskatchewan, only to be forcefully dispersed again following the Northwest Resistance (1885). Government legislation and policies (scrip, treaties, the Indian Act, residential schools, and child welfare systems) further dispossessed the Métis of our land, kinships, culture, and spirituality. From scattered communities, the Métis Nation is reclaiming our sovereignty and re-establishing our connections to our homeland in central Canada. But I am getting ahead of myself again.

Métis, Anishinaabe, and Midewiwin protocol teaches me to first introduce myself so that we may know how we are related through place, clan, family, and spiritual community. Knowing how we are connected helps us understand our roles, responsibilities, and mutual obligations if we aim to be good relatives – whether our ancestors have been here for millennia, settled here in the last few hundred years, or are newcomers who have just arrived. The Midewiwin understand we are all related – we must figure out how and behave accordingly.

My ancestors on my father's side came originally from France in the 1600s, settling first in Quebec with some later moving to Manitoba to pursue agriculture. I grew up in the French, Catholic farming community of Ste-Geneviève, Manitoba, where my father's family settled generations earlier. Many of my relatives still live there. On my mother's side, we have Métis-Métis (i.e., Métis marrying Métis) ancestry dating back seven generations. My ancestors Bostonnais (Pierre) Pangman Jr and his wife, Marie Wewejikabawik, were a founding family of St Laurent in the early 1800s.[2] A renowned bison hunter, and one of four North West Company-designated "Chiefs of the Halfbreeds" ("Captains of the Hunt," along with Cuthbert Grant Jr), Bostonnais was one of the first to be arrested for ignoring the Pemmican Proclamation issued by the first governor of the Red River colony.[3] Two dozen of my ancestors were issued scrip but, due to the legacy of colonization, we no longer carry memory of what happened to our scrip or the land promised to us.[4] While many Métis were pushed out of Manitoba after 1870, my ancestors were among those who chose to stay, facing oppression brought by white settlers from English Ontario and a foreign government that disregarded the terms of confederation. My mother grew up in St Laurent; many of my relatives still live there and speak *Michif* (Indigenous language composed especially of Cree verbs and French nouns). Before further discussing Métis dispossession, let us consider the meanings of *diaspora* and Indigenous diasporas.

DEFINING *DIASPORA*

In its simplest definitions, diaspora means the dispersal of a people from an original homeland (Butler 2001, 189); "to scatter people as seed is scattered for planting" (Lilley 2006, 33). More complicated definitions offer checklists for identifying a diasporic people. William Safran (1991) suggests the following criteria: dispersal to one or more locations, collective mythology of homeland, alienation from homeland, idealization of return to homeland, and ongoing relationship to homeland. Kim Butler agrees with three of these basic features of a diaspora – dispersal to two or more locations (scattering), some relationship to an actual or imagined homeland (foundation from which diasporan identity may form), self-awareness of the group's identity – and adds a fourth feature: its existence over at least two generations (multigenerational) (2001, 192). Yet Butler is quick to critique checklists as reifying identity since identity is never fixed. She proposes a shift away from defining whether a group qualifies as a diaspora, and instead focuses on five dimensions of diasporan *analysis*: (1) reasons for, and conditions of, the dispersal; (2) relationship with the homeland; (3) relationship with the hostland; (4) interrelationships within communities of the diaspora; and (5) comparative studies of different diasporas (195). She distinguishes between micro-diasporas (multiple destinations within a nation) and macro-diasporas (encompassing several nation-states) (196).

The term *diaspora* now describes several categories of people: expatriates, expellees, political refugees, alien residents, immigrants, and ethnic and racial minorities (Safran 1991, 83). Some suggest that white settlers who voluntarily left Europe to colonize foreign lands can be considered a diaspora (Lilley 2006). Steven Vertovec (2000), in agreement with James Clifford (1994) and Phil Cohen (1993), worries that the concept of diaspora is being too widely appropriated and risks becoming ineffective; the overuse and under-theorization of the term is threatening its descriptive usefulness (6). If everyone is diasporic, the term loses its meaning.

This resonates with a long-standing problem afflicting the Métis: when biological determinism (blood quantum, racial mixing) is used to define Métis (i.e., anyone with any degree of Indigenous and non-Indigenous ancestry including white people with one Indigenous ancestor 200 years ago), the unique history, culture, languages, and nationhood of the Métis is erased. If everyone is Métis, that term too becomes meaningless. The problem deepens when such individuals create organizations claiming to represent the Métis Nation, obtain intervenor status in high-level court cases impacting our nation, and demand section 35 Aboriginal rights. In eastern Canada, there is now an explosion of white settlers newly self-identifying as "Métis" in adulthood after finding one Indigenous ancestor in their genealogy from hundreds of years ago (or fabricating one); this type of white privilege, ethnic fraud, and cultural appropriation impedes Métis Nation sovereignty (Andersen 2014; Gaudry 2016; Gaudry 2018; Gaudry and Leroux 2017; Leroux 2019). With this in mind, let us take a closer look at the relationship between Indigenous peoples and diasporic discourse.

INDIGENOUS DIASPORAS

Scholars increasingly believe colonial dispossession experienced by Indigenous peoples can indeed be described as diasporic; exploring this relationship exposes tensions that can further the discourses of diaspora and Indigenous nationhood. James Clifford argues the following: "Diasporas are dispersed networks of peoples who share common historical experiences of dispossession, displacement, adaptation, and so forth ... [Thus d]ispersed [Indigenous] tribal peoples, those who have been dispossessed of their lands or who must leave reduced reserves to find work, may claim *diasporic* identities. Inasmuch as their distinctive sense of themselves is oriented toward a lost or alienated home defined as aboriginal (and thus 'outside' the surrounding nation-state)" (1994, 309). As Ian Lilley (2006) points out, Clifford acknowledges that describing Indigenous experiences of dispossession as diasporic is contentious, given Indigenous claims that "stress continuity of habitation, aboriginality, and often a natural connection to the land" (34). Canadian courts have ruled that in order to identify the existence of section 35 Aboriginal rights (Constitution Act, 1982) and Aboriginal title to land, an Indigenous community must prove continuation of habitation in the disputed area and control over the region (to the exclusion of other Indigenous groups) before foreign (European/Canadian) rule was established. The historic mobility of many Indigenous groups (Métis included) across vast traditional territories, and the dispossession resulting from colonization, can make this challenging. This also risks perpetuating harmful stereotypes of Indigenous people as frozen in time; proving "aboriginality" and a "natural connection to the land" raises the familiar authenticity debate. To justify our rights to the courts, Indigenous people must prove our authenticity. Often, we are expected to conform to stereotypes of 1800s Plains Indians – "But, you don't look like an Indian/ Métis!" Here, Lilley encourages us to take Clifford's advice: "'in addressing the spectrum of indigenous separations from, and orientations to, homeland, village or reservation, we need to complicate diasporic assumptions of 'distance'"; "Indigenous diasporas need not involve dispersal over large distances or across major political boundaries" (2006, 36). Let us consider examples of Indigenous diaspora over varying distances.

Discussing Australian Indigenous people, Mitchell Rolls reminds us that "most Aborigines are not on their land, in their country, or whatever term you prefer. They are elsewhere, and they are elsewhere (urban populations for example) in large numbers. And children's children's children are born in that elsewhere" (2001, 17). Hokulani Aikau offers the example of Indigenous Hawaiians "who have been exiled from their homeland and who carry their own history of dispossession, exploitation, and expropriation with them as they settle in the diaspora" (2010, 479). Aikau explains that Polynesian Latter-day Saints (in this case, Indigenous Hawaiians colonized by white Mormons) moved to Utah in the late nineteenth century to establish a religious homeland (Iosepa) in the traditional territory of the Skull Valley Goshute Nation (who had already been displaced by white Mormons) (483, 486). Aikau challenges the belief that Indigenous people become "less native" the longer they live away from their homeland; Indigenous identity (including relationship to homeland and genealogy) is carried with us through dispossession and migration. Commenting on their complex relationship with land in Utah, Aikau describes a major event in the Iosepa festival where Hawaiian Latter-day Saints clean the cemetery where the bones of their ancestors are buried in Goshute soil. Aikau warns that "making … [a Hawaiian] Indigenous claim to land in Utah, even when done with an Indigenous framework … is predicated upon forgetting a prior indigenous relationship to the same land, namely that of the Skull Valley Goshute tribe" (492). This raises the potential for, as Benjamin Smith says, "identity claims of diaspora people [to] be rejected by other Indigenous people who have remained on their country" (quoted in Lilley 2006, 35). The Goshute are not the only ones who could make such a claim.

For several years, former regional Assembly of First Nations (AFN) chief Isadore Day (and former chief of Serpent River First Nation) has denied Métis rights to land and potential revenue from resource extraction in Ontario (Newlove 2016; Raby 2010).[5] The Métis descendants of signatories to Treaty 3 (1875 adhesion) have a legitimate claim to land in Ontario; this legitimacy deepens when we consider the Supreme Court of Canada ruling in *R. v. Powley* ([2003] 2 SCR 207), which declared section 35 Métis hunting rights in Sault Ste Marie, Ontario. Treaty 3 is the only historic treaty that Métis were permitted to sign as a collective; where does this leave Métis rights to land in other parts of Canada?

The history of the Métis Nation is intricately tied to colonization, dispossession, forced dispersal and relocation, settlement, and policies of segregation, marginalization, and assimilation that continue to impact Métis people, including our relationships with spirituality. By the late eighteenth and early nineteenth centuries, the Métis were recognized as a distinct Indigenous people in what would become Manitoba. However, we were punished for negotiating the confederation of Manitoba. John A. Macdonald sent Colonel Garnet Wolseley and the Red River Expeditionary Forces (RREF) to ensure a smooth transition from the Métis provisional government to a provincial government. The RREF wreaked havoc for two years (physically assaulting Métis men, raping Métis women, and preventing Métis participation in elections) before being reigned in (Fiola 2015). Many Métis also grew tired of waiting for land promised in the Manitoba Act and moved out of province after seeing the corruption of the scrip system.

When Métis attempted to establish a new homeland in what would become Saskatchewan, they were again pushed out by a colonial government and replaced by white settlers. Métis took up arms (Northwest Resistance, 1885) only after the failure of repeated peaceful attempts to gain an audience with the Canadian government. Again, the Métis were punished for trying to protect their nation; they would become "the forgotten people/road allowance people" during a dark period of oppression lasting until after World War I. The government refused to let Métis collectively into the Numbered Treaties signed across Canada (1871–1921). The Indian Act (1876) excluded Manitoba Métis from registered Indian status and the associated benefits. Métis people were not spared from the residential school system and the Sixties Scoop; both forcefully removed thousands of Indigenous children from their families, placing them in white institutions and homes where their language, culture, and spirituality were forbidden. The Métis were dispossessed of our lands, culture, bison governance system, and spirituality, and were scattered throughout Canada and the northern United States. Many of us continue to live in or near our homelands, yet our sovereignty is denied by colonial governments and by many settlers, newcomers, and diasporic peoples who moved here.

DISPOSSESSION OF MÉTIS SPIRITUALITY

Several factors have historically influenced Métis relationships with spirituality, including ancestry, the presence or absence of a Euro-Canadian father, and proximity to Euro-Canadian towns, city centres, and other Indigenous communities. French policy and the North West Company encouraged intermarriage between European settlers and Indigenous women, while the Hudson's Bay Company officially discouraged this (Van Kirk 1985). French Catholic priests were supportive of intermarriage if Indigenous people converted to Catholicism and married in a church. Métis have a long history of interconnection with the Catholic Church; priests often joined us on our bison hunts, wintered with us, and delivered religious instruction to us (Fiola 2015; Huel 1996). While some Métis requested a priest in their community, the pressures to convert to Christianity became overwhelming and most Métis were not free to practise Indigenous spirituality. In fact, the Canadian government effectively made Indigenous ceremonies illegal for three-quarters of a century following the 1885 Resistance (Pettipas 1994). Colonial legislation and systems, as discussed above, created forced divisions between Métis and First Nations kin (Fiola 2015). Métis were constantly told by government and church that we are wholly different from First Nations. While Métis are distinct from First Nations, such colonial tactics ignored our kinship relationships; many of us internalized these messages. Divisions are worsened by resource extraction and government refusal to honour Aboriginal title and rights, which pit us against each other. We have forgotten the kinship relationships, and historic alliances and treaties between our peoples.[6]

One impact of such colonial efforts is the disconnection of Métis people from Indigenous spirituality. After generations of forced assimilation, many Métis believe that Métis people only go to church and First Nations people go to ceremony; this ignores First Nations conversion, and spiritual syncretism, it erases historic Métis participation in ceremonies, and it discourages Métis from participating in ceremony, which is our birthright (Fiola 2015 and forthcoming). Such internalization (and syncretism) can be heard in an interview I conducted with a Métis citizen named Benny who states, "There's Michif [Métis] people I've known that have a Catholic funeral for somebody but cut their hair off and put it in the coffin; I had an old woman once say to me 'No, to be Michif is to be Catholic! Now could you please pull the car over, I have to bury some medicines'" (Fiola 2015, 166).

Many Métis (and First Nations) people have also internalized Eurocentric patriarchal beliefs regarding gender. Victorian ideals of womanhood began to replace the power and authority Indigenous women held in many Indigenous nations, including property and marriage rights and political influence (Anderson 2000). Colonization shattered the respect that many Indigenous nations held for other genders and sexualities (Fiola 2020; Wilson 2008; Jacobs, Thomas, and Lang 2007). The sacredness of women and two-spirit people is acknowledged in Anishinaabe Creation Stories and in the important roles held by such individuals in spiritual ceremonies (Fiola 2020). Today, we are living a colonial legacy of lateral violence whereby women and two-spirit people are told, sometimes by respected elders, that "women's subordination to men is traditional," and that "homosexuality did not exist on Turtle Island until white people brought it here" (Fiola 2020).

Darren Préfontaine, Todd Paquin, and Patrick Young (2003) say it is impossible to discern a common Métis religion or spirituality. I argue that Métis spirituality can be understood as a continuum with Indigenous spirituality on one end, Christianity on the other, and syncretism in between (Fiola forthcoming). While much has been written about Métis relationships with Christianity (Gareau 2021; Huel 1996; McCarthy 1990; Widder 1999), almost nothing has been published regarding Métis relationships with Indigenous spirituality (Fiola 2015 and forthcoming; Ghostkeeper 1986). Despite this, Métis people are increasingly reconnecting with Indigenous spirituality (Fiola 2015 and forthcoming).

REKINDLING KINSHIP, SPIRITUALITY, AND NATION-TO-NATION RELATIONSHIPS

Grappling with the relationship between Indigenous experiences of dispossession and who counts as diasporic peoples, Clifford asks the following: "Should we think of a continuum of indigenous and diasporic situations? Or are there specifically indigenous kinds of diasporism? Lived dialectics of urban and rural? On *and* off the reservation? Island *and* mainland native experiences? ... It is crucial to recognize patterns of visiting and return, of desire and nostalgia, of lived connections across distances and differences." He continues, "What traditional practices allow one to feel rooted without being localized? ... How do moving people take their roots with them...? And are there specifically indigenous kinds of homes away from home?" (2001, 470). Yes, Indigenous peoples have traditional practices that remind us we are connected (rooted) no matter how far we travel or are forcibly relocated.

Midewiwin Anishinaabe Creation Stories teach us that we are born of the soil of the earth and given life through spirit (Benton-Banai 1988). We are connected through our ancestors to the beginning of human life. This does not change when we relocate. The clan system means that we have family wherever we go (Dumont 1985). Kinship relationships give our lives meaning; they teach us about who we are, our roles and responsibilities to our communities and beyond. *Bezhik mide, Métis kwe ndaaw, biizhew nidoodem* (I am a first-degree Midewiwin, Métis woman who belongs to the lynx clan). All over Turtle Island, I will have Métis, First Nations,[7] Midewiwin, or clan relatives who could welcome me. In areas without a lynx clan, another clan will be considered closely related to the lynx with mutual kinship obligations. The same goes for visitors who travel through my territory and those who move here (ideally, they would be invited or our peoples would have come to an agreement for cohabitation). Good neighbours, and good humans, learn each other's clan system and figure out how we can relate for *mino-bimaadiziwin* (good, healthy, balanced life).[8] Our Creation stories teach us that all humans are related as children of *Gizhi Manidoo* (Creator); it is our responsibility to figure out how to live peaceably. Importantly, our kinship relationships extend beyond humans to animals, spirit beings, and to the land.

There are many challenges to *mino-bimaadiziwin* and understanding our kinship relationships; however, due to the legacy of (ongoing) colonization that has disconnected Métis and other Indigenous peoples from ourselves, our families, our communities, our nations, our clan systems, our governance systems, and our ceremonies, we were forced to forget and to assimilate. Today, many of us no longer have memory of our family's clans, have never heard our Creation Stories, have never participated in ceremony. We have internalized the stories, beliefs, and values of white settlers. Euro-Christian patriarchal beliefs that disparage two-spiritedness and relegate women and dark skin to a lower class were not our beliefs.[9] Thankfully, our resilience is stronger than (neo)colonization; we never gave up, and never will.

Beginning especially in the post-World War II era, Indigenous peoples on Turtle Island have been undergoing a rebirth of our cultures and regaining pride in our identities. The civil rights movement and minority movements, such as the Red Power Movement, encouraged a remembering of our ancestral ways, including ceremony. We are increasingly seeking out elders and knowledge holders who retained some of that knowledge; we are relearning our languages; remembering our subsistence and cultural pursuits; rebuilding our relationships with place, with our earth, with each other. Midewiwin believe this time of reconnection was prophesied (Seven Fires Prophecy) before white people arrived on Turtle Island (Benton-Banai 1988; Fiola 2015).

Along with a return to ceremonies, we are remembering and nurturing our nation-to-nation relationships. As in the pre- and early-colonial periods, we invite those living in our homelands to build nation-to-nation relationships with us; we expect our sovereignty as self-determining Indigenous nations to be recognized and have demonstrated a willingness to acknowledge yours. This can be seen in the early treaties between Indigenous and settler peoples on Turtle Island, especially the Two Row Wampum belt.[10] Our cultures and histories contain the building blocks of our nation-to-nation relationships and can help us be good neighbours today. We can also look to traditional Indigenous governance models, such as confederacies, for how to welcome visiting nations into our homelands while both sides retain sovereignty. Of course, not every group will be acknowledged as sovereign within our homelands, but there is protocol for sharing land, resources, and respecting each other's systems. Indigenous governance systems held women in high esteem – for example, Haudenosaunee Clan Mothers selected male chiefs, removed their chieftainship, declared war, or a return to peace (Haudenosaunee Confederacy n.d.). In governance systems across many Indigenous nations, women participated in decision-making and had rights to their bodies, homes, property, children, and land. Today, it is often women and young people on the front lines of our self-determination efforts and efforts to protect the waters, earth, and children, though the media prefers to interview our conspicuous male leaders wearing large headdresses. These men certainly have a role to play, but need to take care not to co-opt our struggles for their personal recognition and ego (often becoming loud spokespeople overshadowing the women and youth who began the efforts in the first place). Our men have also been impacted by colonization. The Indian Act band council system forbade Indigenous women from participating in governance until 1951 (First Nations and Indigenous Studies 2009); some Indigenous men internalized the colonial belief that women are not fit to be leaders. We are actively decolonizing ourselves and unlearning settler ways that distanced us from *mino-bimaadiziwin*. In fact, since colonization has impacted all peoples, we would all benefit from decolonizing unhelpful beliefs in a collective effort to strive for *mino-bimaadiziwin*. The same goes for the discourse on diaspora and relationships between Indigenous peoples, settlers, and newcomers (whether they arrived voluntarily, sought refuge, or were forced to relocate).

DECOLONIZING DIASPORIC DISCOURSE

Celia Haig-Brown, a non-Indigenous scholar, encourages "each reader to respond to the question, 'Whose traditional land are you on?' as a step in the process of decolonizing our countries and our lives" (2009, 4). She encourages us to ask "not only where do people of the diaspora come *from*, but where have they come *to*?" (5). In a similar vein, Aikau says the members of the Hawaiian Indigenous diaspora in Utah (on Goshute land) need to decolonize their stories and relationships: "In substantiating this identity [of Polynesian Saints in Utah], we delete, erase, and silence those aspects of stories that would ask us to question the authority and decision of church leaders [to move onto Goshute land in the first place]" (2010, 496). She reflects critically on how we claim land and suggests "a process of unsettling our settler-colonial tendencies ... Which has the potential to reconnect us to the Goshute tribe ... Unsettling settler-colonialism is also about returning land to native peoples." She encourages Indigenous Hawaiian Latter-day Saints in Utah to go beyond understanding their claims to the land for their own benefit and to "work with the Skull Valley Goshute tribe to help them reclaim their land. Doing so could mean we do not get to expand the footprint of the Iosepa historical site, but it might be a first step in re-establishing a relationship with the people whose land has nourished us spiritually, emotionally, and physically" (498). This gives me hope and reminds me of the Métis and Anishinaabeg who are also trying to decolonize our relationships and to remember how we shared lands and territories before disruption by foreign occupation and governance.

In the early nineteenth century, the Plains Cree (Nêhiyawak), Assiniboine (Nakota), Saulteaux/Chippewa (Anishinaabeg), and Métis (Michif) joined together in a military alliance known as the Iron Alliance (Fiola forthcoming; Innes 2013). As newcomers to the Plains, the Anishinaabeg and Métis needed to be "brought in" to the area and alliance; this occurred via Sundance ceremony in 1820. At that Sundance – said to be the largest ever on the Plains, with fourteen centre poles and 1,500 dancers! – a song given by Creator to the ceremony-leader, Many Eagle Set, was shared to commemorate the "Unity of the People" (Spalding 2004, 16). At that time, those nations agreed to an alliance against the Dakota and the Hudson's Bay Company (Spalding 2004; St-Germain 2015). The gathering joined the nations of the alliance together as one people who would use the

Sundance to survive into the future and for their children. Fast forward to the summer of 2004, delegates from the Métis Nation of Ontario (MNO) and the Manitoba Metis Federation (MMF), among others, came in ceremony to the Turtle Mountain Indian Reserve in Belcourt, North Dakota to be gifted that song, again commemorating their nation-to-nation relationship. There, Francis Eagleheart Cree, great grandson of Many Eagle Set and keeper of the song among the Chippewa of Turtle Mountain, gifted the song to Tony Belcourt who is now considered keeper of the song for the Métis.

Fast forward again to 2016, and we witness another effort to strengthen the relationship between the Métis and Anishinaabe nations. According to Isaac Murdoch, one of the organizers of the Painted Hand Ceremony gathering in Serpent River First Nation,[11] a purpose of the gathering was to revisit, feast, and nourish old treaty arrangements between the Métis and Anishinaabe nations, including relationships forged by Chief Shingwauk and the Métis in the Sault Ste Marie region in the 1800s, and the Iron Alliance further west. Murdoch reminds us that our identity as Indigenous peoples is rooted in the land, not in political organizations or governments, whether Indigenous-run or not. He believes that the emphasis on difference between Métis and Anishinaabe peoples is a result of a rights-based agenda that pits us against each other for scraps of power/rights handed out by the Canadian government. Murdoch suggests instead that we highlight our kinship relationships and our similarities, which can be seen in our languages and ceremonies, including sweat lodge, pipe ceremonies, fasting, face painting, tattooing, and pictographs.[12]

These efforts to nurture a sovereign nation-to-nation relationship between the Métis and the Anishinaabe nations can teach us about "relational sovereignty" (Clifford 2001, 483) between Indigenous nations living in our homelands (or forcibly relocated onto the homeland of another Indigenous nation), as well as between Indigenous nations and settlers/newcomers/diasporic peoples now living in our homelands. Again, this does not mean that everyone who comes to live in Indigenous lands will be accorded sovereignty. Indeed, many Indigenous peoples today do not recognize the legitimacy of the Canadian government – choosing instead to identify with Anishinaabe, Haudenosaunee, or Michif nationhood, for example. In 1996, the Royal Commission on Aboriginal Peoples (RCAP) recommended that Canada recognize inherent Indigenous self-government (which could take many forms) and encouraged a return to a nation-to-nation relationship as was envisioned via the Two Row Wampum. RCAP suggested the inclusion of an Aboriginal Order of Government, called the First Peoples' House, alongside the House of Commons and the Senate, in Parliament (volume 2, chapter 3, section 3). RCAP explained that the First Peoples' House would be composed of Indigenous leadership representing the Indigenous population of Canada and would advise the other two houses on matters affecting Indigenous peoples. While a good step, this does not go far enough; the other two houses retain more power and could make decisions affecting Canada without Indigenous input.

Exciting conversations are being had envisioning a truly nation-to-nation relationship between Indigenous peoples, settlers, newcomers, and diasporic peoples in Canada. Discussions between discourse on diaspora and Indigenous sovereignty can contribute understanding. As Sophie McCall suggests, theories of diaspora may offer vital insights into the history of displacement of Indigenous peoples in Canada and into the experiences of mixed-race, urban, and off-reserve Indigenous people "who may or may not maintain strong ties to a sovereigntist nation based on a defined territory" (2012, 22). On the other hand, McCall states, "Indigenous sovereigntist perspectives may help articulate community-based processes of participatory citizenship." McCall encourages us to resist the tendency to hierarchize diasporas and instead to "build coalitions between disparate minority histories and to participate in a model for relational history writing … We might garner a better understanding of sovereignties-in-motion, or confederacies, and develop new ways of conceptualizing Native nationalisms that address the wide range of relationships that Aboriginal peoples have to their ancestral territories." After all, she states, "diasporic and Indigenous-sovereigntist standpoints share the desire to challenge settler nationalisms and expose the exclusions that have produced Canadian citizenship" (ibid.). Moreover, "diasporic and Indigenous communities share common experiences of loss, uprooting, and adaptation; they emphasize in a comparable manner the importance of maintaining the homeland and dreaming of one day 'returning' to the homeland; and they strategically 'bypass an opposition between rootedness and displacement'" (27). Indigenous and diasporic communities can learn much from each other's struggles to retain a connection to our respective homelands.

Relationship to homeland is complicated by the fact that most Indigenous peoples in Canada now live in urban areas (Urban

Aboriginal Peoples Study 2010). As discussed above, the Métis were dispossessed of our lands in Manitoba after 1870, then again from our lands in Saskatchewan after 1885. We are now scattered throughout Canada and the northern United States. Except for eight Métis settlements in Alberta, the Métis do not have a federally recognized, constitutionally protected land base (Métis Settlements General Council n.d.). Sovereignty and self-determination are nearly impossible without a land base. The Métis Nation was attacked on all fronts by colonial forces and pressured to assimilate politically, economically, and spiritually; we are now rebuilding our nation on all fronts. This includes no longer fearing self-identification as Métis,[13] remembering our kinship relationships with our First Nations relatives, finding our way back to the spiritual lodges, and relearning our Indigenous languages. Along with First Nations, we are also remembering the sacredness of our women and two-spirit community members and reclaiming our roles in politics, economics, ceremony, and so on.

Métis lawyer and popular blogger Chelsea Vowel illustrates these multilayered efforts of contemporary Métis self-determination in her decision to move from Montreal back to her family's home territory in Alberta despite not having a job waiting for her or money to build a house, and having three daughters. She contemplates what it means to move back home when you are Métis: "This move will mean accepting poverty again. It will mean gruelling work building a home by hand, the way people did in my grandfather's time. It also means returning to the support of my community, returning to the land, the medicines, the lakes. It means having the tools I need to ensure my children learn their culture and language in the place where those things live. It means access to the kind of cultural continuity I have been unable to access here in Quebec" (Vowel 2016). What Vowel lists here – community, land, medicines, lakes, language, culture, and cultural continuity – amounts to Métis spirituality. Indigenous spirituality is more than specific ceremonies; it is an all-encompassing way of life. Regarding the dialogue about Indigenous relocation happening in Canada, Vowel further explains that while many Métis people left our home communities and territories for many reasons, Canadians need to recognize "the battles we [Métis] fight in order to go home ... Canadians aren't asking us what we want. You'd be surprised how many of us would say *we want to go home*" (emphasis added).

Whether intentionally or not, Vowel also reminds us that some Indigenous people do not identify as "Canadian"; we (Métis included) were here in our birthlands before confederation. And, while some of us were open to joining confederation and treaty-making, a history of broken promises exposes Canada's ongoing refusal to acknowledge Indigenous sovereignty. Therefore, today, some Indigenous people continue to self-identify with their nation (e.g., Métis Nation, Anishinaabe Nation, etc.), rather than as Canadian citizens. This is an act of self-determination and a push for a nation-to-nation relationship with Canada.

Also worth repeating here is the harm inherent in the trend whereby settlers self-identify as Métis since Canada was built by Indigenous and settler nations, and therefore the nation and its inhabitants must be "Métis." Such logic, espoused for example by John Ralston Saul in *A Fair Country* (2009), is based on biological determinism (i.e., Métis = anyone with any degree of real or imagined Indigenous racial mixture), and ignores distinct Métis history, languages, culture, and nationhood. Such a trend can be understood as a settler "move to innocence" (Tuck and Yang 2012), which conveniently homogenizes Indigenous and settler people into one body politic, erases Indigenous sovereignty, and justifies settler occupation of Indigenous lands. When settler Canadians are encouraged to self-identify as Métis based on such flawed reasoning, it threatens Métis sovereignty by swelling our numbers and enabling settlers to "speak as Métis," weighing in on issues affecting the Métis Nation (Andersen 2014; Gaudry and Leroux 2017; Gaudry 2018; Leroux 2019).

Returning to Vowel, the question becomes: In what ways can settler, newcomer, and diasporan allies assist Métis (and other Indigenous) people in *going home* – in reconnecting with and reclaiming our homeland? Insight can be gained by Aikau's suggestion that diasporic Hawaiian Latter-day Saints living in Utah decolonize their relationship to the land and to the Goshute people and help them reclaim their homeland even if it means the Latter-day Saints cannot expand Iosepa. Similarly, how can settler, newcomer, and diasporan allies support Indigenous self-determination and reconnection to our languages, cultures, and ceremonies, including remembering the sacredness and power of our women and two-spirit community members? Whether you believe Indigenous experiences and diasporas are mutually intelligible or not, the more these issues are understood by people engaged with the discourse of diaspora – indeed, by all settlers, newcomers, and diasporic peoples in Canada, as well as by Indigenous peoples ourselves – the better neighbours we will become while living in Canada, on Indigenous lands, and honouring the sovereignty of Indigenous peoples, including the Métis Nation.

NOTES

1 Spiritual way of life practised among the Anishinaabe and other Indigenous nations that includes sacred knowledge, scroll teachings, and ceremonies. Other terms for Anishinaabe include Ojibwe, Saulteaux, Chippewa; it can also mean all original (Indigenous) peoples.

2 Along with the Chartrands, the Lavallées, and the Sayers (St-Onge 2004, 4). Today, St Laurent remains a well-known Red River Métis community.

3 The Pemmican Proclamation, precursor to the Battle of Seven Oaks, was a law forbidding the export of bison products (including pemmican, the staple fur trade food) from the colony without the governor's written permission, thereby inhibiting Métis livelihood (Fiola 2010).

4 Because of Métis efforts, Manitoba became the fifth province of Canada; section 31 of the Manitoba Act (1870) promised 1.4 million acres for the Métis. The Canadian government devised the scrip system to distribute this land: a corrupt lottery system that dispossessed most Métis of their land (Fiola 2015; Augustus 2008; Murray 1993). The Supreme Court of Canada declared that the Crown failed in its constitutional duty when distributing land promised to the Métis in the Manitoba Act (*Manitoba Metis Federation Inc. v. Canada (Attorney General)*, [2013] 1 SCR 623). Louis Riel called the Manitoba Act "the Manitoba Treaty" and the "Métis Treaty" and highlighted the nation-to-nation relationship between the Métis and the Crown (Gaudry 2016).

5 @ChiefDay. "Has MNO (Metis Nation of Ontario) made Agreements Regarding 'Energy East' in Ontario, on #TreatyLand? Have Treaty Regions been Notified?" Twitter, 5 January 2015. https://twitter.com/chiefday/status/552737562929958915.

6 For example, the Iron Alliance between Plains Cree, Assiniboine, Saulteaux, and Métis peoples in central "Canada" in the early 1800s (Fiola forthcoming; Innes 2013).

7 In addition to Métis ancestors, I have Anishinaabeg (Saulteaux) and Nêhiyawak (Cree) ancestors; these communities could claim me today based on my genealogy as well as on the kinship relationship-building I have done in Anishinaabe communities such as Roseau River, Hollow Water, Shoal Lake, and Bad River, and in the Nêhiyaw spiritual community of the Blacksmith Spruce Woods Sundance family.

8 Midewiwin Anishinaabeg believe that all peoples, at one time, had a clan system; many have since forgotten. Clans can be relearned through family history and archival research, and through prayer, ceremony, and petition to Spirit.

9 These beliefs are not shared by all Euro-descended settlers; however, these are the dominant beliefs that have been promulgated in our lands – indeed, across the earth.

10 Pre-contact, many Indigenous nations practised wampum diplomacy (Gehl 2014); this continues today. Wampum belts were made of shells (later beads), leather, and sinew with patterns sewn into them representing the terms of agreement in a treaty. The Two Row Wampum was exchanged between the Haudenosaunee and the Dutch in the early seventeenth century in what would become New York, and again in the mid-eighteenth century between the Anishinaabeg and the British in the Niagara region. It illustrates a white background with two parallel purple lines; one represents Indigenous peoples and our ways, and the other represents white peoples (newcomers) and their ways. The lines never intersect, thus representing our nation-to-nation relationship: both sides agreed not to interfere in the affairs of the other; both sides retain sovereignty politically, economically, spiritually, and so on.

11 Recall that former Serpent River chief Isadore Day disregards Métis rights to land in Ontario (above). Isaac Murdoch is the biological brother of Isadore Day. Out of respect, Murdoch does not discuss his brother's position. *Miigwetch* (thank you) to Isaac for our phone conversation, on 30 December 2016, regarding the Painted Hand Ceremony.

12 Murdoch is respected for his research on ancient pictographs and bringing them into the present – for example, the image of Thunderbird Woman that appeared on banners at the Standing Rock Indian Reservation gathering to protect the waters from the Dakota Access Pipeline. He and fellow artist Christi Belcourt (Métis) reproduced several pictograph images and encourage protectors from all over to freely use them in their defence of the earth.

13 It bears repeating that white settlers are co-opting the history of Métis dispossession and claiming that Indigenous identity in their family (i.e., one literal or fictional Indigenous ancestor in their family from centuries ago) was also suppressed and is now resurfacing. Perpetuating biological determinism (Métis = mixed stereotype), they are specifically claiming a Métis identity. Therefore, Métis efforts to rebuild our nation today also involve untangling such claims from those of legitimate descendants of the historic Métis nation who were dispossessed.

REFERENCES

Aikau, Hokulani. 2010. "Indigeneity in the Diaspora: The Case of Native Hawaiians at Iosepa, Utah." *American Quarterly* 62, no. 3 (September): 477-500.

Andersen, Chris. 2014. *'Métis': Race, Recognition, and the Struggle for Indigenous Peoplehood*. Vancouver: University of British Columbia Press.

Augustus, Camie. 2008. "Métis Scrip." *Our Legacy*. University of Saskatchewan Archives. http://scaa.sk.ca/ourlegacy/exhibit_scrip.

Benton-Banai, Edward. 1988. *The Mishomis Book: The Voice of the Ojibway*. Hayward, WI: Indian Country Communications.

Brydon, Diana. 2000. "It's Time for a New Set of Questions." *Essays on Canadian Writing*, no. 71: 14–25.

Butler, Kim. 2001. "Defining Diaspora, Refining a Discourse." *Diaspora: A Journal of Transnational Studies* 10, no. 2: 189–219.

Clifford, James. 1994. "Diasporas." *Cultural Anthropology* 9, no. 3: 302–38.

– 2001. "Indigenous Articulations." *The Contemporary Pacific* 13, no. 2: 468–90.

– 2007. "Varieties of Indigenous Experience: Diasporas, Homelands, Sovereignties." In *Indigenous Experience Today*, edited by Marisol de la Cadena and Orin Starn, 197–224. New York: Berg Publishers.

Dumont, James. 1985. "Aboriginal Government: A Research Paper Prepared for the Roseau River Tribal Council." ISHKOTE Institute of Research and Learning, Three Fires Society and Roseau River Anishinabe First Nation, Manitoba.

Fiola, Chantal. 2010. "Stories from a St. Laurent Founding Family: Experiences in Red River Metis Family History Research." In *The Land between the Lakes*, edited by St Laurent History Book Committee, 506–11. Altona, MB: Friesen's History Book Division.

– 2015. *Rekindling the Sacred Fire: Métis Ancestry and Anishinaabe Spirituality*. Winnipeg: University of Manitoba Press.

– 2020. "*Naawenangweyaabeg Coming in*: Intersections of Indigenous Sexuality, Spirituality, and Feminism." In *In Good Relation: History, Gender, and Kinship in Indigenous Feminisms*, edited by Sarah Nickel and Amanda Fehr, 138–53. Winnipeg: University of Manitoba Press.

– Forthcoming. *Returning to Ceremony: Spirituality in Manitoba Métis Communities*. Winnipeg: University of Manitoba Press.

First Nations and Indigenous Studies. 2009. "The Indian Act." *Indigenous Foundations*, University of British Columbia. http://indigenousfoundations.arts.ubc.ca/the_indian_act/.

Gareau, Paul L. 2021. "Mary and the Métis: Religion as a Site for New Insight in Métis Studies." In *A People and a Nation: New Directions in Contemporary Métis Studies*, edited by Jennifer Adese and Chris Andersen, 188–212. Vancouver: University of British Columbia Press.

Gaudry, Adam. 2016. "Are the Métis Treaty People?" Lecture, *Weweni Indigenous Scholars Speaker Series*, University of Winnipeg, 6 January. https://www.youtube.com/watch?v=oU8b5QFB53g.

– 2018. "Communing with the Dead: The 'New Métis,' Métis Identity Appropriation, and the Displacement of Living Métis Culture." *American Indian Quarterly* 42, no. 2: 162–90.

Gaudry, Adam, and Darryl Leroux. 2017. "White Settler Revisionism and Making Métis Everywhere." *Media Indigena with Rick Harp*. Podcast audio, 23 July. http://app.stitcher.com/splayer/f/85465/50886939.

Gehl, Lynn. 2014. *The Truth That Wampum Tells: My Debwewin on the Algonquin Land Claims Process*. Winnipeg: Fernwood Publishing.

Haig-Brown, Celia. 2009. "Decolonizing Diaspora: Whose Traditional Land Are We On?" *Cultural and Pedagogical Inquiry* 1, no. 1: 4–21.

Haudenosaunee Confederacy. n.d. "Clan Mothers" (accessed 1 August 2017). http://www.haudenosauneeconfederacy.com/clanmothers.html.

Hogue, Michel. 2015. *Metis and the Medicine Line: Creating a Border and Dividing a People*. Regina, SK: University of Regina Press.

Huel, Raymond. 1996. *Proclaiming the Gospel to the Indians and Métis*. Edmonton: University of Alberta Press.

Innes, Robert. 2013. *Elder Brother and the Law of the People: Contemporary Kinship and Cowessess First Nation*. Winnipeg: University of Manitoba Press.

Leroux, Darryl. 2019. *Distorted Descent: White Claims to Indigenous Identity*. Winnipeg: University of Manitoba Press.

Lilley, Ian. 2006. "Archaeology, Diaspora and Decolonization." *Journal of Social Archaeology* 6, no. 1: 28–47.

McCall, Sophie. 2012. "Diaspora and Nation in Métis Writing." In *Cultural Grammars of Nation, Diaspora, and Indigeneity in Canada*, edited by Christine Kim, Sophie McCall, and Melina Singer, 21–41. Waterloo, ON: Wilfred Laurier University Press.

McCarthy, Martha. 1990. *To Evangelize the Nations: Roman Catholic Missions in Manitoba 1818–1870*. Winnipeg: Manitoba Culture Heritage and Recreation Historic Resources.

Métis Settlements General Council. n.d. "Home Page" (accessed 1 August 2017). http://www.msgc.ca/.

Murray, Jeffrey. 1993. "Métis Scrip Records: Foundation for a New Beginning." *The Archivist* 20, no. 1: 12–14.

Newlove, Nigel. 2016. "Métis to Isadore Day – 'We Don't Agree with You.'" *NationTalk*. http://nationtalk.ca/story/metis-to-isadore-day-we-dont-agree-with-you-aptn.

Pettipas, Katherine. 1994. *Severing the Ties That Bind: Government Repression of Indigenous Religious Ceremonies on the Prairies*. Winnipeg: University of Manitoba Press

Préfontaine, Darren R., Todd Paquin, and Patrick Young. 2003. "Métis Spiritualism." *The Virtual Museum of Métis History and Culture*. Gabriel Dumont Institute. http://www.metismuseum.ca/media/db/00727.

Pulitano, Elvira. 2007. "'One More Story to Tell': Diasporic Articulations in Sally Morgan's *My Place*." In *The Pain of Unbelonging: Alienation and Identity in Australasian Literature*, edited by Sheila Callingwood-Whittick, 37–56. Amsterdam: Rodopi.

Raby, Rosalind. 2010. "Treaty Power Struggle behind Métis and First Nations Disagreement." *Midnorth Monitor*. http://www.midnorthmonitor.com/2010/06/29/treaty-power-struggle-behind-metis-and-first-nations-disagreement.

Rolls, Mitchell. 2001. "The Meaninglessness of Aboriginal Cultures." *Balayi: Culture, Law and Colonialism* 2, no. 1: 7–20.

Royal Commission on Aboriginal Peoples. 1996. "Section 3: Implementing an Aboriginal Order of Government." In *Final Report*, vol. 2, chap. 3. Ottawa: Government of Canada.

Safran, William. 1991. Diasporas in Modern Societies: Myths of Homeland and Return. *Diaspora: A Journal of Transnational Studies* 1, no. 1: 83–99.

Saul, John Ralston. 2009. *A Fair Country: Telling Truths about Canada*. Toronto: Penguin Canada.

Spalding, Tom. 2004. "Métis Receive Sundance Song." *Métis Voyageur: The Publication of the Métis Nation of Ontario* (September and October): 1, 16.

St-Germain, Marc. 2015. Michif Song Ceremony, Belcourt, ND, 2004. YouTube video. https://www.youtube.com/watch?v=ew3gpTKDQlA.

St-Onge, Nicole. 2004. *Saint-Laurent, Manitoba: Evolving Métis Identities, 1850–1914*. Regina, SK: Canadian Plains Research Center, University of Regina.

Tölölyan, Khachig. 1996. "Rethinking Diaspora(s): Stateless Power in the Transnational Moment." *Diaspora: A Journal of Transnational Studies* 5, no. 1: 3–36.

– 2012. "Diaspora Studies: Past, Present and Promise." Working paper. International Migration Institute, University of Oxford. https://www.imi.ox.ac.uk/publications/wp-55-12.

Tuck, Eve, and K. Wayne Yang. 2012. "Decolonization Is Not a Metaphor." *Decolonization: Indigeneity, Education and Society* 1, no. 1: 1–40.

Urban Aboriginal Peoples Study. 2010. "Main Report." *Environics Institute*. http://www.uaps.ca/wp-content/uploads/2010/04/UAPS-FULL-REPORT.pdf.

Vertovec, Steven. 2000. "Religion and Diaspora." Paper presented at *New Landscapes of Religion in the West Conference*, University of Oxford, 27–9 September. http://www.transcomm.ox.ac.uk/working%20papers/Vertovec01.PDF.

Vowel, Chelsea. 2016. "What it Means to Move Back Home When You're Métis." *TVO.org*, 16 May. http://tvo.org/article/current-affairs/shared-values/what-it-means-to-move-back-home-when-youre-metis.

Widder, Keith. 1999. *Battle for the Soul: Métis Children Encounter Evangelical Protestants at Mackinaw Mission, 1823–1837*. East Lansing: Michigan State University Press.

Contributors

RIMA BERNS-MCGOWN, PhD, is the member of provincial parliament for Beaches-East York in Toronto and the official opposition critic for poverty and homelessness. Before she was elected, Rima was a researcher and lecturer in diaspora studies at the University of Toronto. Born of a mixed background in South Africa, Rima has a long history of writing about and advocating for systemic change that creates equity and societies that truly work for everyone who lives in them.

ANDREA A. DAVIS is associate professor of Black cultures of the Americas, former chair of the Department of Humanities, and former interim director of the Centre for Research on Latin America and the Caribbean at York University in Toronto. Her research focuses on the literary productions of Black women in the Americas. She is particularly interested in the intersections of the literatures of the Caribbean, the United States, and Canada, and her work encourages an intertextual cross-cultural dialogue about Black women's experiences in diaspora.

KEN DERRY is associate professor of religion (teaching stream) in the Department of Historical Studies at the University of Toronto Mississauga. His academic focus is on the ways in which modern cultural products relate to more "traditional" religious beliefs and practices. He is particularly interested in connections between religion and violence in Indigenous literature and film, and in popular culture. With John Lyden he co-edited *The Myth Awakens* (2018), the first book on *Star Wars* by scholars of religion. Ken has also written about pedagogy in relation to grading, course design, and humour, and in 2013 received the UTM Teaching Excellence Award.

CHANTAL FIOLA is Michif (Red River Métis) with family from Saint Laurent and Ste-Geneviève, MB. She is the author of *Rekindling the Sacred Fire: Métis Ancestry and Anishinaabe Spirituality*, which won her the John Hirsch Award for Most Promising Manitoba Writer and the Beatrice Mosionier Aboriginal Writer of the Year Award. Her follow-up book, *Returning to Ceremony: Spirituality in Manitoba Métis Communities* (University of Manitoba Press) will be released in fall 2021. Chantal is an associate professor in the Department of Urban and Inner-City Studies at the University of Winnipeg. She is two-spirit, Midewiwin, a Sundancer, and lives with her wife Nicki and their daughter in Winnipeg.

NADIA Z. HASAN has a PhD in political science with a specialization in transnational feminism. She works in the non-profit sector on civil liberties and human rights issues related to Muslims in Canada. In the non-profit space, Nadia works to build community-academic relationships to produce and mobilize knowledge that addresses systemic racism, Islamophobia, and hate. She is the co-author of "Under Layered Suspicion: A Review of CRA Audits of Muslim-led Charities," a SSHRC-funded project that examines how Muslim charities are profiled at the intersection of national security and financial regulation. Nadia's doctoral research critically analyzed epistemologies of women's engagements with Islam in Pakistan and the Pakistani diaspora. Nadia was a founding member of the South Asia Group and has taught courses in South Asian Studies, religion, gender, and feminism.

SAILAJA V. KRISHNAMURTI is an associate professor of religious studies and women and gender studies at Saint Mary's University, Halifax. Her research and teaching explore religion, race, gender, and migration in the South Asian diaspora and in global culture. Sailaja has previously taught at York University and the University of Toronto. Sailaja holds a PhD in social and political thought and a graduate diploma in Asian Studies (York, 2008). She also holds an MA in English literature (University of Victoria, 2000). She is the author of several refereed articles and book chapters, and co-edited a collection of essays, *Organizing the Transnational: Labour, Politics, and Social Change*.

BECKY R. LEE is professor emerita and senior scholar in the Department of Humanities at York University. Her research and teaching are concerned with the intersection of religion and gender in the past and the present. In addition to book chapters and articles in journals, including *Method and Theory in the Study of Religion*, *Journal of Family History*, and *Gender and History*, she is the co-editor of *Canadian Women Shaping Diasporic Religious Identities* (Wilfrid Laurier Press 2016).

LINA SAMUEL, PhD, is an assistant professor (teaching faculty) in the Department of Sociology at McMaster University, Hamilton. Her research examines intergenerational cultural retention and the construction of diasporic identities among South Asians in Canada. She has published her research in a number of books and scholarly journals, including *South Asian Diaspora* and the *Journal of Intercultural Studies*. Her current research projects include the challenges of elder-care among elderly immigrants within the South Asian diaspora in Canada. She teaches in the areas of work and occupations, social inequality, gender, family, immigration, and race and ethnicity.

HENRY SHIU is the inaugural Shi Wu De Professor in Chinese Buddhist Studies at Emmanuel College of Victoria University, University of Toronto. His area of research specialization lies in the theory of the *tathāgatagarbha* or Buddha nature, and he has also focused his studies on Mahāyāna Buddhism in India, China, and Tibet, particularly on the historical and doctrinal development of the Madhyamaka and Yogācāra traditions. His other research interests include contemporary Engaged Buddhist movements, Buddhist chaplaincy, Buddhism in Canada, and Western classical music.

CARY TAKAGAKI currently teaches at York University in the Department of Languages, Literatures & Linguistics, and has taught at the University of Western Ontario and the University of Toronto. He holds a PhD from the University of Toronto in East Asian Studies. His research concerns premodern Japanese religious institutions and the Japanese diaspora in Canada during the late nineteenth and early twentieth centuries.

JULIE VIG is an assistant professor in the Department for the Study of Religion at the University of Toronto. Her research focuses on premodern Sikh and Punjabi cultural production and how it relates to wider cultural worlds and networks of pre-modern North India

(c. 1500–1850). Her particular focus is on gurbilās literature and its interactions with Brajbhasha literature. She has secondary research interests in the reception of early modern Sikh texts in the colonial period, and women, gender, and sexuality within the Sikh tradition.

PREET KAUR VIRDI is an independent researcher and writer based in New York City. Her research concerns the migration and socio-legal status of non-Western women in Western legal jurisdictions, focusing on culture, religion, and gender. She completed her PhD at SOAS, University of London, and taught at John Jay College of Criminal Justice, City University of New York (CUNY) before temporarily leaving the academy in 2020 to champion the complex medical needs of her infant daughter amidst the global coronavirus pandemic.

Index